MW0616452

MAKING HOLLYWOOD HAPPEN

No. 478695.

Certificate of Incorporation.

I HEREBY CERTIFY that

FILM FINANCES LIMITED

is this day Incorporated under the Companies Act, 1948,
and that the Company is Limited.

Given under my hand at London, this Twenty-fourth day of
February One thousand nine hundred and fifty.

J. D. TODD

Registrar of Companies.

MAKING HOLLYWOOD HAPPEN

The Story of Film Finances

Charles Drazin

THE UNIVERSITY OF WISCONSIN PRESS

The University of Wisconsin Press gratefully acknowledges the cooperation
and assistance of Film Finances in the preparation of this book.

The University of Wisconsin Press
728 State Street, Suite 443
Madison, Wisconsin 53706
uwpress.wisc.edu

Gray's Inn House, 127 Clerkenwell Road
London ECIR 5DB, United Kingdom
eurospanbookstore.com

Printed in the United States of America
This book may be available in a digital edition.

Library of Congress Cataloging-in-Publication Data

Names: Drazin, Charles, 1960- author.
Title: Making Hollywood happen: The Story of Film Finances / Charles Drazin.
Description: Madison, Wisconsin: The University of Wisconsin Press, [2022] |
Includes bibliographical references and index.
Identifiers: LCCN 2021041566 | ISBN 9780299337001 (cloth)
Subjects: LCSH: Film Finances (Firm)—History. |
Motion picture industry—Finance—History. |
Independent films—Finance—History.
Classification: LCC PN1993.5.AI D739 2022 | DDC 791.4309—dc23
LC record available at https://lccn.loc.gov/2021041566

To all the filmmakers who have worked with

FILM FINANCES

over more than seventy years

Contents

Please reply to:

   5, Hanover Street, W.1.

                           26th September, 1950.

The Westminster Food,Office,
14, Grosvenor Gardens,
S.W.1.

Dear Sirs,

     This Company is shortly taking over a
suite of offices in 34, South Molton Street,
London, W.1. and I should be glad if you would
forward me the necessary application forms for
office tea and milk permits.   We have no
permits at present as, since the Company's
formation some six months ago, we have had no
offices of our own.

     There will be four persons working
full-time in the offices to start with, but it
is expected that this number may shortly be
increased.

                    Yours faithfully,
                    for FILM FINANCES LIMITED.

                    Susan Durnford.

Preface

This book offers a brief history, decade by decade, of the completion guarantor Film Finances, which in the 1950s pioneered the financial tool that facilitated the growth of independent production—first in Britain and then around the world. A completion guarantee is a guarantee to the financiers of a film, whether lender, distributor, or equity investor, that the film will be completed by an agreed date and delivered at no additional cost. It provides the certainty that gives investors the confidence to engage in an otherwise notoriously unpredictable process.

Undertaken at the suggestion of Film Finances itself, the book had been intended to mark the seventieth anniversary of the company's incorporation in London on 24 February 1950, but the publication had to be put off due to the unfolding global health crisis; 24 February 2020 turned out to be a very poor day for celebration. The most significant film industry headline that day was the conviction of Hollywood mogul Harvey Weinstein on two felony counts of sexual assault. Otherwise, it was the rapid spread of COVID-19 that dominated the headlines. Only two weeks later, on 11 March, the World Health Organization declared the outbreak to be a pandemic. As country after country went into lockdown, the film industry was only one of many industries to grind to a halt. All of a sudden, the priority for Film Finances became, as for many other businesses, not to celebrate its history but to do whatever it could to continue its history.

With hindsight, Film Finances' difficult anniversary has a curiously fitting irony. The company was founded as the result of a crisis when the post–World War II British film industry was on the verge of collapse; and its subsequent continued existence has depended on its ability to negotiate the unforeseen in one of the riskiest of all industries, where crisis has often seemed the natural order.

For the title of this book, I have borrowed part of Film Finances' own company slogan, "Making Hollywood Happen since 1950." It contains only a modest degree of exaggeration, capturing the epic scale of a company that has over seven decades played an important role in the production of approximately eight thousand films, including many of the most celebrated ever made. It has guaranteed films that have been the recipients of countless Oscars, including six Academy Awards for Best Picture, but, besides making Hollywood happen, it has also played an important role in the development of film production around the world.[1]

Before we go back to the very beginning of what has been a long, eventful journey, it is worth pausing to consider where that journey has reached today. Film Finances is a global business with offices in the United States, Britain, Germany, Scandinavia, Canada, Australia, and South Africa. Its completion guarantee facilitates the production of more than two hundred films and TV shows annually, with a total budget value of billions of dollars. It is no exaggeration to claim that the story of Film Finances is also the story of the international independent film industry.

The word "independent" requires some explanation. It is used in this book to refer to film companies that are not controlled by the major studios and play an active part in securing financing for their productions. It is an imprecise, relative concept, with the exact meaning of both "major" and "independent" shifting according to time and place. But one defining characteristic is that a major will not only finance the production of films but also distribute them. The largest of today's majors, Disney, started out as an independent, which distributed its first feature-length films in the 1930s through United Artists. A turning point that marked its transformation into a major was when it began to distribute its own films in 1953.

When Film Finances started out, its principal center of operations was London. The "independents" that it most often worked with in the 1950s were British production companies, which were nonetheless mostly dependent for the distribution of their films on three large—or major—British corporations, the Rank Organisation, British Lion, and the Associated British Picture Corporation. In the next decade these British "majors" began to retreat from the scene as the even more major Hollywood studios, with their global reach, invested more heavily in British production. The last British film corporation of any significant size disappeared in 1986 with the sell-off and demise of Thorn-EMI Screen Entertainment (the successor company to the Associated British Picture Corporation).

Various names have been coined over the years to capture the attributes of a constantly changing production infrastructure—"major," "instant major," "mini-major," "major independent," "indiewood," and so on.[2] Yet the company that has played arguably the most significant part since World War II in making an independent film industry possible—whether in Britain, Hollywood, or elsewhere—eluded the attention of film historians for the first sixty years of its history.

When Film Finances invited me to explore its old files in the spring of 2009, I had never heard of the company. Yet it had recently guaranteed the film that had won that year's Best Picture Oscar, *Slumdog Millionaire*, and the archive box I was shown as an example of its work contained files for one of the most famous movies ever made, *Dr. No* (1962), the first film in the James Bond franchise.

I was astonished to find a complete set of papers documenting the production of an iconic movie but even more surprised to learn that the company had kept the files for every film it had guaranteed since 1950. Including scripts, budgets, production schedules, daily progress reports, and call sheets, as well as correspondence with the filmmakers concerned, these files, taken together, were an unparalleled treasure trove that offered an in-depth overview of the postwar history of independent production in the English-speaking world.

Film Finances was too busy meeting the challenges of the films it was involved with in the present to have much time to think about the ones it had guaranteed in the past. But having discovered its past, it was keen to document and celebrate it. In the months that followed, we began to retrieve from commercial storage files that had been quietly accumulating over sixty years. Many of the oldest—still tied up in pink ribbon—had remained unopened since they had first been archived.

Lacking space in its small Mayfair office, Film Finances borrowed a room from the De Lane Lea postproduction house in Soho, where over a period of about a year, three interns—Wes Fleuchaus, Olivia Parkes, and Schuyler Ransohoff—compiled a catalog of all the films that the company had guaranteed though the first thirty years of its history.[3]

On 12 October 2012, Wes, Olivia, Schuyler, and I gave the first public presentation on the Film Finances archive to a gathering of film historians and scholars. The booklet of facsimile documents that we handed out included a progress report from the forty-fourth day of shooting of *The African Queen* on the Nile near Lake Victoria ("Jack Cardiff ill today. Ted Moore took over lighting."); a typically bumptious letter from the producer-director Michael Powell introducing his latest project ("May I venture to mention our title. It is, as you see above, 'Oh—Rosalinda!!' not 'Oh, Rosalinda,' which is as if one said, 'Oh, Rosalinda, whip down the street and get a pound of Stork, will you?' *Our* 'Oh—' is meant to convey shock."); a report from the company's consultant John Croydon on *Zulu* ("Am I being too prophetic when I remember our dreadful experience on a film called *O.H.M.S.* when one soldier, in the heat of the moment, mistook one of his companions, simulating death, for a dummy and stuck his bayonet right through his body?"); and a letter from Cy Feuer, the producer of *Cabaret*, sharing his delight at the film's positive reception ("It has its faults, as have all other projects, but all-in-all, 'it works.'").

But what we shared that day was not even the tip of the tip of the iceberg. Film Finances subsequently agreed to allow a team of film historians to explore its pre-1980 files. The result was a special issue of the *Historical Journal of Film, Radio and Television* that was published in 2014.[4] Since then, many other film historians have been granted access to an astonishingly rich archive that gives a unique insight into the history of the postwar independent cinema, but this is the first book to tell the story of Film Finances itself.

MAKING HOLLYWOOD HAPPEN

Minutes of the first Meeting of Directors

of Film Finances Limited held at 3, Finch

Lane, London, E.C.3. on Monday the

thirteenth day of March 1950, at 3.30 p.m.

Present:

    W.B. Cullen   (Director) (In the Chair)
    A.H.P. Hope   (Director)
    R.E.F. Garrett (Director)

In Attendance:

    Messrs. Thomson, Sammons, McKelvie
    and Croft.

REGISTRATION

1. It was reported that the Company had been registered

on the twentyfourth day of February 1950 and there were

produced to the Meeting

    (a) the Certificate of Incorporation.

    (b) a print of the Memorandum and Articles of

        Association as registered, and

DIRECTORS

    (c) a Memorandum signed by the Subscribers to

        the Memorandum of Association of the Company

        appointing the following persons as the First

        Directors of the Company -

            WILLIAM BENJAMIN CULLEN

            ALBERT HENRY PETER HOPE

            ROBERT EDMUND FRANCIS GARRETT

and IT WAS RESOLVED that Mr. W.B. Cullen be and he is

hereby appointed Chairman of the Meeting.

(1)

IN THE BEGINNING

The 1950s

Film Finances was incorporated in London on 24 February 1950, but its story really began many years before when a young, movie-mad, twenty-five-year-old faced for the first time the challenge of finding the money to make a film.

Bobby Garrett, the founder of Film Finances, started out at the top. Born in 1910, he belonged to a family that was part of the Bowring insurance dynasty. In the 1930s, he inherited a fortune, which he used to set up an independent production company with Otto Klement, a Jewish film producer who had fled Nazi Germany.

The founder of Film Finances, Bobby Garrett, as a young film producer in the mid-1930s.

The British film industry was then riding a wave of confidence that had begun with the worldwide success of Alexander Korda's *The Private Life of Henry VIII* in 1933. New studios were being built, production companies were starting up, and the City was investing in the dream of a Hollywood in Britain. Garrett-Klement Pictures was a beneficiary of these boom years.

The new company aimed to make films for the world market with international box office stars. In 1935, it announced an ambitious production program of six films. It made two of them in 1936—*Romance and Riches* (also known as *The Great Adventure*), starring Cary Grant; and *A Woman Alone*, with Anna Sten. Although largely unknown today, back in the 1930s Sten was as famous as Grant; she was the Hollywood star whom movie producer Sam Goldwyn was going to turn into the "New Garbo."

It was an impressive start, but neither film was a box office success. Garrett-Klement Pictures lost money and, as the industry entered a severe slump, it struggled to find the finances to make any more films.

World War II then intervened. Garrett joined the Royal Air Force (RAF) Volunteer Reserve, rising to the rank of wing commander. Fluent in German, he joined the Government Code and Cypher School at Bletchley Park, where, as deputy head of the Air Section, which decoded enemy air force communications, he became, in Prime Minister Winston Churchill's memorable phrase, one of "the geese that laid the golden eggs and never cackled."[1] Although Garrett kept his role as a senior intelligence officer secret until his death, his name can be found today on the Bletchley Park Roll of Honour.

After the war, Bobby Garrett went back into the film industry. He set up an independent production company called Constellation Films with producer Anthony Havelock-Allan, who is perhaps best known today for producing David Lean's films *Brief Encounter* (1945), *Great Expectations* (1946), and *Ryan's Daughter* (1970).

It wasn't good timing. Although the British film industry had enjoyed a boom during the war years, the return of peace had brought another slump. The two big corporations, the Rank Organisation and Associated British Picture Corporation, had incurred huge losses on production and were cutting back. The result was a major structural shift in the nature of the British film industry. Rather than invest directly in film production themselves, the big corporations now minimized their exposure to risk by relying on independent producers, who were expected to finance their films through a combination of government subsidy and bank loans secured on the strength of a distribution guarantee. But banks were reluctant to lend to independent producers in a climate where production costs had spiraled and box office returns were increasingly uncertain.

Bobby Garrett experienced the difficulties of financing firsthand when he and his partner Anthony Havelock-Allan were making their first movie together in Italy, a historical picture called *Shadow of the Eagle* (1950).

The greatest obstacle had been to find some institution or individual of means who could guarantee to the bank that the film would be completed. For while the risks of a film exceeding its budget were only too obvious, it was only once the completed film had been delivered that the distributor would pay the advance agreed under the distribution contract, with which the producer could then reimburse the bank. To guarantee the completion of *Shadow of the Eagle*, Garrett had relied on wealthy individuals he had met through accountant Bill Cullen, a close personal friend he had known since he first entered the film industry in the 1930s. To insure the production itself, he turned to Peter Hope, of the Lloyd's broker Tufnell, Satterthwaite. It was after

On the set of the costume drama *Shadow of the Eagle*, 1950. Garrett can be seen in the background (*second from left, chin on his hand*) with his business partner Anthony Havelock-Allan (*far left*), looking on nervously as director Sidney Salkow (*foreground center*) and cinematographer Erwin Hillier (*foreground left*) discuss the next shot.

NOTES ON PROPOSED SCHEME TO SET UP A COMPANY
FOR THE PURPOSE OF GIVING GUARANTEES OF
COMPLETION TO SELECTED FILM PRODUCERS

Proposal

It is suggested that, subject to certain safeguards, the
giving of film guarantees of completion is a good business risk
offering reasonable profits to the guarantors.

The principal safeguards are:

(1) That the producer should have a satisfactory record in
the matter of delivery of his pictures at or under their
agreed budgets.

(2) That the producer should be sufficiently able, administrat-
ively and technically, to ensure that all operations
connected with the making of the film are under efficient
control.

(3) That the producer's integrity should be undoubted.

(4) That the producer's budget should contain sufficient
financial margin and his schedule sufficient time margin to
allow for those reasonable but unforeseeable delays to which
any film could be subject. Some account should also be
taken of the reliability of the senior technical personnel
it is proposed to employ. (Appendix "A" contains an outline
of the way in which a pre-production budget is arrived at
and the method by which a film production is usually
financed)

(5) That the production should not be one in which unknown
hazards are likely to be encountered.

(6) That where possible the producer himself should bear part
of the risk of any over-cost.

(7) That the guarantors should have at their disposal an
efficient organization both to examine a proposition
initially and to keep in touch with its progress at all
stages of production. (Appendix "B" contains an actual pre-
production budget together with the final cost of the same
picture and notes showing why individual items were in
certain cases larger or smaller than expected)

(8) That as a last resort the guarantors have the necessary
power to take over the production themselves.

The business plan for Film Finances, August 1949.

discussions with Cullen and Hope that Garrett wrote a business proposal for the world's first specialized completion guarantor.

Dated 3 August 1949, the memorandum on which Garrett sketched out the original idea for Film Finances still survives in the company archives.[2] As in the case of most successful businesses, the idea was simple. When a producer makes a film, he or she must borrow money from a bank, but the bank will lend money only to the producer who can give a guarantee that, if the film costs more than originally intended, it will still be completed and delivered to the distributor without the bank having to provide more money. Garrett's idea was to create a company that could offer such a guarantee. If it sounded like car insurance, it was different in that Garrett's team of experts would do their best to make sure that the production did not crash in the first place: they would vet each proposition, satisfy themselves as to the competence of the filmmakers, monitor their progress, and, in the very last resort, even take over the production themselves. It was different, too, from conventional insurance in that when Film Finances did provide the extra money to finish a film, then the company had a right to recoup its investment from the eventual revenues of the film.

Garrett's notes turned out to provide an effective blueprint for a company that would continue to operate according to the same principles seventy years later. He listed the "principal safeguards" in eight numbered points. The only one that might cause a wry smile today is his requirement "that the producer's integrity should be undoubted," but then it was a comment made in the aftermath of a war when officers and gentlemen were not so difficult to find.

Indeed, several of them could be found among the business associates, family members, and wealthy friends that Garrett, Cullen, and Hope persuaded to back the new venture. There were twenty-seven original investors who subscribed for 127,000 shares of one pound each (US$2.80).[3] The Honourable Frederick Fergus MacNaghten, who received ten thousand shares, belonged to the landed gentry. A London lawyer, he succeeded in 1951 to the ninth baronetcy of Bushmills House, County Antrim. The family's ancestral seat was at Dunrave Manor near the Giant's Causeway. George Wigham-Richardson, who also took ten thousand shares, was from a prominent shipbuilding family (Swan Hunter & Wigham Richardson had built the *Mauretania*) and was an underwriting member at Lloyd's. Frederick Newman (fifteen thousand shares) was an accomplished batsman who had played first-class cricket for Surrey between the two world wars. He had been the private secretary to the retail magnate and philanthropist Sir Julien Cahn. Joseph Vecchi (five thousand shares) was a well-known restaurateur, who owned the Hungaria restaurant, a famous haunt for high society and show business. The restaurant possessed a deep cellar that had enabled Vecchi during the war to promote it as "bomb-proof, splinter-proof, gas-proof and BOREDOM PROOF." Located in Lower Regent Street near Piccadilly Circus, the Hungaria hosted the annual general meetings of Film Finances' early years. The extraordinary completeness of Film Finances' archives means that we can piece together its early days with a great degree of detail. Every letter, receipt, or estimate was routinely filed away, making it possible to build up a picture of a company whose identity was forged amid the austerity of a country still recovering from the worst war the world had known, when the dividing line between public and private had become blurred.

Exactly two months after the company's incorporation, with an authorized share capital of £100,000 ($280,000), the first film it guaranteed—a mystery thriller called *The Woman in Question*, starring Jean Kent, Dirk Bogarde, John McCallum, and Susan Shaw—went on the floor at the Rank Organisation's Pinewood Studios on Monday, 24 April 1950. The front page of *Variety* that week offers some index of the low ebb the British film industry had then reached. "Every Rank Studio Is Dark for First Time since He Entered Pix Industry," ran its headline.[4] Film Finances had literally turned the lights of the British film industry back on.

The budget for *The Woman in Question* was £129,986 ($363,961). Shooting was completed on 29 June 1950, only one day ahead of schedule but £18,362 ($51,414) under budget.[5] A significant factor that accounted for this large savings, the report on production costs explained, was a delay in the commencement of shooting that was "used to plan each shot in great detail, and this resulted in smooth floor shooting."[6]

When there was a claim on Film Finances' guarantee, the company drew on consequential loss insurance from the Lloyd's insurance market, which was obtained through Peter Hope's brokerage firm, Tufnell, Satterthwaite. The chief Lloyd's underwriter that Tufnell, Satterthwaite dealt with, Morris Herbert Lee, was also one of the original investors in Film Finances.

For the first few months of its existence, Bobby Garrett had been running Film Finances from his office at Constellation Films on Hanover Street, but on 16 October 1950 the new company moved into a suite of offices on the third floor of 34 South Molton Street, on the north side of Mayfair. The Bond Street Underground Station was at one end of the street, Claridge's hotel at the other.

We can reconstruct the look and atmosphere of the office from the documentation relating to its upkeep—a sketch plan for its refurbishment, quotes

DAILY PRODUCTION AND PROGRESS REPORT

DAY Monday	DATE April 24th, 1950	REPORT No. 1
PRODUCTION No. J.F.L.220	PRODUCTION "THE WOMAN IN QUESTION"	DIRECTOR A. Asquith
ALLOTTED DAYS 48 plus 1 Location	ELAPSED DAYS 4 Tests 1	STATUS Up to schedule
DATE STARTED 24th April, 1950	ESTIMATED FINISHING DATE 29th June, 1950	FINISHED DATE

TIME		SCRIPT REPORT			WHERE WORKING

TIME		SCRIPT REPORT	Number	Minutes	WHERE WORKING
					TO-DAY
COMPANY CALLED	8.30	SCENES IN ORIGINAL SCRIPT	251		Int. Ext.
TIME STARTED	9.20	SCENES PREVIOUSLY TAKEN	-		Int. Astra's Bedroom,
LUNCH CALLED	1.00	SCENES TAKEN TO-DAY	2	2.53	Landing and Stairs
TIME STARTED	2.00	TOTAL TAKEN TO DATE	2	2.53	"C" Stage
FINISHED	6.23	BALANCE TO BE TAKEN	249		
		ADDED SCENES TAKEN TO-DAY	-	-	TO-MORROW
		ADDED SCENES TAKEN TO DATE	-	-	Int. Ext.
STILLS PREVIOUSLY -		RETAKE SCENES TAKEN TO-DAY	-	-	Int. Astra's Bedroom,
TO-DAY 2		RETAKE SCENES TAKEN TO DATE	-	-	Landing and Stairs
TOTAL 2					"C" Stage

STAR & LEADS	Worked	Held	Rehearsed	SMALL PART	Worked	Held	Rehearsed	EXTRAS & STAND-INS NUMBER & RATE	Worked	Held
JEAN KENT	1							Stand ins:		
SUSAN SHAW	1							Joyce Radcliffe @ £2.15.6		
								Elvira Fordyce @ £2.15.6		
CALLED FOR COSTUME FITTING ONLY										
BOBBIE SCROGGINS										

ACTION PROPS Number and Kind	EFFECTS
Practical gas fire	
Parrot	

	PICTURE FOOTAGE				SOUND FOOTAGE	
	GROSS B. & W.	GROSS COLOUR	PRINT		GROSS	PRINT
			B. & W.	COLOUR		
PREVIOUS	3303	-	2692	-	-	-
TO-DAYS	2510	-	710	-	3010	750
TOTAL	5813	-	3402	-	3010	750

No. OF CAMERAS	KINDLY INDICATE REASON FOR TIME LOST, EXCESSIVE FOOTAGE OR SCENES, ETC.: ALSO INDICATE WHEN STARTING OR FINISHING WITH ANY ARTISTE.
TO-DAY 1 N.C.32 TO-MORROW 1	SHOOTING STARTED TODAY
SLATE NUMBERS 1 - 6	3303' of Picture footage has been used on Tests.
SCENE NUMBERS 63, Alt.63, 63A, 63B, 64, 64A	Please note extra quarter hour worked.

CORRECT:

Assistant Director

PRODUCTION MANAGER

Report No. 1. The camera turned for the first time on a production guaranteed by
Film Finances on 24 April 1950.

for decoration, receipts for office furniture. There were several letters concerning the building's rickety elevator, which had an iron lattice inner door that would often bounce open again when it was slammed too hard, so that the elevator would not operate and staff would find themselves having to walk up four flights to Film Finances' office. The presiding note was one of dilapidation and disrepair. The agreement to install the telephone, "on behalf of the Post Master General," came in an envelope marked "On His Majesty's Service" and warned that "in view of the pressure of work already on hand it may be some weeks before service can be provided."[7] Rationing was still in force. An application had to be made to the Westminster Food Office for tea and milk permits, while the office kettle was hired from the London Electricity Board.

Bobby Garrett started the business with only his secretary, Susan Durnford, from Constellation Films. His first priority was to put together a team. In the original business proposal, he had written that the company would vet each proposition with "a good intelligence service and an expert examination of the details of the production submitted."[8] The person who took on this role, almost from the very beginning, knew more about practical production than just about anyone else alive.

Born in 1907, John Croydon had entered the film industry in 1931 during the early days of sound. He had started out as a location accountant at Gainsborough Studios, then the following year became a studio manager at Gaumont-British, working with many of the most well-known directors of the time, including Alfred Hitchcock and Michael Powell. In 1936, he became a construction manager for Metro-Goldwyn-Mayer (MGM), contributing to the three big-budget films that Hollywood's most glamorous studio was making in Britain, *A Yank at Oxford* (1938), *The Citadel* (1938), and *Goodbye, Mr. Chips* (1939). When World War II began in 1939, he moved on to Ealing Studios, where he worked as a line producer. Known as "the studio with the team spirit," the wartime Ealing had under the supervision of its production head Michael Balcon served as a school to a generation of talented young filmmakers who would go on to make the comedy classics for which Ealing is still remembered today— *Whisky Galore* (1949), *Kind Hearts and Coronets* (1949), *Passport to Pimlico* (1949), *The Man in the White Suit* (1951), and *The Ladykillers* (1955). The revered mentor for these filmmakers was the great Brazilian director Alberto Cavalcanti, who had been a key figure in the 1920s French avant-garde and then the British documentary movement of the 1930s. At Ealing, the films he directed included the classics *Went the Day Well?* (1942) and *Dead of Night* (1945). John Croydon was his close collaborator and producer.

John Croydon, Film Finances' production consultant.

In 1946, Croydon was hired by the Rank Organisation as a head of production to bring the Ealing ethos of teamwork to its Highbury studio, which had been established with the object, in Croydon's own words, "of giving promising artistes, writers, composers and directors opportunities to develop their talent."[9] When in 1949 the studio became the first casualty of the Rank Organisation's massive cutbacks in production, Croydon took this ethos to Film Finances instead.

But Croydon's first experience of Film Finances was as a client. He was the freelance producer of a comedy called *One Wild Oat* (1950), the third film that the company guaranteed. Starring Robertson Hare and Stanley Holloway, the film is little known today, but it is notable for the first appearance in British pictures of a young Audrey Hepburn.

John Croydon (*left*) with the great Brazilian director Alberto Cavalcanti, with whom he had worked closely during the 1940s at Ealing Studios.

The day before *One Wild Oat* went on the floor at Riverside Studios, Hammersmith, on Wednesday, 3 May 1950, Croydon attended a board meeting of Film Finances, at which he discussed the terms on which he would become a consultant to the company. It was agreed that he would investigate each proposition in return for a fee. Never an actual employee, he continued meanwhile to work as an active producer. His first full report for Film Finances, dated 8 June 1950, was on a production of *Tom Brown's Schooldays*: "The intention of the unit is not to use an Art Director as most of the sets are reproductions. I have already told their Production Manager that I think such an idea is nonsense."[10] The tone of this first report was typical of the way Croydon would continue, as he went on over the next thirty years to write more than a thousand reports. Plain-spoken and direct, he set out to articulate the production challenges of each film with as much accuracy as he could muster. In the form of a private and confidential letter, usually addressed to Bobby Garrett, he was able to offer Film Finances that most rare but priceless asset of the unvarnished truth.

A young Audrey Hepburn in her first appearance in a British-made picture: *One Wild Oat* (1950). Produced by John Croydon, it was the third film to receive a completion guarantee from Film Finances.

The following month, Garrett took stock of the company's early progress. In a memorandum to his codirector Bill Cullen dated 10 July, he wrote that he was satisfied with the way it had consolidated relations with the principal financiers and standardized the necessary documentation. But, he argued, "our ultimate success will still mainly depend on two things: (a) the efficiency of our initial intelligence on a proposition; and (b) the up-to-the-minute policing of that proposition."[11] Whereas he thought that the new system under which John Croydon investigated each proposition was "working well," there was a clear need now for a full-time member of staff who could closely monitor the production period of each film under guarantee, checking progress reports and cost statements against the original budgets and schedules. Such policing, he wrote, "would enable us to see at as early a date as possible and in its correct perspective the 'red light' if ever it begins to show." As one reads through this memorandum, perhaps what stands out most, as with many other of the early documents, is the "stiff upper lip" manner of this "Keep Calm and Carry On" generation. "I emphasise the importance of correct perspective,"

Garrett went on, "as whereas we want to take all possible precautionary measures we should avoid 'flaps.'" The ability to avoid "flaps" was a not unimportant reason why the company would still be carrying on seventy years later.

The next day, 11 July, on John Croydon's recommendation, Garrett interviewed Maurice Foster, who had worked as Croydon's personal assistant at Ealing Studios. Thirty years old, Foster was a qualified accountant who had been responsible at Ealing for not only the scheduling and costing of productions but also the supervision of their progress. Recommending his employment to his fellow directors Cullen and Hope, Garrett wrote, "He seemed to me a keen man and one who had acquired considerable experience of the kind which we need."[12]

Two years later, as the company continued to grow, Film Finances hired Bernard Smith, who had worked as a production accountant for the Rank Organisation. Like Garrett, Smith had served in the RAF during the war, when he had flown as a navigator in Stirling and Lancaster bombers. Film Finances' entire operational team—Garrett, Foster, Smith, Croydon, and a couple of secretaries—could easily have fitted into a Lancaster bomber itself, yet each year during the 1950s it was guaranteeing as many as thirty feature films.

Bernard Smith, a production accountant from the Rank Organisation, joined Film Finances in 1952. During World War II, he had served as a navigator in the RAF.

The other mainstay of Film Finances' first generation was Prince Alessandro Tasca di Cutò, a Sicilian aristocrat who had been forced to earn his own living after his father had squandered the family fortune. Since the war, Tasca had worked as a consultant to the Anglo-American film companies that had been coming to Italy in ever-increasing numbers. Garrett had first met him in Venice in 1949 when Tasca was a production adviser during the shooting of *Shadow of the Eagle*. So many films were being shot in Italy that in 1952 Garrett invited him to become Film Finances' representative there. "What this company as a guarantor requires," he wrote to him, "is an adviser who can from time to time be called upon to undertake examination of a project from what might be termed the 'Italian' point of view."[13] To give an idea of the sort of thing he had in mind, he enclosed with his letter two of John Croydon's reports. "I was amazed at the exactness with which they are handled," commented Tasca when he replied a week later to accept the job. "I can assure you that no Italian film is ever handled with such thoroughness."[14]

By the end of the 1950s, Italy had become such an important center of international filmmaking that Film Finances established an Italian completion guarantor, the Società Finanziaria Garanzie e Controlli (SFGC), with Tasca as its chief adviser. The first film to be guaranteed was *Vengeance of Hercules* (*La vendetta di Ercole*, 1960). But the routine fare of SFGC included not only so-called sword-and-sandal epics and Spaghetti Westerns but such prestige productions as Michelangelo Antonioni's *Red Desert* (*Il deserto rosso*, 1964), Gillo Pontecorvo's *The Battle of Algiers* (*La battaglia di Algieri*, 1966), and Pier Paolo Pasolini's *The Gospel According to St. Matthew* (*Il vangelo secondo Matteo*, 1964). In the latter, Tasca can briefly be seen playing the part of Pontius Pilate.

Like John Croydon, in addition to his role as a consultant to Film Finances, Tasca also continued to work in various freelance production roles, one of which included running Orson Welles's European production company.

A chart of Film Finances' first year of business enables us to follow the progress of what turned out to be an encouragingly positive beginning to its history. By the end of 1950, the company had guaranteed fourteen films, of which only two went over budget. It was a lucky beginning. As the odds evened out over the decade that followed, the pattern was of about one film in every five involving a claim. But when there was a claim, it was a rare film that would exceed an overage of 10 percent. Film Finances' great achievement over the decade was to play a leading part, through its supervision but also its production advice, in bringing to the British film industry a system of disciplined, well-planned film production. An essential part of this system was the requirement for a contingency fund to be made available within the budget. Originally 5 percent of the total direct costs of the production, this figure would rise over the years to a standard 10 percent.

Once Film Finances had proved its long-term viability, the complexion of its ownership changed. In 1954, when a large number of shares became available, Garrett reorganized the shareholding to include several prominent film industry figures. Among the independent producers who took stock in the company at this time were Sydney Box, James Carreras, Joseph Somlo, Herbert Wilcox, and John Woolf. They became invaluable sources of advice and influential support for a business that had quickly become, in Garrett's own words, "something of a key institution in independent finance."[15]

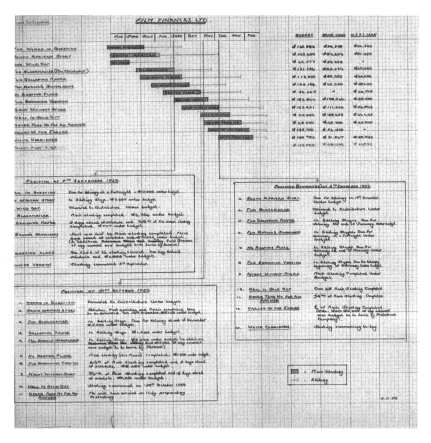

Chart showing the progress made on the first fourteen films under Film Finances guarantee, 2 November 1950.

Although the perspective of Film Finances would become increasingly more international in the decades that followed, what is striking about this first decade of business is its Britishness. In their subject matter but also their financing, the majority of the 1950s films that Film Finances guaranteed in its first decade reflected a British film industry relying on home funding to turn out films for primarily home consumption. The standard pattern for financing, stated time after time on Film Finances' appraisal report for each film, was "70% Discountable Distribution Guarantee, with investments from NFFC and Producers." The "NFFC" stood for the National Film Finance Corporation, the state bank that the British government had been compelled to create in 1948 as an emergency measure to prevent the complete collapse of film production in Britain. Although its existence had been intended to be temporary, this instrument of state support became a quasi-permanent feature of the British film industry, only eventually being abolished in 1985.

What this relatively simple pattern of financing meant in practice was that an independent production company would secure a guarantee from a British distributor—the main ones were Rank, Associated British Picture Corporation, and British Lion, but there were many smaller ones too—to advance 70 percent of a proposed film's budget on its completion. With this distribution guarantee, the producer could then borrow the 70 percent from a bank and put together the 30 percent remainder of the financing—the "end money"— from a combination of a producer contribution in the form of an investment or, more likely, a deferment of fees, and a loan from the National Film Finance Corporation, which would normally cover the lion's share of the end money. The loans of the bank and the NFFC were both protected by Film Finances' guarantee to provide whatever extra funds were required to complete the film.

A random sample of these 1950s films reflects the output for the most part of an industry fashioning mainstream, popular entertainment for the same general audience that had gone to the cinema in the previous decade and would be content to stay at home in front of the television during the next. It was a genre-oriented, commercial cinema that operated within the fairly narrow box office requirements of the major distributors, producing thrillers, comedies, and a notably large number of war films that celebrated Britain's exploits in a World War II that was still within recent memory. Films such as *Angels One Five* (1952), *Above Us the Waves* (1955), or *Reach for the Sky* (1956) may be little remembered today, but they commanded huge audiences when they first came out.

It was a cinema that was for the most part a recognizably "British" cinema, funded by British money, which showed an outward continuity with the British

Reach for the Sky (1956), the story of World War II ace pilot Douglas Bader, was typical of the mostly British-financed, mainstream films that Film Finances guaranteed during its first ten years.

cinema of previous decades. But it had been sustained only by a profound change in the industrial system, as now independent producers acted as contractors for corporations that rarely any longer directly financed production in the way they had done before 1950.

This structural reform underpinned the creation of Film Finances, which came into being to facilitate loans for independent producers who did not have the capital means to guarantee such loans themselves. But while the completion bond was developed in the context of the British film industry, it was potentially significant anywhere there were independent producers who needed financing.

Hollywood in 1950 was still dominated by the major film studios, which remained the prime source of production financing, but the American film industry was also undergoing huge structural change. To the extent that these upheavals involved independent producers, Film Finances soon found that it had an important role to play there too.

During the war, Hollywood had enjoyed a boom time, with surging box office revenues. The easy availability of financing from banks for what was perceived to be a hugely profitable industry encouraged many of Hollywood's most famous filmmakers to break away from the major studios to establish their own independent production companies. The aptly named Liberty Films, for example, was founded in 1945 with the purpose of producing, independently of the established studio system, the films of star Hollywood directors Frank Capra, George Stevens, and William Wyler. But with the return of peace, Hollywood soon found itself facing its own crisis.

Liberty's first production, *It's a Wonderful Life*, turned out to be its last. The film is today of course a treasured classic, but when it was first released at the end of 1946, it was a box office failure. Struggling to cope with the financial fallout, Liberty sold out to Paramount in 1947.

A ruling of the US Supreme Court a year later forced the Hollywood majors to sell their theater chains, which led to the eventual breakup of the studio system. It seemed on the surface to be the independents' great opportunity. But after the boom of the wartime years, box office revenues were now in decline. The advent of television, as well as currency and quota restrictions imposed on many of Hollywood's foreign markets, added to the widespread sense of turmoil. The provision of production financing to independents, which had in the boom years been a dependable business, now seemed a risky activity fraught with danger. Amid the concerns about the underlying profitability of the industry, banks began to impose such Draconian conditions on loans that most producers struggled to meet them.

"Bell Tolls for Indie Producers," ran a *Variety* headline in May 1948. The story claimed, "Except for the handful of solidly established independents . . . the knell is heard sounding for this type of production."[16] A year later *Variety* reported, "The only two banks in the country that are still actively lending for production are Bank of America in Los Angeles and Chemical Bank & Trust in New York. Bank of America, however, is asking for 100% guarantee of loans from most producers, which means the indie must have a backer with plenty of cabbage."[17]

This drying up of financing for independent producers had a disastrous knock-on effect on their principal champion, United Artists, which, lacking product to distribute, was now incurring huge weekly losses. In an attempt to turn around its fortunes, the owners Charlie Chaplin and Mary Pickford made an innovative deal with New York lawyers Arthur Krim and Robert Benjamin to take over the management of the company. Krim and Benjamin were made trustees of all sixteen thousand shares of United Artists and were granted an option to purchase half those shares for a nominal one dollar per share if they succeeded in any one of the next three years to get the company back into the black.

The Chicago financier Walter Heller & Co., which had participated in the restructuring negotiations, agreed to provide the working capital for this new management team to help get United Artists back on its feet again. But it brought to the partnership an attitude of extreme caution, which reflected its reevaluation of the realities of film financing. Milton Gordon, one of the Heller executives involved in the negotiations, explained the calculation that underlay the financing agreement: "I made a survey of all the pictures then being distributed by United Artists. . . . I found that the million-dollar minimum gross was a thing of the past, but actually that seven pictures had gone through United Artists that year which had grossed as little as $400,000 to $450,000. Accordingly, we moved our sights down, and decided that instead of $600,000 based on a gross of a million, the safe area for an ordinary program picture was a loan of no more than $200,000."[18]

The financial restructuring that Heller agreed with United Artists reflected a fundamental downgrading of the banks' assessment of the profit potential of the film industry. "A single average picture without any distinguishing elements has departed from the 'area of predictability' and cannot be regarded as a good risk," Gordon explained.[19] Indeed, the readiness of the banks to finance even a better-than-average picture depended on the degree to which a producer could demonstrate having taken measures to defend increasingly narrow profit margins. One of these measures, Gordon explained, was a completion guarantee, "in the form of cash or a responsible person or studio to insure that a pic will be completed even though the cost exceeds the budget estimates."[20]

Another measure was to spread the risk through coproduction. The existence of Film Finances' completion guarantee played a critical role in facilitating a new practice in the 1950s of independent producers from Hollywood entering into coproductions with European partners. Both partners were able not only to benefit from sharing the production costs but also to take advantage of the incentives that many European governments had introduced to support their film industries.

The first instance of Film Finances supporting such a partnership occurred in January 1951, when American company Telinvest approached Film Finances about its intention to participate in a coproduction with British company Mayflower of a film called *So Little Time*. Set during World War II, it told the story of a German officer who falls in love with a Belgian woman when he is billeted in a requisitioned château. While Mayflower would bear the "below-the-line" costs in British pounds sterling of actually making the film in a British studio, Telinvest would provide the "above-the-line" costs in US dollars of the then Hollywood-based director Compton Bennett and Hollywood star Van Heflin. (As it turned out, Van Heflin turned down the role, and the British actor Leo Genn took his place.)

Beyond this specific Mayflower deal, Telinvest, which had made a fortune in the United States through selling TV distribution rights for old feature films, had ambitious plans for a much more extensive program of coproduction. Partnerships with established British production companies offered Telinvest a means of acquiring new product, while the benefit for the British partner was the opportunity, through Telinvest's dollar investment, to secure the services of the big Hollywood stars, which the stringent currency controls of the time would otherwise have made impossible.

Within weeks of Telinvest's inquiry, Film Finances had agreed to guarantee two more Anglo-American productions that had been set up in a similar fashion. Both films were to be distributed in the United States by United Artists, which would help the American production companies cover their dollar costs through its refinancing agreement with Walter Heller & Co.

Another Man's Poison (1951) was a thriller starring Bette Davis and her actor husband, Gary Merrill, who had recently appeared opposite her in *All About Eve* (1950). The director was Irving Rapper, who had directed Davis in four films, including *Now, Voyager* (1942). British company Daniel Angel Productions was responsible for the below-the-line sterling cost of making the film in England, and independent producer Douglas Fairbanks Jr. for the above-the-line dollar cost of the Hollywood stars and director.

The other film was *The African Queen* (1951). While British producer John Woolf's company Romulus would make the film, using British sterling, Sam Spiegel's Horizon Enterprises would pay the dollar cost of director John Huston and the stars Humphrey Bogart and Katharine Hepburn.

In this case, Film Finances guaranteed only the above-the-line dollar costs of the director and stars because the British producer John Woolf, who had a considerable personal fortune, exceptionally undertook to make himself liable for any overage that might occur on the sterling budget for making the film. He wished to give as much support as he could to one of Hollywood's most acclaimed directors. So it was natural that he should seek to preempt any possible negative impact of the completion guarantor seeking to minimize costs if

Messrs. Walter E. Heller & Co.,
105, West Adams Street,
CHICAGO,
Illinois.   May, 1951.

Dear Sirs,

        Whereas :-

(a)   Horizon Enterprises, Inc. of 650 North Bronsten Avenue,
Los Angeles, California (hereinafter called "Horizon") has
entered into an Agreement dated 17th April, 1951, with
Rolulus Films Limited (hereinafter called "Romulus") which
Agreement as from time to time amended by any further
Agreement between the parties is hereinafter referred to as
"the Production Agreement".

(b)   Under the terms of the Production Agreement Horizon
is obliged to provide certain services and facilities for
the purpose of production of a cinematograph film entitled
"THE AFRICAN QUEEN" (hereinafter called "the said Film"),
including the services of John Huston as Director and
Katherine Hepburn and Humphrey Bogart as star artistes.

(c)   You have agreed to advance to Horizon to enable Horizon
to carry out its obligations under the Production Agreement
the sum of 60 000 dollars and you have procured United
Artists Corporation of Delaware (hereinafter called "United
Artists") to guarantee to Katherine Hepburn the payment of
or before the 15th December, 1951 of the sum of 65,000
dollars.

        NOW in consideration of the foregoing we hereby agree
with you as follows :-

1.   If the production of the said film shall not have been
completed within the time permitted by the Production
Agreement and in accordance with the provisions therein
contained, we shall procure the completion of the production
of the said film forthwith in accordance with such provisions.

2.   If notwithstanding the completion of production of the
said film as aforesaid a positive print and an original
negative of the same shall not have been delivered to you or
Technicolor Limited (as the case may be) on or before 1st
June, 1952 in accordance with the provisions of the Production
Agreement, we shall forthwith procure the delivery to you
of the same.

                                        P.T.O.

First page of Film Finances' letter agreement with the Chicago bank Walter Heller &
Co., May 1951. Heller was the principal financier of United Artists, distributor of *The
African Queen* (1951), a landmark in international independent film production.

the film went over budget. Film Finances was only a year old. The challenge that still lay ahead of it was to prove to the industry that its involvement was ultimately much more likely to support rather than undermine a film's quality.

After several days' delay caused by the difficulties of setting up the Technicolor equipment in the jungle and heavy tropical rains, *The African Queen* began location shooting in the Congo on Monday, 28 May 1951. The first sequence the crew shot was an early scene in which Katharine Hepburn's character, Rosie, buries her brother after their mission station has been burned down, and then boards the *African Queen* for the first time.

From a logistical perspective, the substance of the film was straightforward— mostly a man and a woman on a boat. But the production offered plenty of examples of the unforeseen incidents that can push even the most well-organized films to exceed their budgets. There was the day the boat sank when the unit had to spend the morning pulling it up again. There was the entire week lost to illness when famously the only members of the unit to stay healthy were Humphrey Bogart and John Huston, whose love of whisky defeated the bugs in the bottled water. Back in England, where shooting recommenced in Isleworth Studios on Monday, 23 July, two whole days were lost when the leeches that were supposed to cling to Bogart's body as he pulls the *African Queen* through the reeds stubbornly refused to live up to their names. After sixty-one days on location in Africa, and fifty-five days at Isleworth and Shepperton, the last day of shooting took place at Whipsnade Zoo, where the camera unit spent the day taking animal shots.

The African Queen opened in the United States at the Wilshire Theatre in Los Angeles on 26 December 1951. Sam Spiegel used the occasion to urge independent producers to take advantage of the production incentives that had been introduced in Europe, notably production funds in the UK and Italy levied on box office takings. Recalling the experience of making the picture two months later, when it opened in New York, Humphrey Bogart commented, "The four of us, Katie, myself, Huston and Spiegel, we were a little company, a kind of task force for independent production. That's one reason why we feel a sense of accomplishment. It wasn't like doing a picture over here."[21]

According to *Variety*, *The African Queen* was the sixth most successful film at the US box office in 1952, grossing more than $4 million.[22] An important element in United Artists' return to financial health, the success of *The African Queen* was a timely shot in the arm for independent film production. Bogart, who had his own film production company, Santana, expressed the view that it had helped break the Hollywood mold: "I'll even go this far and predict that

PRODUCTION PROGRESS REPORT		REPORT No. 4I Loo.

PRODUCTION "THE AFRICAN QUEEN"   DATE Saturday, 30.6.51

DIRECTOR JOHN HUSTON

SHOOTING SCHEDULE	BEGIN	FINISH	TOTAL DAYS	DAYS TO DATE
ESTIMATED	24.5.51			
ACTUAL	27.5.51			33

WHERE WORKING (STUDIO — STAGE — SET — LOCATION)
ON LOCATION - UGANDA - MURCHISON FALLS

TIME

CALL	7.30a.m.
1st SET UP COMPLETED	-
LUNCH—FROM	I.00p.
TO	2.00p.
UNIT DISMISSED	6.00p.
TOTAL HOURS	9½ hrs

SCRIPT SCENES

	SCRIPT		EXTRA		RETAKES	
	NUMBER	MINUTES	NUMBER	MINUTES	NUMBER	MINUTES
PREVIOUSLY TAKEN	I08	34.I4	I		4	I.05
TAKEN TO-DAY	-	-			-	-
TAKEN TO DATE	I08	34.I4	I		4	I.05
TO BE TAKEN	233					
TOTAL SCRIPT SCENES	54I					

CONTRACT ARTISTES

NAME	W	s/n	RE

The following members of the Unit are sick and confined to bed :-

Katharine Hepburn
Jack Cardiff
Ted Moore
John Mitchell
Kevin McClory
George Stephenson
Ernie Webb
Eileen Bates
George Frost
Rodney Chilton
Ernie Rayner
Tommy Frewer
John Kotze
George Minassian

SMALL PARTS

NAME	DAILY RATE

STAND INS		CROWDS	
NAME	RATE	NUMBER	RATE

ACTION PROPS AND EFFECTS	SLATE NUMBERS	SCENE NUMBERS

B & W PICTURE — NEGATIVE FILM FOOTAGE — SOUND

WASTE	RESERVE & N/G	PRINT	TOTAL		TOTAL	PRINT	RESERVE & N/G	WASTE
				PREVIOUSLY USED	12,630	11760	870	
				USED TO-DAY	-	-	-	
				TOTALS TO DATE	12,630	11760	870	

STILLS	PREVIOUSLY TAKEN	Prod: 74 Pub: I04 Ref: 85	TAKEN TO-DAY	-	TAKEN TO DATE	Prod: 74 Pub: I04 Ref: 85

REMARKS

No shooting due to sickness.

STATUS	DAYS	OVER UNDER
PREVIOUSLY REPORTED	32	
TO-DAY	I	
TO DATE	33	

SIGNED GEOFFREY INNES

Production progress report for *The African Queen*, 30 June 1951, reflecting a day of sickness in the jungle.

not too many years from now the major studios will disappear completely, just serving as outlets for independent productions. That way, they'll function nominally, renting out space and players to these new outfits. . . . Hollywood can't make any real money now, what with television cutting in, and the result will be less theatres and a concentration of dollars on better pictures. The banks still aren't playing ball with the independents, but it's getting easier."[23]

One reason why it was "getting easier" was Film Finances' completion guarantee, which had given the banks the necessary confidence to lend without fear of the budget overcosts. The two films that Huston directed after *The African Queen*—*Moulin Rouge* (1952) and *Beat the Devil* (1953)—were both independent coproductions made with Film Finances' support.

And the independent financiers of the film that Huston directed after *Beat the Devil* must have regretted that they hadn't secured Film Finances' support. The budget of *Moby Dick* (1956) was $2 million. According to Huston, the production, which was shot at Shepperton and on location off Fishguard in South Wales, had to contend with not only the "worst weather in the history of the British Isles" but also some serious errors in its setup.[24] To serve as Captain Ahab's ship the *Pequod*, the filmmakers had fitted out an old three-master with engines beneath the poop deck that were too small for the size of the vessel. As Huston recounted, "All of these deficiencies, along with the bad weather, created a nightmare of problems. The high poopdeck made us a plaything to the winds, and we were knocked around so much as to be almost spinning at times. We had to keep the engines running constantly to maintain headway, and this meant we couldn't record dialogue because of the noise. It was just one thing after another."[25] The final cost of production was $4.4 million, a colossal figure for the time.

As the years passed, the film industry came to appreciate that Film Finances' guarantee not only offered a protection against overcosts but also brought with it a production expertise that often anticipated the errors of set-up that led to the overcosts in the first place.

Even the industry's most experienced and highly regarded filmmakers discovered that they had lessons to learn. In the 1940s, with the aid of huge budgets from the Rank Organisation, Michael Powell and Emeric Pressburger had been responsible for some of the most ambitious and spectacular films ever made in Britain, including *A Matter of Life and Death* (1946), *Black Narcissus* (1947) and *The Red Shoes* (1948). When in 1954 they approached Film Finances for a guarantee of completion for *Oh—Rosalinda!!*, their new adaptation of the operetta *Die Fledermaus*, the negotiations got off to a bumpy start.

After a difficult start, Michael Powell came to appreciate Film Finances' technical expertise. Nearly all his films, from *Oh—Rosalinda!!* (1955) onward, had a guarantee from the company.

Michael Powell sent a shooting script, budget, and schedule to Bobby Garrett with the comment, "We hope you enjoy reading the script. Everyone else has." The tone was of someone writing to his bank manager, full of a rather patronizing arrogance to which it was difficult not to take exception. "We hope you know the music of *Die Fledermaus*, because the score will be one of the glories of the film."[26]

In the report that he wrote on the material, John Croydon did not trouble to conceal his irritation: "I take it that Powell phrases his letter in his own inimical childish fashion as he probably thinks that our knowledge of film production is nil, and feels that he should mount the lecture platform for our benefit." Expressing the view that Film Finances should turn down Powell and Pressburger's project, he went on, "If we were to enter into this Guarantee of Completion, we should have egotistical, unpractical and intolerable clients." As regards the script, he seemed to be pleased to be able to disappoint Powell's expectations: "I may be in a minority of one but as we have apparently been asked to express an opinion about the script—I do not like it. However, it is not our place to express our likes and dislikes."[27]

Croydon complained that what Powell called a schedule was actually no more than a list of sets with cast and scene numbers from which it was impossible to estimate how long the script would take to shoot. The budget was even worse. "I must confess that I am completely baffled by it. It does not seem to bear any comparison with reality. I will give you a few instances." He went on to list the instances in lettered paragraphs, *a* to *z*, and, running out of letters, had to continue in numbers, 1 through 8. "I am sure that having read through the above comments on the budget, you will agree with me that we enter the realm of fantasy."[28]

Since Powell and Pressburger had previously relied on what was virtually a blank check from the Rank Organisation to foot their production costs, it was perhaps hoping for too much to expect their budget to be anything else. The challenge was gently to bring them back down to earth. Garrett's instinct was to make the venture viable if he possibly could. So he asked Maurice Foster to work with Powell and Pressburger on producing an accurate schedule, cross-plot, and budget. A month later Foster submitted these to Croydon on Powell and Pressburger's behalf. "I would ask you to forget my own association with the project and examine the papers as a normal proposition put up to us," he wrote. "I shall certainly not resent any criticisms that you may have."[29]

Although there was of course no shortage of criticisms, Croydon's overall response this time was much more positive. Foster had helped Powell draw up an excellent working budget. Croydon wrote, "I hope, therefore, that the Producer will continue his very close collaboration with us, so that as the picture comes together it will be possible to relate final arrangements with this budget. . . . The papers are certainly realistic, and do not in any way indulge in the blunders, indicative of lack of knowledge, which was prevalent in the first set of papers I considered."[30]

A mutual respect now existed between the two parties. Film Finances was impressed by the energy and time that Powell had put into mastering the budget and schedule, while Powell offered a generous acknowledgment of their help that more than compensated for his previous arrogance. Thanking them for the offer of a completion guarantee, he wrote on behalf of himself and Pressburger, "We would like to say how much we admire the thorough methods of your representatives, their sympathetic approach to technical problems, their wide knowledge of the film-business, and their personal interest in quality and personality. In the past we have often found that a so-called 'realistic

MICHAEL POWELL AND EMERIC PRESSBURGER
PRODUCTIONS LIMITED

CABLES: ARCHERS, LONDON

TELEGRAMS: ARCHERS, KENS, LONDON.

DIRECTORS { MICHAEL POWELL.
EMERIC PRESSBURGER.

Tel. Western 2516.

PLEASE REPLY TO :-

1, St. Mary Abbot's Place
London, W. 8.

Film Finances Limited,
34, South Molton Street,
London, W.1.

27th
September,
1954.

Dear Sirs,

"Oh - Rosalinda!!"

We are obliged to you for your favourable letter of
September 22nd and note the many detailed remarks you emphasize
regarding the production, which summarize our recent discussions
with you.

Perhaps you will allow me to comment in detail upon
some of your numbered remarks, while agreeing in principle with
them all.

No. 2: We presume that you only ask to know details
of Distribution Agreements when they affect the financing of the
production.

No. 5: I understand the undertaking that the salaries
etc. will not exceed in aggregate the sum allocated in the budget.
But I don't understand the reference 'should this amount be exceeded,
any such additional amount etc'. Forgive me. I thought that this
was what the Guarantee of Completion was for, should an excess on
this amount cause the total cost to go over budget. I am sure I
am being dumb. Please explain.

No. 8: We understand that it would be satisfactory
to study the set and costume designs before agreeing the final
budget, but who will pay for this? Because they would have to be
commissioned from Hein Heckroth. Once the budget is agreed and
preparation has started I quite understand the need for close
examination of the designs over the next two months or so while
the Design of the film is being prepared and executed.

/over

A characteristically enthusiastic letter from Michael Powell, 27 September 1954,
ending with an explanation of how the title of his new film should be pronounced.

Film Finances Limited   27th September, 1954

       No. 9: We are making a detailed scenario of the
8 - minute Overture Ballet. Here again, of course, Heckroth's
designs will be of importance.

       No. 20: We propose to take this up with the Board of
Trade now and would appreciate your advice in the matter.

       We would like to say how much we admire the thorough
methods of your representatives, their sympathetic approach to
technical problems, their wide knowledge of the film-business, and
their personal interest in quality and personality. In the past we
have often found that a so-called 'realistic approach' to schedule
and budget was depressing and deadening to the creators of the film:
your representatives' methods, on the contrary, stimulate and encourage
us.

       May I venture to mention our title. It is, as you
see above, "Oh - Rosalinda!!" not "Oh, Rosalinda", which is as if
one said 'Oh, Rosalinda, whip down the street and get a pound of
Stork, will you?' Our 'Oh - ' is meant to convey shock: the gentleman
has, as it were, instinctively covered his eyes, while still, of
course, peeking through his fingers. Then, his breath returning, he
ejaculates " - Rosalinda!!" giving every syllable full value, lingering
on the two last and topping the whole delightfully shocking experience
off with (please!) two exclamation marks, thus:

O H - R O S A L I N D A !!

            Yours sincerely,
          For and on behalf of:
   MICHAEL POWELL AND EMERIC PRESSBURGER PRODUCTIONS

Michael Powell

     MICHAEL POWELL

MP/DBW.

approach' to schedule and budget was depressing and deadening to the creators of the film: your representatives' methods, on the contrary, stimulate and
encourage us."[31]

Oh—Rosalinda!! went into production at the Associated-British studios in
Borehamwood on 24 January 1955 at a total budget of £276,328 ($773,718).
It may have been less than half the amount that the Rank Organisation
had expended on *The Red Shoes*, but Film Finances had taught Powell and
Pressburger how to make that money go much further. The last of the weekly
"summary of production costs," for the week ending 1 October 1955, shows
that the production was about £2,000 ($5,600) under the estimated cost. The
team went on routinely to rely on completion guaranties for the remainder
of their films, including *Battle of the River Plate* (1956), *Ill Met by Moonlight*
(1957), and, made without Pressburger, Michael Powell's *Peeping Tom* (1960).

As the 1950s drew to a close, Film Finances could look back on a decade in
which it had not only returned stability to the British film industry but also,
through its involvement in the revival of United Artists, contributed to a fundamental paradigm shift in Hollywood. Once United Artists had returned
to financial health and enjoyed the renewed confidence of the banks, it then
began to provide the independent producers whose films it distributed complete financing for their projects. Over the period from 1953 to 1957, when
United Artists was releasing an average of fifty films a year, the number of such
independently produced films rose from twenty a year to forty-seven.[32]

The other Hollywood majors soon followed United Artists' lead. The 1950s
was a decade of transformation in which, shorn of their theater chains, one
by one the Hollywood majors closed down their in-house production depart-
ments and cut the payroll of in-house talent, whether producers, directors,
or stars. Instead, they became effectively the backers of quasi-autonomous
production units, even if in practice those "independent" producers yielded
up the ownership of the projects they brought to the studios in return for 100
percent financing and a profit participation. In 1949, of the 234 films released
by the eight Hollywood majors, "independents" produced about 20 percent of
the total. Only eight years later, in 1957, the "independents" accounted for
58 percent of the 291 films that the majors released.[33]

The degree to which these "independents" lived up to their name was in
practice very limited, and the studios continued to exert immense control, but
it was an index of the degree to which independence had become everyone's
ideal.

METRO-GOLDWYN-MAYER
PRESENTS
A MODERN LOVE STORY!

ELIZABETH TAYLOR • RICHARD BURTON

LOUIS JOURDAN • ELSA MARTINELLI
MARGARET RUTHERFORD • MAGGIE SMITH
ROD TAYLOR AND ORSON WELLES IN

The V.I.P.s 'A'

In PANAVISION and METROCOLOR

CO-STARRING
LINDA CHRISTIAN • WRITTEN BY **TERENCE RATTIGAN** • DIRECTED BY **ANTHONY ASQUITH** • PRODUCED BY **ANATOLE DE GRUNWALD**

CHAPTER 2

SWINGING LONDON

The 1960s

Every year Bobby Garrett would give a speech in which he offered Film Finances' shareholders an overview of the company's fortunes. After he had considered the specific challenges and opportunities for Film Finances, he liked to step back and offer a few comments on the state of the film industry as a whole. A notable trend of the new decade was the way in which the industry was making fewer but more expensive pictures. If through the 1950s the company had on average been guaranteeing thirty pictures each year, the number had dropped in the 1960s to little more than twenty each year.

With the competing pull of television, the moviegoing public had become much more discriminating. "The first result of this was that receipts on a great number of films proved disastrous," Garrett observed.[1] As investment became confined to "fewer but more ambitious projects," the routine program picture of the past became an endangered species. To succeed in the cinema, every film had to seem in some way special.

The higher budgets that this more ambitious cinema required were beyond what British financiers were prepared to support. During the first half of the 1960s, loans from British banks for independent producers dried up, and the National Film Finance Corporation, which had been a mainstay of British production, became dormant. The situation became so serious that for a brief time in 1963 Film Finances concluded that without some radical reorganization of the industry, it would have to give up providing completion guaranties altogether. The only major distributor in Britain that continued to engage in financing on any substantial scale was the Rank Organisation, although it was extremely conservative in the projects it backed and often sought to share the cost with an American company.

This collapse of British finance during the 1960s might have made Film Finances' annual general meetings rather bleak affairs were it not for the other

FILM   FINANCES   L::ITED

STATEMENT OF TRADING

Year to 23rd Feb.	No.of Films	Fees Received	Rebates	N.C.B.	Net Fee	O/Hs	Balance	Claims	Recoveries
1951	14	53,644	-	800	52,844	25,000	27,844	(2) 22,846	12,446
1952	19	57,538	3,489	9,086	44,963	25,000	19,963	(2) 59,915	44,000
1953	37	132,203	19,017	13,696	99,490	25,000	74,490	(9)104,349	97,379
1954	35	102,926	11,886	10,438	80,602	25,000	55,602	(5) 59,061	24,589
1955	33	137,864	19,959	9,385	108,520	25,000	83,520	(6) 68,222	22,082
1956	31	131,548	10,970	7,510	113,068	25,000	88,068	(8)144,882	63,050
1957	33	136,423	7,510	21,938	106,975	25,000	81,975	(6) 90,015	7,519
1958	33	152,026	9,436	16,130	126,460	25,000	101,460	(9)157,726	42,016
1959	20	119,032	13,848	21,341	83,843	25,000	58,843	(3) 45,752	-
1960	33	190,820	10,102	31,655	149,063	25,000	124,063	(5) 37,500	1,585
1961	20	61,320	8,762	4,735	47,823	25,000	22,823	(5) 44,429	3,600 Possible 4,553
1962	21	141,555	-	31,628	109,927	25,000	84,927	(4)102,579	- Possible 58,400
	329	1,416,899	114,979	178,342	1,123,578	300,000	823,578	937,276	318,266 Possible 62,953

Chart indicating Film Finances' business record over the first twelve years of trading, 1950–62.

significant trend that Garrett often singled out in his speeches: the hugely increased presence of the American majors in British film production. At the annual general meeting of 1965, he offered the following rosy assessment:

> On the whole, the atmosphere is much more optimistic. A good film can take a considerable amount of money and this is encouraging worthwhile production. Although it is unlikely that the number of films which your Company will be asked to guarantee in the years to come will ever be on quite the same scale as it was some years ago, nevertheless, the individual cost of such films, and in consequence the premiums receivable, will be on the average much higher. At the same time, with enlarged experience, we can look forward to better planning and furthermore, that if films should exceed their budget, the prospect of their recovery should be higher than hitherto.[2]

One reason why Hollywood was turning to Britain and Europe in the 1960s was its realization that it had lost touch with its audience. Many of the movie

9th November, 1962.

M. Silverstein, Esq.,
Metro-Goldwyn-Mayer Pictures Ltd.

Dear Mr. Silverstein,

    Mr. Maurice Foster has told me that you would like to have
a letter from us with regard to our capacity to undertake a
guarantee of completion on "VERY IMPORTANT PERSONS" which we
appreciate has a budget of $3,000,000.

    It is not our practice as a private company to issue the
Accounts of this or its associated companies. I think the best
thing I can do is to point to our record. We have been in
existence for twelve years, during which time we have given
guarantees of completion in respect of 350 films whose budgets
in aggregate have amounted to over £45,000,000 and in no case
have we failed to deliver. At the same time in the course of
fulfilling our guarantees we have had to make advances in excess
of £1,000,000 which figure I think speaks for itself. Your
company has, of course, records of those films in which we have
invested, which include in recent years "Action of the Tiger",
"Tom Thumb" and "Swordsman of Siena".

    I would point out what you probably already appreciate
and that is that the prime purpose of a guarantor is to provide
overcosts on a picture and that the liability of repayment in
the event of non-delivery is a very remote contingency and one which
in practice is largely covered by the various insurances effected.
We appreciate however that large scale pictures are capable of
having proportionately large overcosts and I can assure you,
therefore, that we approach such pictures with a good deal of
caution.

    In the case of "VERY IMPORTANT PERSONS" I would not be frank
with you if I did not say that we would not consider this a good
risk from our point of view were it not for the fact that 1) it
is an all-studio picture and, 2) that you yourselves are providing
if needs be, a first loss cushion of $300,000 (for which however
we halve our fee). Under these circumstances however we regard

/2.

Letter from Bobby Garrett, 9 November 1962, in which he explains to the president
of MGM International, Maurice "Red" Silverstein, why MGM can depend on Film
Finances' guarantee for *The V.I.P.s* (1963). It starred Elizabeth Taylor, the first woman
ever to earn $1 million for appearing in a movie.

moguls from Hollywood's golden age were still in charge. They green-lit old-
fashioned movies that took little account of the massive changes in popular
culture that the decade was ushering in. Movies such as *My Fair Lady* (1964),
Mary Poppins (1964), and *The Sound of Music* (1965) commanded massive family audiences, but they took little account of a younger, more sophisticated
filmgoing public that had come of age. While in Hollywood a long-established
group of filmmakers continued to make movies much in the same way as they
had over the previous two decades, in Europe a new generation had come to

the fore, making films that reflected back to audiences their own contemporary world, with a spontaneity of style and a readiness to challenge the stale
conventions of the past.

When a young Robert Evans started out as an executive at Paramount in the
mid-1960s, he was sent to London as head of European production. "That's
where the action is," he was told. "Writers, actors, directors. It's fresh, not stale
like Hollywood."[3] The producer and star of *Bonnie and Clyde* (1967), Warren
Beatty, who would make the key breakthrough in Hollywood's belated efforts
to become relevant again, recalled the attitude of a more discerning American
audience that had emerged during the 1960s: "The movies that were really
attracting the attention of people who were kind of smart were those of the
Nouvelle Vague and the neo-realists and all those guys in Woodfall."[4]

The "guys in Woodfall" were director Tony Richardson and playwright John
Osborne. In collaboration with Canadian producer Harry Saltzman, they had
formed independent production company Woodfall to exploit the success of
Osborne's landmark play *Look Back in Anger*, which Richardson had staged at
London's Royal Court Theatre in 1956. As principal figures of what the British
press had labeled the "Angry Young Man" generation, they aimed to carry its
spirit of creative renewal into the cinema.

After filming adaptations of *Look Back in Anger* and Osborne's follow-up
play at the Royal Court, *The Entertainer*, Woodfall achieved a major commercial breakthrough in 1960 with its production of the film *Saturday Night and
Sunday Morning*. Other British production companies soon joined Woodfall
in creating a "New Wave" of realist films that sought to hold up a mirror to
contemporary life.

Behind the scenes, facilitating this rejuvenation in the British cinema, was
Film Finances. Its completion guarantee underpinned the financing of a remarkable roll call of films, including many of the most influential of the period—
Room at the Top (1959), *A Taste of Honey* (1961), *A Kind of Loving* (1962), *Billy Liar*
(1963), *The Servant* (1963), *Darling* (1965), and so on. In addition to providing
the essential guarantee, it also operated as a de facto school for filmmakers,
making available its production expertise to the often inexperienced filmmakers who produced and directed these films.

In his memoirs, Tony Richardson described *The Entertainer* (1960), starring Sir Laurence Olivier, as a key moment in his development "because all the
ideas and convictions I was to work with afterwards were crystallized in its
making."[5] He was determined that the film should be made on location to

Julie Christie, who won the
Best Actress Oscar for her
performance in *Darling* (1965).

the extent possible. He disliked studios because, as he put it, "their artificial conditions produced artificiality in acting and image."[6]

Helping him put his taste for realism into practice was John Croydon, who joined the production as an associate producer but also acted as an impromptu location manager (the film's producer Harry Saltzman having neglected to hire one).

Richardson chose to shoot the film in the Lancashire town of Morecambe, where his parents lived. "We haven't a word that doesn't need post-synch," reported Croydon, "mainly because of the location sites we use."[7] But he knew who in the Shepperton sound department could best help Richardson achieve the semblance of natural sound that he wanted. In this way, he reconciled the gulf between innocence and experience.

"In his disobedience of film convention," Croydon observed afterward, "I found on *The Entertainer* that the technicians seem to admire his work and his personality and consequently came to the rescue time after time."[8] When Woodfall sought a completion guarantee for *A Taste of Honey*, Croydon had no hesitation in supporting Richardson's insistence on shooting the film entirely on location. He wrote to Garrett,

Director Tony Richardson (*right*) talks with actors Rita Tushingham and Paul
Danquah during the production of *A Taste of Honey* (1961).

My experience of him tells me that Richardson is a hard worker with a basic
sense of responsibility, and provided he has someone who is prepared to jog his
elbow from time to time over this sense of responsibility, a man who takes considerable care, curiously enough, not to damage the conventions any more than
he has to. I think one has to remember that he comes from a Lancashire family
where a spade is called a spade and is an instrument with which to dig! I think

that once he has determined on a course of action he will stick to it and so far as film production is concerned, once he has determined his plan he will follow it through, and it is up to his executive people to make sure that the plan is feasible and lies within the available money before the production commences.[9]

The newly revitalized industrial framework of the British cinema, with its shift of initiative to small, independent production units, was much more able than Hollywood to be responsive to a society in the throes of change. Not directly answerable to monolithic corporations, nor so hampered by the self-censorship of a blatantly out-of-date Motion Picture Production Code, independent producers in Britain benefited from an organic relationship to the zeitgeist of a postwar world that was going through a revolution in popular music, fashion, and art as well as social values more generally.

Hollywood's way of catching up was to buy the vitality that it struggled to generate spontaneously. Still remembering the last time the film industry went bust, British financiers were too cost-conscious to be able to offer much resistance. When Woodfall made *The Entertainer*, the financing of the film was secured only on the basis that the producers—and even the star of the film, Sir Laurence Olivier—defer their salaries. The commercial success of *Saturday Night and Sunday Morning* did little to change the atmosphere of parsimony. While Woodfall's chief British backer Bryanston had been prepared to approve the modest budgets of such realist, contemporary films as *Saturday Night and Sunday Morning*, *A Taste of Honey*, and *The Loneliness of the Long Distance Runner* (1962), it did not agree to the much higher budget that Woodfall needed to make the period film *Tom Jones* (1963). So Woodfall turned to United Artists instead.

Although United Artists took the precaution of asking Film Finances to guarantee the budget of more than £400,000 ($1.3 million), a new psychology quickly became apparent as Woodfall, departing from the agreed production plan that had been the basis of Film Finances' guarantee, made the most of the opportunity to film on the more lavish scale that the resources of a major Hollywood company made possible. Closely following the production, which was shot on location in the West Country, Bobby Garrett wrote to the line producer Michael Holden to express his concerns.

While observing that "Tony Richardson should be congratulated on some extraordinarily fine material," Garrett questioned the shooting of a hunt sequence that had been scheduled for two days but had been expanded so far beyond two days even to include the use of a helicopter for two weeks that

Albert Finney waits patiently to be "hanged" while cinematographer Walter Lassally checks the light during the production of *Tom Jones* (1963).

had not been envisaged in the original proposition. "All of this would be fine if in fact the picture in other respects was reasonably on schedule."[10]

Garrett sent a copy of the letter to the head of United Artists' British office, George Ornstein, with this accompanying note:

> We have hitherto found Woodfall a most business-like concern and Tony Richardson one of those directors who knows what he is doing and what he can do. He is also a director who is capable, like most really good directors, of compromising when needs be. I am wondering, and I hope I am wrong in this, if there may not be a slight tendency on this occasion, now they are connected with a big company operating on the scale that UA do, rather than with a minor British company such as Bryanston, that they may be getting the sort of feeling (which you and I have noticed among certain other producers) that cost does not matter very much any more. I may be maligning him in this, but I thought it might be worth passing the observation on to you.[11]

THIS AGREEMENT is made the _16th_ day of _July_ One
thousand nine hundred and sixty-two BETWEEN   WOODFALL FILM
PRODUCTIONS LIMITED   whose registered office is at 23 Albemarle
Street London W.1. (hereinafter called "the Producer" which
expression shall include where the context admits its successors
assigns and licensees) of the one part and ALBERT FINNEY   care of
MCA (England) Limited of 139 Piccadilly London W.1. (hereinafter
called "the Artiste") of the other part
    NOW IT IS HEREBY AGREED   as follows:

1.   THE   Producer hereby engages the services of the Artiste and
the Artiste agrees to render his services as a film Artiste in
the manner hereinafter mentioned playing the part of "Tom Jones"
in a film provisionally entitled "TOM JONES" (hereinafter called
"the film")

2.   (a) THE   Artiste's engagement shall be deemed to have
commenced on the Fourteenth day of May One thousand nine hundred
and sixty-two and shall subject to the provisions for suspension
and determination hereinafter contained continue for a period
(hereinafter called "the said period") from such day as aforesaid
until the Producer notifies him that it relinquishes first call
upon his services or completes the shooting of his part in the
film (whichever is earlier) and thereafter subject to the prior
professional commitments for extra scenes retakes post-synchronisa-
tion re-recording and the like

      (b) During the said period the Producer shall be exclusively
entitled to the Artiste's entire services

3.   (a) THE   Producer shall pay to the Artiste as inclusive
remuneration for all services to be rendered by him hereunder
the following sums:-

      (i) for the film a sum of Nine thousand pounds by equal
weekly instalments in respect of the first twenty weeks of the
said period and in respect of any weeks after the twenty weeks
of the said period and in days in any incomplete week thereafter
at pro rata weekly and daily rates of £450 and £75 respectively
together with sums at the same daily rate in respect of any
days after the said period upon which the Artiste renders services
at the Producer's request

      (ii) Sixteen and two-thirds per centum (16⅔%) of the total

Albert Finney's contract for *Tom Jones* (1963), showing that in addition to a salary of £9,000, he was entitled to "16⅔ percent of the total net profit of the film." On its first release in the United States alone, *Tom Jones* received $16 million in rentals.

The tone of careful understatement belonged to that of a man whose early career ambition, before he went into the film industry, was to be a diplomat. It is impossible to know for sure, but when Garrett wrote of "certain other producers," it is likely that he was thinking of another independent production that United Artists had asked Film Finances to guarantee at about the same time. The producers of the first James Bond film, *Dr. No*, Harry Saltzman and Albert "Cubby" Broccoli, were—in a similar fashion to Woodfall—spending on a scale beyond what the agreed budget had allowed.

In any case, Garrett's observation went to the nub of how, in financial terms, an independent film differed from a studio film. The only sustainable basis for genuinely independent production, where a producer could not count on the deep pockets of a corporation to pay for his second thoughts, was to respect a well-thought-out plan. Under a completion guarantee, any departures from such a plan should take place only in response to the unforeseen, or to the degree that the overall budget afforded the latitude. Film Finances existed to help filmmakers cut their coat according to their cloth, not to make a different coat.

If there was a tendency for Hollywood films to be much more expensive than independent films, it was not just a matter of the greater resources available to a studio but because the production framework was at the mercy of many more people who had the power to change their minds, although often not for the reasons that mattered most to the filmmakers themselves.

The underlying principle of the guarantee came into issue when *Tom Jones* began to go well over budget. Film Finances warned United Artists that it would have to exercise its right to take over the production of the film to bring costs back under control. United Artists agreed instead to make itself responsible for the overcosts, which had clearly resulted from a much more ambitious production plan than had originally been agreed.

As *Tom Jones* went on to become a big box office hit on its release in the United States, United Artists would have thought the extra expense (of approximately £100,000) more than justified. A genuinely groundbreaking film, it was an extraordinary hybrid that married the documentary realism of such earlier Woodfall films as *Saturday Night and Sunday Morning* and *A Taste of Honey* to the cinematic flair of the French New Wave. It was an adaptation of a classic eighteenth-century novel but made with a contemporary feel that anticipated the individualistic, newly permissive spirit of a society that was undergoing revolutionary change.

Whereas the film received a mixed critical reception on its opening in London, the US reviewers gave it a uniformly ecstatic reception. "They've brought *Tom Jones* to the screen in all its lusty brawling sprawling human comedy and given us one of the most delightful movies of recent years," declared Judith Crist in the *New York Herald Tribune*, while Bosley Crowther, in the *New York Times*, lauded "a wonderfully energetic and entertaining film" that was "as fast as a Keystone comedy and as loaded with cinema techniques and calculated stunts with the camera as the most arty film of the French New Wave."[12] His review went on to suggest the gauntlet that the film threw down to Hollywood: "The method of this achievement is going to be pondered and studied for a long time, and cinema students are going to marvel at the boldness of the method as much as the boldness of what is shown."[13] *Tom Jones* went on to win four Academy Awards, including Best Director and Best Picture. The Oscar for Best Foreign Language Film that year went to Federico Fellini's *8½*. The emcee for the presentation ceremony, Jack Lemmon, wound up the evening with the comment "When in Hollywood, do as the British and the Romans do." But in practice it was easier for Hollywood to go to Europe, where it could find not only the talent that was winning new audiences to the cinema but also a resurgent culture that was making these places exciting in themselves.

With the weight of a phenomenally successful franchise to keep it in the memory of subsequent generations, *Dr. No* is today a far better-known film than *Tom Jones*, but in 1961, when United Artists concluded a financing agreement with British-based producers Harry Saltzman and Cubby Broccoli to adapt a series of films "based upon the so-called James Bond Stories," it must have seemed a very speculative venture.[14] The future of the original agreement depended on the box office performance of the first film that the producers put into production, which was in the nature of a prototype. United Artists would exercise its option to make the next film in the agreement only if the prototype turned out to be a success.

United Artists proceeded with considerable caution. The distribution agreement gave it approval of director, principal artists, script, budget, and production schedule. Advancing a budget of approximately £320,000 ($1 million)—large for a British production but modest by Hollywood standards—it stipulated that the film should count among the quota of British films that government legislation required it to distribute in British cinemas but also that it should qualify for a British production subsidy. The underlying rationale of the agreement was to provide a framework for the economic, cost-effective development of a new product that had yet to be tested in the market.

The completion guarantee from Film Finances gave United Artists the certainty that the film would be made for a fixed cost according to the terms of the distribution contract, but it also provided the means of efficient control and supervision, as Film Finances was able to bring to bear its accumulated experience of local filmmaking conditions.

Film Finances already knew the principal personalities extremely well. It was familiar with Harry Saltzman through Woodfall, which Saltzman had left only after the completion of *Saturday Night and Sunday Morning*. Indeed, it was this film's success that had enabled him to buy the rights to the Ian Fleming novels. Before Woodfall, Film Finances had guaranteed the very first feature film that Saltzman had made after coming to Britain, a 1956 Bob Hope comedy called *The Iron Petticoat*, and even before that a TV series that he had produced in Italy called *Captain Gallant of the Foreign Legion* (1955–57).

Film Finances' connection with Cubby Broccoli went back to the earliest years of the company. In 1951, Broccoli had set up the British-based Warwick Pictures with fellow American Irving Allen. Following the success of its first film, *The Red Beret* (1953), starring Alan Ladd, Warwick went on to produce a series of films with Hollywood stars but made in England that were distributed by Columbia. Nearly all of them had been guaranteed by Film Finances, and many of them had involved overcosts.

If Film Finances must have had some sense of dealing with "the usual suspects," as it evaluated the first proposition of Saltzman and Broccoli's new company, Eon Productions, that sense can only have been strengthened by their choice of director. Terence Young had built up a reputation for exceeding his budget on several pictures he had directed for Warwick, as well as many other pictures that Film Finances had guaranteed besides.

Offering an overview in his report on *Dr. No* (1962), John Croydon commented, "I had liked the script and the look of the papers until I heard that Terence Young was to be the director!" He went on, "I believe that under normal conditions the schedule could be accepted; that a certain amount of under-budgeting is present, but would not take too much to rectify, but I must confess to alarm at the combination of Broccoli, Saltzman and Young in charge of the picture."[15]

Film Finances went on to secure a slight upward adjustment of the budget and further protected itself by insisting that Terence Young defer his salary, but the "combination," pressing to extract the maximum out of an adequate but still tight budget, led to significant overcosts that caused Film Finances to make the rare decision of taking over the film to ensure due economy on the postproduction phase of the picture.

Film Finances quickly recouped its investment of £59,000 ($165,200) from the box office receipts of the film, which achieved a worldwide gross of $6 million. The prototype had clearly paid off, but it gave little indication of the scale of success that the subsequent movies, repeating the formula, would soon go on to achieve. Produced on a budget of $2 million, *From Russia with Love* (1963) grossed $12.5 million worldwide, while *Goldfinger* (1964), on a budget of $3 million, grossed $46 million.

Although the original financing agreement had anticipated that Film Finances would go on to guarantee the other films in the series, the box office success of

CABLE ADDRESS·ALLEN FILMS

Warwick Film Productions, Inc.
RKO Studios⬛⬛⬛⬛⬛⬛⬛⬛⬛⬛⬛⬛⬛⬛⬛ 780 No. Gower
HOLLYWOOD 38, CALIFORNIA
HOLLYWOOD ⬛⬛⬛⬛ 9-5911

May 14; 1952

Peter Hope, Esq.
FILM FINANCES LTD.
34 South Moulton Street
London W. I., England

My dear Peter:

Irving Allen, who is producing "THE RED BERET" for RKO, is coming over to England within the next few days and will be getting in touch with you.

The film is being financed 100% by RKO but they will nevertheless require an English guarantee of completion, which I hope you will be able to provide.

I shall be over myself in about a fortnight's time, as we are still at work here polishing up the script. In the meantime, give my love to Bob Garrett, and look after yourself.

Sincerely,

TERENCE YOUNG

TY:pw

Letter from director Terence Young introducing Warwick Film Productions to Film Finances, 14 May 1952. Young made the introduction when the American company, wishing to take advantage of British production incentives, decided to make *The Red Beret* (1953) in England.

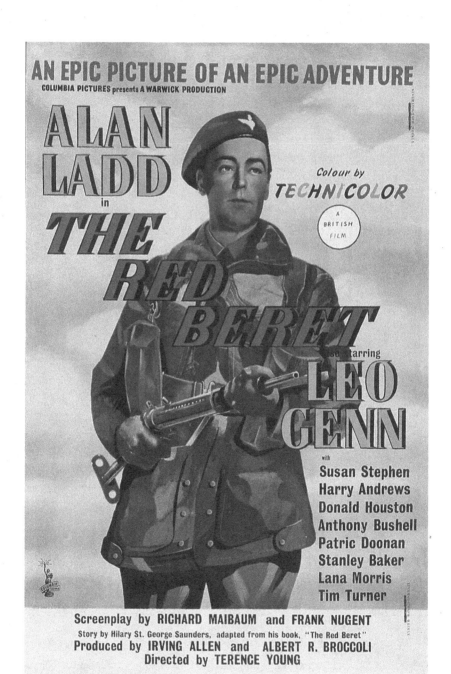

Poster for James Bond film producer Albert "Cubby" Broccoli's first British production, *The Red Beret* (1953).

Dr. No meant that United Artists was prepared to dispense with the security of the guarantee as it invested ever greater sums of money in the subsequent films. Once the blueprint for a clearly profitable commodity had been established, the guarantee was no longer such an essential tool.

When Harry Saltzman set up a new company, Lowndes Productions, in 1964 to introduce to the screen a downbeat, deglamorized Bond in the form of Michael Caine as Harry Palmer, the venture was in the nature of a prototype once again. Bank of America advanced the £309,000 ($865,200) budget on the strength of distribution contracts from Rank Film Distributors and Universal but, lacking any reliable index of the film's future commercial prospects, required a completion guarantee from Film Finances.

It was Film Finances' accumulated expertise and knowledge of the key personalities that made it best placed to manage the uncertainties of production. Among its archived papers for *The Ipcress File* (1965) can be found a rough sheet of foolscap summarizing the principal elements of risk.[16] Underneath the name "Harry Saltzman" were listed the Bond films *Dr. No*, *From Russia with Love*, and *Goldfinger*, with the information that they had all gone over budget. Then came the name of the director, Sidney Furie. His previous three films were *The Young Ones* (1961), *The Leather Boys* (1964), and *Wonderful Life* (1964), of which only the last had gone over budget. Named too were the principal actors Michael Caine and Nigel Green. "As far as known their record is good," the summary said, although it went on to note, "None have yet worked together."

Film Finances made it a condition of the guarantee that "an Administrative Producer of a certain standing" be appointed to the production.[17] "This picture is one which will require a great deal of on the spot practical management from the producer," Bobby Garrett confided in a company memorandum, "which we do not think Harry has either time or, for that matter, the temperament to give it—I need say no more."

Garrett took care to keep close track of progress to the very end. "My dear Harry," he wrote as the film approached the end of its shooting schedule, "Rumour—that often lying jade—has it that although main shooting has finished on the film you may still need to shoot some additional scenes. I appreciate you have a certain amount of money in hand, but I would be glad if you would get in touch with us before anything further is done."[18]

Completed within budget, *The Ipcress File* turned out to be another successful prototype. Michael Caine went on to appear in two Harry Palmer sequels, *Funeral in Berlin* (1966) and *Billion Dollar Brain* (1967), neither of which

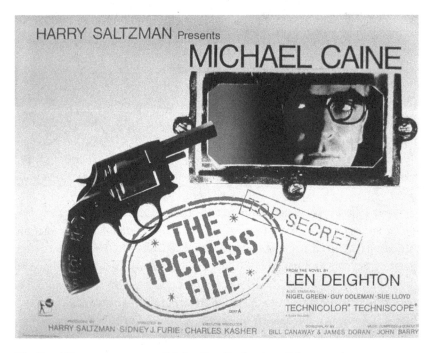

The Bond films were so successful that Eon Productions did not need to return to Film Finances for a completion guarantee. But when Harry Saltzman wanted to make *The Ipcress File* (1965), a guarantee was a necessary condition of the picture's financing.

required guaranties from Film Finances, but also many other iconic movies (including *Zulu* [1964], which Film Finances did guarantee) that established him as one of the most significant new box office stars of the 1960s.

Tom Jones's triumph at the 1964 Oscars ceremony marked the moment at which Hollywood as a whole could see that the social and cultural transformation of contemporary Britain was itself a great subject for the movies. Only a week before the ceremony, the Beatles had achieved the astonishing feat of holding the top five positions in the Billboard Hot 100. Just as British pop music seemed to be conquering America, it looked as though British movies were beginning to do so too.

United Artists made the most of its head start. At the beginning of March 1964, after the Beatles got back from their first tour of America, they began to shoot *A Hard Day's Night*, the first of three movies that they had signed up to make for the company. But Beatlemania was only a small part of the much

Film producer Harry
Saltzman, mid-1960s.

Michael Caine (*right*) and Stanley Baker in *Zulu* (1964). Film Finances guaranteed
Baker's production of the film for independent producer Joe Levine's Embassy
Pictures.

larger revolution that was turning Britain into an international showcase. Two years later, in April 1966, *Time* magazine dubbed London the "city of the decade." A cover feature on the city coined an irresistible new nickname: "Youth is the word—and the deed. . . . The London that has emerged is swinging." The piece captured this newly swinging London at its pinnacle, providing the basis for countless treatments: "This spring, as never before in modern times, London is switched on. Ancient elegance and new opulence are all tangled up in a dazzling blur of op and pop. The city is alive with birds (girls) and Beatles, buzzing with minicars and telly stars, pulsing with half a dozen separate veins of excitement. The guards now change at Buckingham Palace to a Lennon and McCartney tune, and Prince Charles is firmly in the long-hair set."[19]

The other Hollywood studios lost no time in coming to London, where they were able to take advantage of a pool of fresh talent and lower production costs. Out of their readiness to harness the spontaneity that was already there emerged some of the most well-known movies of the decade—*Blow-Up* (1966), *Far from the Madding Crowd* (1967), *2001: A Space Odyssey* (1968), *Oliver!* (1968), *If. . . .* (1968), *The Italian Job* (1969), and so on. But as evident were the efforts of Hollywood executives to repeat a successful formula.

Within months of the success of *Tom Jones* at the 1964 Academy Awards, Paramount recruited *Dr. No* director Terence Young and producer Marcel Hellman to make *The Amorous Adventures of Moll Flanders* (1965). The concern seemed not to attempt to be original but, on the contrary, to flaunt all the elements that had made its model a success. Consciously aping the style of *Tom Jones* to appeal to the huge audiences that flocked to that film, it turned out to be an undistinguished, quickly forgotten production even although Paramount had committed twice as much as the *Tom Jones* cost to its budget.

The imperative for Hollywood was to embrace the genuinely new, which required deferring to the taste of a younger generation. Robert Evans's description in his memoirs of being sent to Britain as a young studio executive to run Paramount's London office captures well the nature of the revolution: "Paramount's executives in London were overage, overpaid, and over-British. To my face they bowed, to my back they laughed. Within a month, I fired half of them. The others knew their days were numbered. I was too new at the game to be sure of what I wanted. But I knew what I didn't want—which was everything my Dark Age compatriots were excited to see get to the screen."[20] While "one of the old guard's pet projects" was the $6 million musical *Half a Sixpence*, Evans admired a much less expensive picture set against the background of contemporary London: "Paramount had released, almost by mistake, a beautifully written 'little' picture called *Alfie*, starring an unknown Cockney actor named Michael Caine. So what if *Alfie* cost less than John Wayne's asking price and captured the imagination of the world."[21]

Whichever way around such Hollywood-backed movies came into being, whether it was a producer approaching a studio with an idea or the studio taking a property it already owned to a producer, Film Finances played a central role as the studios relied on its detailed knowledge of the British film industry to provide the supervision and control that they struggled to provide themselves.

A familiar experience for Bobby Garrett during the 1960s was to explain to a newly arrived Hollywood executive how the completion guarantee worked. In August 1964, over a "delightful lunch," Garrett chatted to Paramount's head of British production Howard Harrison about *The Amorous Adventures of Moll Flanders*, which Paramount had put into production that summer without a guarantee. Using it as an example to illustrate the way in which Film Finances' involvement could help encourage disciplined, cost-effective production, Garrett stressed that it was "important psychologically with regard to the producer, and in order to make it possible for us to keep control of things and if needs be play the heavy, that any private arrangements between Paramount and ourselves in respect to finance should not be known to the producer."[22] This was the *Tom Jones* lesson. The perception of British producers that Hollywood had deep pockets had to be discouraged.

The retreat of British financing was a familiar backdrop to these meetings. The following year, Garrett wrote to Elmo Williams of 20th Century-Fox concerning the comedy thriller *Modesty Blaise* (1966), which 20th Century-Fox had picked up from British Lion. "We had arranged originally to give a guarantee of completion in respect of this film, and I hope that now it has come to your company that we shall be able to offer you the same service."[23] Although in the end Film Finances did not guarantee *Modesty Blaise*, it went on to guarantee many of the British-made 20th Century-Fox films that followed.

In January 1966, Jay Kanter arrived in London as head of European production for Universal. His specific reason for contacting Garrett was to inquire about the possibility of Film Finances guaranteeing *Fahrenheit 451*, which François Truffaut was about to begin shooting at Pinewood, but it was an occasion to discuss the giving of guaranties more generally.

Garrett offered Kanter the following overview of the basic procedure:

When we are approached with regard to a guarantee we naturally assume that the distributor is requiring one in good faith and in our financial planning we notionally pencil this in as a risk which might arise within the next six months. When we have received the production papers, these are independently examined by three people and, of course, at the same time our lawyers look into the various legal documents. As soon as we have examined the papers we like to meet the Producer, Director, and possibly the Associate Producer, and other senior technicians and put to them any criticisms we have, and at the same time have an opportunity of learning from them how various things are to be done (which of course are not always clear from the actual papers themselves). In many cases, as a result of this meeting, we are able to accept the proposition as it stands, but in some others we find that there are certain deficiencies. . . . In addition to giving guaranties of completion, in view of our close touch with the industry here we are frequently able to give useful advice as to costs, personnel, etc to producers, particularly those who may be making their first picture in this country.[24]

Garrett repeated the tutorial the following month when Gerry Blattner of Warner Bros. asked to be "put in the picture with regard to our standard arrangements."[25] By the end of that year, most of the Hollywood majors were relying on Film Finances to guarantee their British-made movies.

During the 1960s, Film Finances tended to guarantee midrange budgets—in Hollywood terms, up to about $3–$4 million. But as long as sufficient adjustment was made in the spread of risk, Film Finances was prepared to consider some of the biggest movies of the day. Few came bigger than *The Battle of Britain* (1969), which producers Harry Saltzman and Benjamin Fisz (best known for producing *The Heroes of Telemark*) brought to Film Finances in 1966 as a project they then hoped to make for Paramount—it would eventually be financed by United Artists.

An internal memorandum of notes on the production, dated 9 September 1966, singled out the producers as the greatest element of risk, because "our experience with Producers dealing with the major companies without intervention of a 3rd party, i.e. a guarantor, is that they tend to regard their budget as a sort of piece of paper to which in the long run they need pay very little attention."[26] It required only a cursory look at how the studios handled their own productions to understand why producers might take this view.

At about the same time that Film Finances was considering whether to guarantee *The Battle of Britain*, the 20th Century-Fox production of *Doctor Dolittle* (1967)—in which Rex Harrison, the Oscar-winning star of *My Fair Lady* (1964), was playing the title role—had abandoned location shooting in

"BATTLE OF BRITAIN"

1.   This proposition by virtue of its size, of its budget,
its nature and the personalities involved is we feel somewhat out of our class.

2.   We think, however, we could look at it and play a useful
part in controlling the Producers if:-

    a) A substantial first loss was provided by Paramount
       (after we had officially approved the basic budget
       as adequate).

    b) For this, we would be prepared to give back a
       substantial part of our fee, but if it was to be
       efficacious, it would be essential that such an
       arrangement was a purely divided one between
       Paramount and ourselves.

       Our experience with Producers dealing with the
       major companies without intervention of a 3rd party,
       i.e. a guarantor, is that they tend to regard their
       budget as a sort of piece of paper to which in the
       long run they need pay very little attention.

    c) We would favour in the case of the two Producers
       concerned to have their salaries put in escrow.

    d) As a further deterrent, we feel that we should
       apply a penalty clause roughly on the following
       lines: for each 1% by which the final cost exceeds
       the budget plus the guarantee fee, 1% will be deducted
       from the Producers' share of profits.   On paper this
       1% would go to ourselves, but we would suggest that
       in fact the division was on the basis of 80-20 Paramount
       and ourselves.

    e) We feel again having regard to the character of the
       two Producers that the Production should have on it an
       Associate Producer of sufficient strength to, if needs
       be, take over.   In this regard we have in mind Aubrey
       Baring, who apart from his own experience in films is
       also qualified in so far as he fought in the Battle of
       Britain.

The producer Film Finances had in mind to recommend for *The Battle of Britain*
had actually fought in the Battle of Britain.

England after falling weeks behind schedule. Expensive new sets had to be built on the studio's soundstages in Hollywood. When Fox first announced the production in 1964, it anticipated a budget of $6 million, which was a hefty enough sum for the time. But as the studio sought a road show movie that could match its own blockbuster success with *The Sound of Music*, its swelling ambitions for *Doctor Dolittle* created an atmosphere in which the budget spiraled ever upward. "Since this is the most expensive project on our entire program," insisted studio boss Darryl F. Zanuck, "we have got to be positive that the final script will be a masterpiece."[27]

In pursuit of that masterpiece, the studio slid into rolling increases in the budget rather than observe the fixed, underlying plan that a completion guarantee would have required. A $6 million movie eventually became an $18 million movie, but without the desired "masterpiece" ever seeming to come any closer. As the costs escalated, composer Leslie Bricusse penned a spoof song for the producer Arthur Jacobs to be sung to the tune of *The Sound of Music*'s "Sixteen Going on Seventeen." The first verse began, "The budget's sixteen, / Going on seventeen . . ." and the final verse ended: "Now it's nineteen going on twenty / Please will you sign those checks? / Though this film is costing us plenty / Most of it goes to Rex . . ."[28] But *Doctor Dolittle* was only typical of a general tendency among the major studios, which all had plenty of their own examples of films that had veered wildly away from their original production plans as executives gave the nod to any new suggestions that might have seemed to increase the chances of box office success.

The lesson that Film Finances was able to teach the studios during the 1960s was that a disciplined, well-planned production within the framework of a realistic budget was far more likely to release the creativity that led to masterpieces than restrict it.

This lesson was true for all kinds of production. Even the rise of the cult of the *auteur* in the 1960s posed challenges only to the extent that it occasionally encouraged the temptation—as John Croydon would have put it—to "seek perfection regardless of cost." A notorious example was the Italian director Michelangelo Antonioni. Through its Italian subsidiary, the Società Finanziaria Garanzie e Controlli, Film Finances provided a guarantee for *Red Desert*, which went massively over budget when Antonioni decided to stop shooting for five weeks while he waited—in Italy—for the fog, mist, and rain that he considered essential for the look of the movie. "Whatever other lessons one could learn from this," Garrett wrote to Film Finances' Italian representative

Alessandro Tasca, "it is quite clear that one should not give a guarantee for a picture on which the director is in a position to override or pay no attention to his producer."[29]

It was perhaps unsurprising that when Antonioni came to England to make *Blow-Up* (1966), his producer Carlo Ponti did not approach Film Finances for a completion guarantee, nor that this movie, too, should have gone considerably over budget.

The huge influx of investment from Hollywood transformed Film Finances' fortunes. Accustomed to working quietly behind the scenes, Film Finances preferred to shun the limelight, but some indication of the buoyant confidence that it had achieved became apparent on 14 November 1967, when it threw a party for the film industry at the Dorchester Hotel in London to celebrate the signing of the five hundredth film it had guaranteed—*Isadora*, produced by Robert and Raymond Hakim for Universal, and directed by Karel Reisz.

The director of the National Film Finance Corporation, John Terry, gave a speech to express the industry's gratitude to a company that, often going far

Vanessa Redgrave and director Karel Reisz during the making of *Isadora* (1968), Film Finances' five hundredth guaranteed film.

beyond the call of duty, had become "guide, philosopher and friend" to many people present. The job of completion guarantor was "so extraordinarily risky," he quipped, that he was amazed the company had survived to put on a lunch like it did.[30]

"As a barometer of production I would imagine that a company like Film Finances Limited must be a pretty sure guide to what's going on," commented the "Observer" column of the trade magazine *Daily Cinema*.[31] Film Finances' director Peter Hope told the magazine that the company was issuing more guaranties than at any point in its history, and these usually for the much bigger-budget movies that the Hollywood studios were financing. Among the clippings in Film Finances' publicity file from the press coverage of the occasion was an article in the *Financial Times* that described the healthy state of the industry. "Film studios enjoy a boom—thanks to American money," ran the headline. All of Britain's film studios were booked up for months in advance. According to the *Financial Times*, "The conclusion is inescapable: the British film industry is bursting at the seams."[32]

The announcement only a few days later by British prime minister Harold Wilson, on Saturday, 18 November 1967, that Britain was devaluing the pound from $2.80 to $2.40—a massive 14.3 percent—served only to encourage the bonanza, since now the Hollywood studios could make movies in Britain even more cheaply. The perceived potential profitability was such that the following spring, British merchant bank Gresham Trust acquired a 20 percent shareholding in Film Finances and nominated a director to the board. The great prize that everyone had their eyes on was a flotation on the London Stock Exchange. Until recently an obvious obstacle was the abysmal past record of the film industry in Britain, with countless bankruptcies through its history that had lost the City huge fortunes. It meant that, prior to the recent upturn, no sane person would have invested in it. But the scale of American funding was such an unprecedented departure that it led Peter Hope to argue that the earlier history could be safely ignored: "The position has so radically altered in the film industry that it is to the future one must look in this particular business rather than to the past."[33] Gresham Trust's nominee on the board, G. D. Dean, advised caution. "The record of profits leading up to the time of flotation is of paramount importance," he wrote to Bobby Garrett on 19 August 1969, "and in the case of Film Finances where the business would probably be unique amongst quoted companies the quality of this record is particularly important."[34] He recommended that they put off a planned flotation for early 1970 to the following year, explaining, "By delaying it until 1971 I would expect that we would be able to establish a higher P/E [price-earnings] ratio and a better result."

But by early 1970, the landscape had completely changed. Hollywood was going through its biggest financial crisis since the end of World War II. As a result, the studios cut back sharply on their overseas production, drastically slimming down their British programs. When in April 1970 MGM announced its British studio at Borehamwood was closing since it was "no longer viable," it neatly symbolized the ending of an era.[35]

A snapshot of this turning point in Hollywood's fortunes can be found in another article from Film Finances' press clippings file, this one from the London *Times*, dated 31 March 1970:

> Gazing bleakly out over a decaying studio lot cluttered with the relics of past epics, the veteran movie executive heaved a deep sigh and muttered something about a ghost town.
>
> This is Hollywood, 1970, the dream factory where five of the seven major film companies lost a total of something like $150m last year. The movie capital of the world, where only one of every six films distributed in the United States is now made and where "for sale" signs are going up on the great studios.

The financial crisis was only part of the story. Accompanying the article was a still from *Easy Rider* (1969), an independently financed picture made for less than $500,000 that had grossed $60 million for Columbia. Having broken free from the censorship restrictions of the Production Code, Hollywood was beginning to discover that it no longer needed to leave America to find the more realistic, adult stories that appealed to the younger audience. If Hollywood had previously come to Britain to find its filmmaking talent, now the filmmaking talent was going to Hollywood. A topical example of this new kind of career trajectory, with which Film Finances would have been very familiar, was the director John Schlesinger.

Schlesinger had started out in Britain directing three movies for the independent producer Jo Janni, which Film Finances had guaranteed: *A Kind of Loving*, *Billy Liar*, and *Darling*. Then, after making *Far from the Madding Crowd* for MGM in Britain, he moved to America to direct *Midnight Cowboy* (1969). Winning not only the Best Director Oscar for Schlesinger but also the Academy Award for Best Picture at the ceremony on 7 April 1970, the film offered a signpost to a future in which Film Finances would no longer be able to count on British-made, Hollywood-financed movies for its livelihood. The

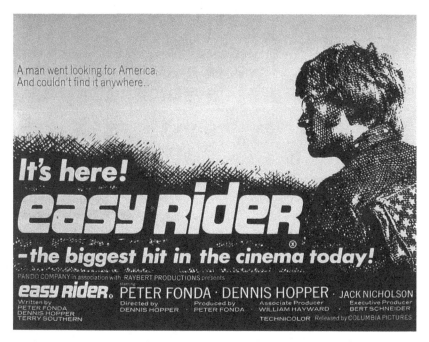

Easy Rider (1969) broke new ground in its financing as well as its subject matter and brought the spirit of independent filmmaking to Hollywood.

great worry was that in 1970 there was very little else to which Film Finances could turn. Completely homegrown projects had become a rarity. So it was perhaps no surprise if the flotation planned for 1971 never actually happened.

With hindsight, the handwriting had already been on the wall back in November 1967 even as Film Finances had invited a booming British film industry to share in its success at the Dorchester Hotel. The following month, *Time* magazine featured on its cover a Robert Rauschenberg collage based on *Bonnie and Clyde*, a film that continued to enjoy huge audiences after its release in Britain earlier that autumn.[36] It coined the phrase "New Hollywood," which would become as resonant a phrase for the approaching decade as "Swinging London" had been for the 1960s.

Jon Voight (*left*) and Dustin Hoffman in *Midnight Cowboy* (1969).

CHAPTER 3

GLOBAL EXPANSION

The 1970s

In the early 1970s, the American producer of *A Hard Day's Night* (1964), Walter Shenson, summed up the postboom mood of the British film industry. "It is a low-profile country now," he commented. "No longer any place for a film-maker to work. For an American, it is impossible to make a film reflecting the British scene, there just *is* no scene today. This place no longer makes news that is of interest to the world. When society is under stress or going through change, the outlines of what's happening are unfamiliar and exciting and the artists are under pressure to react to it all. When we are over-familiar with what has been happening, all that is left is a hangover."[1]

Not only had Hollywood become bored with Britain but even worse, it was losing money in Britain. A series of spectacular flops—which seemed to focus on anything but the "scene"—paved the way to the new decade: *Doctor Dolittle* (1967), *The Battle of Britain* (1969), *Alfred the Great* (1970) . . . As the Hollywood companies quickly ran down their investment in British production, Film Finances was forced to rethink the role it had played through the 1960s as Hollywood's British go-between.

Looking back at the post–World War II cinema in 1980, the *New York Times* film critic Vincent Canby wrote an article that puzzled over the elusive, frontier-defying nature of the cinema that meant that the focus of excitement always seemed to be slipping away elsewhere without easy explanation:

Why is it that some decades appear to be dominated by the films of one country instead of another? Are there particular conditions that suddenly propel one group of nationals to heights of creative activity while other groups languish? When they occur, are those conditions the same in each succeeding country?

Sometimes there are no answers, only questions.

The late 50s and early 60s were dominated by English film-makers like Tony Richardson (*Look Back in Anger, Tom Jones, A Taste of Honey*), Karel Reisz (*Saturday Night and Sunday Morning*), John Schlesinger (*Billy Liar, Darling*) and David Lean (*The Bridge on the River Kwai*). It was a time when Alec Guinness, Peter Sellers, and Terry-Thomas could not make a bad comedy if they tried. Vitality was apparent everywhere. It seemed unstoppable. Then suddenly it stopped. Why?[2]

Film Finances could congratulate itself on the fact that it had provided completion guaranties for five of the seven films Canby had mentioned. But to go forward in the 1970s meant looking beyond Britain, which had become a parochial backwater. Although the film industry in Britain was languishing, new industries were springing up elsewhere and filmmaking was becoming international to an unprecedented degree. For a completion guarantor, there were tremendous opportunities if only they could be seen.

At South Molton Street, the decade began with a timely injection of new blood. In 1971, one of the cofounders of Film Finances, Peter Hope, retired from the company. To fill the vacancy, the remaining cofounder, Bobby Garrett, turned to an Old Etonian, Richard Soames, who had previously worked at the Keith Prowse theater agency. It was, as Soames later recalled, a case of the British film industry's "league of gentlemen" stepping into action. Soames's close friend at Eton, Viscount Royston, was a friend of Bobby Garrett's stepson. When Royston learned that Garrett was looking for someone, he recommended Soames. "If they offer you a job, you should take it immediately," Soames remembered being told. "Bobby Garrett is a real gentleman and he still wears a bowler hat."[3]

But in this new decade, the sight of businessmen crossing Waterloo Bridge with their bowler hats and umbrellas was starting to seem old-fashioned. With the arrival of Richard Soames, who was more than twenty-five years Garrett's junior, a generation gap had opened up at Film Finances, which would become more apparent as Garrett hesitated to embrace the way in which an increasingly cosmopolitan industry was changing. "He was very insular," Soames recalled. "He would never have gone to Cannes in his whole life."[4] Garrett's conception of Film Finances was as a rather august, impartial arbiter that ventured out of its Mayfair retreat to intervene only when necessary. Soames recounted, "He said to me early on, 'You know, you shouldn't become friends with any of these film people, because they'll take advantage of you. We've got to stay away from them.' I thought, 'This is ridiculous! This is the industry we're in!'"[5]

Soames's first taste of Film Finances would have been of a company that was carrying on much as it had done through the 1960s. Hollywood may have been packing its bags, but it had never entirely left. As 1971 began, the two films that were taking up much of Film Finances' time were *Cabaret* and *Straw Dogs*. The production company behind both films, ABC Pictures—usually releasing through the Cinerama Releasing Corporation but in the case of *Cabaret*, through Allied Artists—operated as a quasi-major studio.

The films themselves were in one way typical of the New Hollywood Cinema, with its taste for realism and graphic depiction of sex and violence, but for Film Finances the setup was a familiar one. ABC Pictures, in tandem with the distributors, was providing 100 percent of the financing for both films. Its reason for a completion guarantee was the need to control and supervise, through Film Finances, two productions that not only were being made in Europe, far from its Los Angeles office, but also involved specific reasons why it was important to keep an eye on them.

The director of *Straw Dogs*, Sam Peckinpah, had a reputation for being difficult, and his last film, *The Ballad of Cable Hogue* (1970), had gone considerably over budget. *Cabaret* was produced by Cy Feuer. He was one half of the immensely influential Broadway team Feuer & Martin, who had staged some of Broadway's most successful musicals, but he had no previous experience of producing films. By contrast, Film Finances' accumulated production experience—unparalleled anywhere in the world—amounted now to the more than five hundred feature films it had supervised over its twenty-year history. It had even provided the completion guarantee to the film version of the play on which *Cabaret* was based, *I Am a Camera*—the first film production of the Christopher Isherwood Berlin stories, produced by Remus Films in 1954.

In analyzing the plans for *Cabaret*, Film Finances' consultant John Croydon would have been able, if he had wished, to look through the script and production papers of the earlier film, which included his own detailed report. Then, the Berlin streets and the other German sets had been built at the small Nettlefold studios in Walton-on-Thames, with only a small second unit dispatched to Berlin for a week to film background location footage. The challenge of the *Cabaret* production, which had its base at the Bavaria Film Studios in Munich, was its plan to shoot as much as possible on location. The guiding concept of the film was to cleave to realism. "The picture is not a so-called musical,"

John Croydon
1/23 FITZJOHN'S AVENUE · HAMPSTEAD · NW3 · HAMPSTEAD 8253

October I4th.I954.

R.E.F.Garrett Esqre.,
Film Finances Ltd.,
34,South Molton Street,
London, W.I.

Dear Mr.Garrett,   re: Remus Films Ltd.
                                  "I Am A Camera".

    The production details of this proposition, for which
a Guarantee of Completion is sought, are as follows:-

Producer: J.Woolf.
Associate P roducer: J.Clayton.
Director: Henry Cornelius.
Schedule: IO weeks - as to 9 weeks occupation of Nettlefold
            Studios,Walton-on-Thames, I week occupation of
            British Lion Studios,Shepperton.   There are also
            2 very small 2nd.Unit Locations - one in Berlin
            and the other in London.
Budget: £I56,245, including a Contingency Allowance of
            £5,000 and presumably some form of Cash Cushion
            in view of the rate upon which the Guarantee has
            been calculated.
                There is also an unspecified dollar budget
            to cover the usual U.S.A. Contribution and a Marks
            budget to the extent of £2,956.   Neither of these
            budgets has been taken into account in calculating
            the Guarantee fee.
Finance: Presumably 70% Distribution Guarantee, but no
            further information available.
                There are dollar and marks contributions,
            presumably in cash and for deferments according to
            contract.
Distribution: Independent Film Distributors Ltd.

    I would say that there is nothing inherently difficult
or hazardous about this proposition.   The main question is -
can the Director maintain the necessary speed of production
set out in the X-plot ?   That is mainly a question of the
form of indemnity the Director is prepared to give us.

John Croydon's reports on *I Am a Camera*, 14 October 1954 (*above*), and *Cabaret*,
6 August 1970 (*opposite*).

ABC's representative Lee Steiner explained when he first submitted the papers
to Bobby Garrett, "but rather a picture with music."[6]

    Film Finances negotiated a $200,000 increase in the budget to meet the pro-
duction hazards of shooting on location (the final budget was just over $4 mil-
lion), including Film Finances' fee, but at the same time Croydon's rigorous
assessment saved the producers a considerable cost by anticipating numerous

John Croydon

FLAT 5, 7/8 ST. EDMUND'S TERRACE · LONDON · N.W.8
01-586 0219

6th August, 1970

R.E.F. Garrett, Esq.,
Film Finances Limited,
34 South Molton Street,
London, W.1.

Dear Mr. Garrett,

Re: ABC Pictures/Allied Artists
"CABARET"

This proposition is submitted by Lewis J. Rachmil of ABC
Pictures Corporation, to be produced by Cy Feuer and directed by
Robert Fosse, in Germany (Munich, Cologne and Berlin) for an
existent budget of $3,857,632, which total does not include a fee
for a guarantee of completion or a contingency in the terms in
which we understand one.

The script, based on the Christopher Isherwood story 'I am
a Camera' but adapted from the musical show "Cabaret", is a straight
forward master scene screenplay. The hazards to a guarantee are
obvious and concern the musical numbers, the sequences in the castle
at Cologne and the sort of location which is indicated as being
required in Berlin. It is a long script; I would not like to say
in the ultimate, that it could stand the length of, I would guess
2½ hours, but may be the producers in their wisdom prefer to have
the length upon which to work to determine the final play time.

In fact, in so far as the script and schedule are concerned I
would say that this appears to be the object throughout, and they
appear to have created an inbuilt contingency in as much the the
budget is based on 5 weeks rehearsals and pre-recording of most of the
numbers in London, followed, I am told by Rachmil, one weeks rehearsals
in Munich on the Kit Kat Club set, continuing on to a shooting schedule
of 71 days equalling 14 weeks. No specific schedule has been given
us for the rehersal period but we do have a shooting schedule which
works out to only 62 days shooting, plus 3 days internal location

2/............

potential problems. Little thought, for example, had been given to organizing the moves of the unit from the locations in West Germany to the city of Berlin, then still an enclave within Communist East Germany. To avoid the delays of passing through the Russian checkpoints, the cast and crew could travel by air, but what about the *Cabaret* character Max's car? Whatever route into Berlin was chosen, someone would have to check in advance that it would be allowed to pass without hindrance. The content of some of the location scenes was a cause for concern. As the film was set in the 1930s, would the producer be able to lay his hands on sufficient period transport in all the various locations? One sequence required the portrayal of Nazis writing the word *Jude* on a shop window, while others involved storm troopers creating disturbances in the streets and beating up characters in the story. Who would show the script to the appropriate authorities in advance to check that the necessary permissions would be granted? And so on. Each single point may have been small but had the potential, if unaddressed, to cause significant delay and expense.

On 29 March 1971, *Cabaret* followed *Willie Wonka and the Chocolate Factory* (1971) onto Stage III of the Bavaria Film Studios. Croydon and Bernard Smith, who was now Film Finances' managing director, followed progress on the set closely but also made repeated visits to the various locations. Partly they performed the function of a watchdog over the schedule, but their presence continued to be welcomed as a source of invaluable production advice.

After postproduction in Hollywood, *Cabaret* opened at the Ziegfeld Theatre in New York in February 1972. The influential *New Yorker* film critic Pauline Kael hailed a "great movie musical, made, miraculously, without compromises. . . . [It] is everything one hopes for and more; if it doesn't make money, it will still make movie history. After *Cabaret*, it should be a while before performers once again climb hills singing or a chorus breaks into a song on a hayride."[7]

Cy Feuer, who wrote a letter to Croydon with news of the successful US opening, allowed himself a joke over the expectations that the film would make money: "At the moment my story on CABARET is that it will do $400-million domestic, and considering that musicals are intensely disliked in Europe, I project only $200-million for that area of the world. I'm sure you'll agree that these estimates are on the conservative side, and it will probably do much more in both areas. The above attitude was reached by exposure to the motion picture world after having completed my first picture. It's evidently fun for all concerned to bask in the unreality of projected grosses." But the more important purpose of the letter was to thank John Croydon: "I look back on our association with a great deal of pleasure and I particularly enjoyed our experience together in Berlin. I'll always think of you as the coach who laid out the game plan and then sent me in during the last period to sew up the victory."[8]

Croydon saw the film for the first time at the press show for the London opening in June. "It is a magnificent film," he wrote to his star pupil, "and I am sure that both you and Bob Fosse must be very proud of your achievement. Not only that but it is very nice to see promise fulfilled in this manner; both Bernard and I on our rare visits to you came away with the feeling that you were achieving a cinema landmark. It may well be, too, that all those

FEUER & MARTIN
Productions Inc

March 13, 1972

Mr. John Croyden
Film Finances Limited
34 South Molton Street
London, WIY IHA, England

Dear John:

As you undoubtedly know, CABARET opened very successfully and is
now launched upon an epic-making run as are all successful motion
pictures whose projected grosses are lied about by everybody in
the industry. At the moment, my story on CABARET is that it will
do $400-million domestic, and considering that musicals are
intensely disliked in Europe, I project only $200-million for
that area of the world. I'm sure you'll agree that these
estimates are on the conservative side, and it will probably
do much more in both areas. The above attitude was reached
by exposure to the motion picture world after having completed
my first picture. It's evidently fun for all concerned to
bask in the unreality of projected grosses.

However, the picture turned out extremely well from a creative
point of view, and I'm genuinely pleased with it. It has its
faults as have all other projects, but all-in-all, "it works."
Its reception here has been enthusiastic, and the word-of-mouth
is excellent. I enclose our best review from our toughest
critic. On the other hand, I'm sure you've read Time Magazine
whose critic thought the entire picture was lousy. Please
disregard Time and pay attention to the enclosure which makes
us all appear brilliant.

I look back on our association with a great deal of pleasure,
and I particularly enjoyed our experience together in Berlin.
I'll always think of you as the coach who laid out the game
plan and then sent me in during the last period to sew up the
victory.

It's been quite an experience which, I am sure, will stand me
in good stead. Please convey my regards to Bernie and Bobby.

Best,

Cy Feuer

CF/a
enc.

Letter from *Cabaret* producer Cy Feuer paying tribute to Film Finances' great coach
John Croydon, 13 March 1972.

noughts that were added to the estimated gross will be realized! I sincerely hope so as apart from the fact that *Cabaret* will in a few years move into the archives of memorable films you deserve all the rewards that are coming to you."[9] Those rewards would soon include eight Academy Awards (including Best Director for Fosse, Best Actress for Liza Minnelli, and Best Supporting Actor for Joel Grey), still a record for a film that did not go on to win Best Picture (won that year by *The Godfather*).

Croydon was a coach not only to the filmmakers with whom Film Finances worked but also to the company's new recruit, Richard Soames, who remembered his arrival at South Molton Street as an opportunity to receive from Croydon the most fantastic apprenticeship in the nuts and bolts of practical production. "He taught me everything about filmmaking. We used to have this system of breaking down the script on a day-by-day basis, setup by setup, so we knew more than most directors about how actually to shoot the movie. And then we used to have these meetings, after he had done his report, with the director. And he would say, 'Look, day 25, how are you going to do that? I mean you just can't do it.' So the director scurries through and looks at day 25 and he says, 'You're absolutely right! Hmm. But I think I can catch up on day 26.' 'No, you can't!' And, really, from a director's point of view, it was like going to school, because we'd done much more work on the analysis than anybody normally does."[10]

But it wasn't only technical aspects that had to be considered. While it was still John Croydon in the early 1970s who was pointing out in exhaustive detail what could or could not be done—and assessing the likely cost—the person who then weighed up the risks of giving a guarantee, on the basis of Croydon's reports, was Bernard Smith. Croydon gauged the skill, competence, and expertise of the production team, but his comments were only advisory. It was then up to Smith to make the decision as to whether that team could be relied on to observe the budgetary restraints of the proposition that they had presented for a guarantee, and what specific conditions it might be necessary to impose to make the various risks acceptable. The essential element in making such a decision was one of trust.

Garrett had, by this time, become a somewhat aloof presence. "Bobby read the occasional script, but he didn't actually participate that much," recalled Soames. It was only when there was "a real crisis" that he would get involved, but even then only rarely.[11]

Soames's first crisis at Film Finances concerned a film called *Redneck* (*Senza ragione*, 1973), starring Telly Savalas and the child star of *Oliver!* (1968), Mark

Lester. The production was about to begin shooting in Rome, but the producers had yet to sign a letter that they agreed to the budget and schedule. So Bernard Smith suggested that Soames visit the producers in Rome to secure the necessary letter. Soames arrived on the weekend before the scheduled start of shooting to find "a complete fiasco." The director, Silvio Narrizano, had thrown his boyfriend, who also happened to be the scriptwriter, out on the street naked, and Soames could find no one who was prepared to sign the letter. He recalled, "So I called Bernard about midnight and said, 'What am I going to do? None of these people are going to sign anything and they're starting on Monday. We may have to pull the plug.' So he taught me the greatest lesson ever. He said, 'Look, you're there, I'm here. You do what you think is best.' Finally, I got them to sign something and the film got made."[12]

The successful completion guarantor needed to be a master of production skills, an excellent judge of character, but also, when needed, capable of taking swift, decisive action. Film Finances' Italian representative, Alessandro Tasca, put this aspect of being a guarantor well when he summarized the job as being that of a fireman: "No matter how good you are, no matter how good your budget is, your schedule and everything else, always something will happen. . . . So like a fireman, you don't know where the fire is going to break out, but you have to be ready to rush to it."[13]

～

In spite of the success of *Cabaret*, ABC Pictures closed down its filmmaking division in 1972, after a production program that had in five years failed to generate a profit. It was symptomatic of a wider malaise. The very fact that a New Hollywood had arisen in reaction to the old to some extent indicated the desperation of an industry that had yielded the initiative to the "movie brat" generation through its own lack of confidence about what audiences wanted to see. The rise of the New Hollywood coincided with the majors posting some of the most disastrous losses in their history. "The motion picture companies went through a terrible debacle between 1967 and 1971; collectively, they lost $400-million," wrote Jack Valenti, the president of the Motion Picture Association of America, in 1975.[14]

During the 1950s and 1960s, the term "independent producer," when it came to the production slates of the Hollywood majors, meant in practice someone who produced a motion picture for a fee plus a percentage of the profits but played no significant role in the raising of production finances. The financial crisis of the late 1960s and early 1970s encouraged the newly cash-strapped

Hollywood studios to become more open to cofinancing arrangements that would reduce costs and minimize their exposure to the risks of production.

The result was a revolution in financing during the 1970s as mainstream Hollywood placed increasing dependence on independently produced but also independently financed films. If a striking feature was the degree to which European producers took the lead in this process, it reflected the key structural difference between Hollywood and Europe's film industries in the postwar period: the lack of distributors in Europe with the global dominance and financial strength of the Hollywood majors meant that European producers had long been used to putting together a patchwork of finance on a film-by-film basis, and from many sources. The experience gave them a unique skill set with which to take advantage when the financial crisis of the early 1970s compelled Hollywood to look for nonstudio sources of funding.

Producers in Europe of films with international appeal had long been able to find significant partial financing for their projects through the support of American independent distributors. Among the most well known at the beginning of the 1970s were Embassy, Allied Artists, Cinerama, and American International Pictures, but there were many others. In return for the right to exploit a film in the United States, such a distributor would offer a guarantee of payment that the producer could then use to raise a percentage of the production cost from a bank. The invasion of the Hollywood majors, with their offers of 100 percent financing, had made such deals less frequent in Britain during the 1960s, but it was hardly surprising that there should be a resurgence after the majors began to withdraw.

The producer Josef Shaftel, who was a familiar presence in Film Finances' files from about 1970, provides a good example of the changing pattern. Film Finances already knew him from many years previously. In 1952, as an independent producer in Hollywood, Shaftel had joined forces with British producer Raymond Stross to produce a Georges Simenon thriller, *The Man Who Watched Trains Go By*, which was made in England with a completion guarantee from Film Finances. He spent the rest of the 1950s in Hollywood, where he produced three more films. After a stint as a producer on the successful TV series *The Untouchables*, he then came to Europe in the mid-1960s, where his production company produced two films that enjoyed, in the usual way of the time, 100 percent financing from major Hollywood studios: a crime caper film for MGM, *The Biggest Bundle of Them All* (1968), starring Raquel Welch and Robert Wagner; and a romantic comedy for Paramount, *The Bliss of Mrs. Blossom* (1968), starring Richard Attenborough and Shirley MacLaine.

Cinerama prepared this lavish brochure in 1970 to announce its partnership with London-based producer Josef Shaftel. Its importance as a distributor of independently financed films grew during the first half of the 1970s as the Hollywood majors became increasingly reluctant to invest in European production.

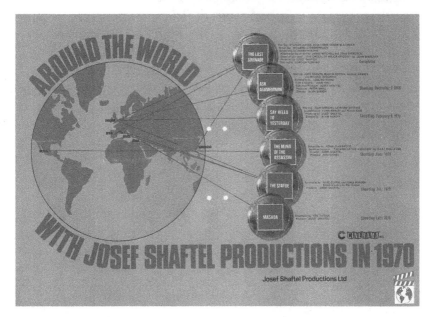

When the following year he managed to raise, independently of the majors, funding for a program of six feature films, it was a novel enough occurrence to receive coverage in the financial pages of the British newspapers, clippings from which were tucked away in the Film Finances publicity file. "Cinerama has now confirmed a deal with film producer Mr Josef Shaftel for making a $14m programme of pictures this year," reported *The Times* of London. "At least two of the films are being jointly financed by Bank of America (85 percent) and Hill Samuel (15 percent). Cinerama guarantees a purchase price for the pictures on delivery and against this the banks put up the cash. Insurance against any of the pictures going over-budget is arranged through Film Finances." Whereas Bank of America had a long-established track record in providing loans for film production, the article pointed out that the merchant bank Hill Samuel was new to the business: "Although the investment at this stage is relatively small, if it proves successful, the bank could be expected to make further incursions into this field."[15]

The much larger budgets encouraged by the presence of the Hollywood majors in the British film industry offered the potential for banks to make significant profit in fees and interest on their loans. So there was an incentive to fill the gap in financing that opened up as the Hollywood studios began to withdraw from Britain at the turn of the decade. The most spectacular deal, which anticipated the shape of things to come, was merchant bank Morgan Grenfell's decision in 1967 to entrust to producer Dimitri de Grunwald a revolving fund of $24 million. Film Finances' agreement in principle to guarantee the ensuing program of films provided the necessary linchpin for the investment.

Born in Saint Petersburg in 1914, Dimitri de Grunwald had fled with his family to England during the Russian Revolution. He was the younger brother of producer Anatole "Tolly" de Grunwald, who had produced several classic British films written by the playwright Terence Rattigan, including *The Way to the Stars* (1945), *The Winslow Boy* (1948), and *The Yellow Rolls-Royce* (1964). After pursuing a successful business career in the pharmaceuticals industry, Dimitri joined his brother's production company in the 1950s and then set out on his own after his brother's death in 1967.

The deal with Morgan Grenfell developed into an ambitious scheme to create a network of distributors around the world that would give independent producers international distribution without reliance on the Hollywood majors. The prototype for the venture was the Western *Shalako*. Starring Sean Connery and Brigitte Bardot, the film was directed in Spain in 1968 by Hollywood veteran Edward Dmytryk. The recent international success of Spaghetti Westerns would have made the hybrid nature of the film less remarkable than it might otherwise have seemed, but British producer Euan Lloyd was unable to persuade any of the Hollywood studios to support the project, in spite of the fact that he already had the commitment of two big international box office stars. So he sold distribution rights territory by territory in return for guarantees of payment on the completion of the film. The practice was already a familiar method of financing films in Europe, but rarely had a producer attempted it on such a massive scale.

With the aid of Paris-based sales agent Albert Carcaro, Lloyd secured guarantees worth $5 million from thirty-six separate foreign distributors. But the critical challenge was to find a bank that would be prepared to issue such a large loan on so many separate undertakings. "I had many financing commitments from many distributors and I had Sean's and Brigitte's agreement to work with me," Euan Lloyd explained in an on-set interview with the *New York Times*. "Edward Dmytryk, the director, was standing by my side from the first day. But I could not find the cash to get going, and all these people were

Sean Connery and Brigitte Bardot in *Shalako* (1968). Its financing arrangement provided an important model for the international independent financing of films during the 1970s.

getting more and more impatient. . . . I knew I was getting nowhere, I had no crews, nothing, just the threat of lawsuits from people with whom I had signed contracts." But then at last Dimitri de Grunwald provided the "elusive element missing in this combination," when Morgan Grenfell agreed to discount the notes, or, as Euan Lloyd put it, "bank the bankers."[16]

De Grunwald used the opening of *Shalako* in the United States in October 1968 to promote the idea for a global network of distributors. "The universality of movie-making is being taken seriously by Dimitri de Grunwald," reported the *New York Times* in an article that explained his plan for "a consortium of companies in more than 30 countries that will cooperate in making films on an international basis."[17]

Indeed, de Grunwald's belief in the universality of moviemaking was such that he was even planning to finance movies made in Hollywood. Early the next year he discussed with Film Finances a program of films that his new company, London Screenplays, wished to support that included several to be made in America. "Naturally we should be delighted, as guarantors, to become generally part of your scheme," Garrett wrote in a letter to de Grunwald dated 4 March 1969. But he went on, with his usual caution, "For the time being, until we learn more about American production from experience we feel we must treat the American films on a different basis. We propose that on these films, after the usual budget has been agreed, yourselves or some other party should enter into an undertaking to meet the first overcost up to the equivalent of 15 percent of the budget, and in return for that we would split our fee with such parties."[18]

Accepting the proposal, de Grunwald immediately asked Film Finances to guarantee *The McMasters* (1970), a Western starring Burl Ives, Brock Peters, and Jack Palance, which was to begin a five-week shoot the very next day in Santa Fe, New Mexico, with a budget of $1.3 million. It became the first film made in the United States to receive a Film Finances guarantee. Directly monitoring the production, but also assuming responsibility for the first overcost, was a small local company called Performance Guarantees, which New York–based film producer Sidney Kaufman had recently set up to take advantage of the nascent market in the United States for independent financing.

Film Finances continued to regard American production as the exception to the rule. Only two weeks later, on 25 March 1969, the producer Sandy Howard, then working for CBS Films, inquired whether Film Finances might be prepared to bond a project to be shot in Los Angeles or New York. Bernard Smith wrote back to explain "that we do not become involved in American domestic films as we feel it is an area that we are not conversant with and the fact that it is too far away to be able to exercise control."[19] At about the same time Film Finances offered a similar response to inquiries from several other American producers, but with hindsight the growing interest was a further sign of an independent industry, beyond the majors, beginning to emerge in the United States. If for the time being the association with London Screenplays continued to offer Film Finances' only experience of filmmaking on the other side of the Atlantic, that would quickly change over the next decade.

In June 1969, Euan Lloyd turned up at South Molton Street with London Screenplays representative Tony Landi to discuss his follow-up to *Shalako*. Adapted from the novel *The Seven File*, by American crime novelist William McGivern, *Chicago 7* was a kidnap story set in the city, with Rock Hudson and Britt Ekland in the starring roles.[20] It was proposed that Film Finances would guarantee the film on the same basis as *The McMasters*, with London Screenplays agreeing to meet the first 15 percent of any overbudget cost. The project soon fell through, but in October 1969 Film Finances sent John Croydon to Los Angeles to explore the viability of Film Finances guaranteeing another London

Richard Thomas and Mary Layne in *Cactus in the Snow* (also known as *You Can't Have Everything*, 1971).

Screenplays project called *A Soldier's Story*, which would eventually be released as *Cactus in the Snow* (and also known as *You Can't Have Everything*, 1971).

Croydon's favorable report gives the impression of a striking personal venture made on the margins of the mainstream industry. The small production company that brought the project to London Screenplays was run by Rudy Durand, whom Croydon described as "a young man, obviously without any production experience at all, but who seems to have contacts with Dimitri de Grunwald in connection with the selling of the London Screenplays films." The thirty-year-old director, Martin Zweiback, was a graduate of UCLA film school "who up to date has failed to obtain a Union ticket but is determined to become a director and has reached his present assignment through writing." Of the script, Croydon wrote, "I found that everyone concerned with it looks upon it as a form of anti-establishment material of a nature which has never yet been presented in relation to the Vietnam war."[21] It told the story of a young American soldier attempting to lose his virginity before he's shipped off to Vietnam.

The essential practical knowledge that made it possible for Croydon to recommend a guarantee came from the line producer, Lou Brandt, who had worked on the popular TV series *I-Spy*. Croydon described him as "a man in the early 40s who has a wealth of production experience, very direct and tough and who in the short time I was with him, impressed me as a man who would retain complete control over the project."[22]

Croydon was witnessing a revolution in the making. *Cactus in the Snow* was an independent movie that had emerged out of the same 1960s counterculture that had been responsible for that summer's sensation *Easy Rider*, reflecting the attitude of a new "movie brat generation" seeking to capture the reality of contemporary America.

Croydon saw an opportunity for Film Finances to take advantage of the moment. On his return to London, he wrote to Bobby Garrett to report on the strong encouragement he had received from producers in Hollywood that Film Finances should open an office there. The only competition was from Sidney Kaufman's Performance Guarantees, which was so notorious for its overbearing supervision that no one wanted to work with it.[23]

But Garrett continued to adopt an attitude of extreme caution. He instinctively regarded Hollywood as a place beyond Film Finances' natural range of operation. He was prepared on an ad hoc basis to guarantee American-made films that some preexisting relationship had brought to Film Finances, but only with stringent additional conditions and under the supervision of a representative who had local knowledge of the industry.

John Croydon

FLAT 5, 7/8 ST. EDMUND'S TERRACE · LONDON · N.W.8
01-586 0219

R.E.F. Garrett, Esq.,
Film Finances Ltd.,
34 South Molton Street,
London, W.1.   22nd October, 1969

Dear Mr. Garrett,

        Whilst I was in Los Angeles everybody I met, without
exception, asked me why Film Finances Ltd. did not open a
Hollywood office for guarantees of completion.

        Partially through the enormous cost of working in the
Hollywood studios, and partially through the comparitive
freedom of operation allowed by the Hollywood union agreements, more and more independent production is being promoted.

        There seems to be no doubt that the introduction of
these cinemobile film units also encourages independent
producers to shoot more and more LOC/INT subjects.

        The fact that most Hollywood major studios are
abandoning their overhead positions and offering what they
call favourable rates for the hire of their studios is only
of advantage to independent producers thinking on terms of
high budget pictures. Independent producers of low budget
films could still not afford the sort of rents the major
studios will be offering.

        When they talk about completion bonds it is also very
obvious that they take as their standard the operation of
Sidney Kaufman. I can only describe him, from the comments
made about him, as one of the most disliked, or best hated,
men on the Hollywood financial scene. Everyone, without
exception, declares that they would go to any lengths to
avoid contact with him.

                                2/......

Letter from John Croydon to Bobby Garrett, 22 October 1969, describing his visit to Los Angeles. At the time, a genuinely independent film industry in Hollywood, where producers raised money independently of the major studios, was still in its infancy.

The *Cactus in the Snow* production began a seven-week shooting schedule at Paramount studios and on location around Los Angeles in January 1970. One of the visitors to the set was the film's financier, London Screenplays' boss Dimitri de Grunwald. He used the occasion to give an interview about his International Film Consortium, which now comprised fifty-nine independent film distributors around the world. The latest coup, he told *Variety* in March, was an agreement with the leisure conglomerate Winthrop Lawrence Corporation to distribute the consortium's films in the US. Describing the consortium as "a sort of United Nations of films," he went on to explain the central role that Morgan Grenfell played: "British banks traditionally shy away from film investments, but apparently the Grenfell people, when it became apparent I wasn't promising the moon and operated in a sane and reasonable manner, believed I had something to offer and agreed to finance me 100 percent. To secure their money, I proposed forming the Consortium."[24]

De Grunwald couldn't help remarking on the atmosphere of gloom he had found in Hollywood, which was experiencing "a loss of confidence to an unprecedented degree."[25] The major studios were in the grip of the financial crisis. Amid heavy losses, they were cutting back their production programs and downsizing. Paramount, where *Cactus in the Snow* was being shot, had put its back lot up for sale. MGM was about to auction off its furniture, props, and costumes. Columbia was selling its studio at Gower Street and Sunset to move in with Warner Bros. in Burbank. The industry's problems seemed so dire that de Grunwald even ventured to suggest that, with his system of pre-sales, he might have found the answer to their difficulties: "I feel like the right person in the right place at the right time."[26]

The comment turned out to be tempting fate. As London Screenplays' production program gathered momentum, Morgan Grenfell began to advance money on what it later discovered were greatly exaggerated estimates of pre-sales. The Winthrop Lawrence Corporation was not the "vigorous American partner" that de Grunwald had claimed but rather a struggling concern with little experience of distribution. It went bankrupt in November 1970, leaving Morgan Grenfell with more than $3 million of suddenly worthless guarantees. In the debacle, Dimitri de Grunwald resigned and Morgan Grenfell took over London Screenplays. Two former executives from Paramount-British were appointed to administer the eight films that had been produced. After they had salvaged what they could, the bank was left with a huge loss on its investment, with estimates ranging between £6 million ($16 million) and £14 million ($34 million). If the City had tended in the past, as de Grunwald put it, to "shy away from film investments," the disaster over London Screenplays encouraged the tendency many times over.

Yet the principle itself of harnessing presales as a security for production was a proven technique that the climate of international filmmaking in the 1970s would cause other producers to embrace with increasing regularity. As they rationalized their businesses, the Hollywood majors were producing fewer and fewer films. The retrenchment led to an increased demand for outside product to supply their worldwide distribution networks.

They were ready now not only to pick up independently financed films but also to entertain cofinancing ventures that, in their previous desire for complete control of copyright, they would have shunned in the past. The weak point of Dimitri de Grunwald's scheme had been the absence of any major Hollywood distributors, but now they were willing to cooperate.

Hollywood's most immediate response to its financial crisis was to take advantage of tax shelters. One of the first such tax-sheltered schemes was the Paramount production of *The Great Gatsby* (1974). A Chicago syndicate of investors, under the name of the "Fitz Service Company," was set up to "provide production services" to "Newdon Productions," which had been created to hold the legal ownership of the film. The "services" amounted to raising $1.8 million of the $6.6 million budget. It offered the basic model for a method of financing that increased at an exponential rate over the next three years.

The high-earning members of such syndicates advanced not more than 25 percent of their investment in cash, borrowing the rest from a bank as a nonrecourse loan that was charged against the future box office receipts of the

Robert Redford in *The Great Gatsby* (1973), one of the first films to take advantage of tax-sheltered financing, which provided a significant financial incentive for independent production during the 1970s.

film. The investors were then able to deduct against tax the full value of their investment (i.e., both down payment and loan) during the year in which they made the investment, although only their downpayment was at risk.[27]

The New York–based partnership of Lester Persky and Richard Bright packaged tax-sheltered deals for twenty-two films that included *The Last Detail* (1973), *Funny Lady* (1975), *Shampoo* (1975), *The Wind and the Lion* (1975), and *Taxi Driver* (1976).[28] "We work on the old-fashioned theory that if you have your own money up, your decisions are more sound," Persky told the *New York Times* in 1976.[29] By 1975 so many Hollywood films had taken advantage of tax-sheltered schemes that they contributed to the funding of approximately half the films produced in the United States.[30] "The availability of this kind of funding is the single most important occurrence in the recent history of the film industry," the CEO of Columbia Pictures, Alan Hirschfield, told *Variety* in 1974. "And if we can continue to attract outside capital . . . it can be the savior of the film industry."[31] The only majors to shun such funding were the three that were in robust enough financial health not to need it—Disney, MCA-Universal, and 20th Century-Fox.

"Necessity dictated that we look to independent producers," commented Columbia's head of distribution, Norman Levy, in 1978.[32] But he pointed out that the industry as a whole had become more enthusiastic about independently financed films. The most successful film at the box office that year was Warner Bros.' *Superman*, which was a negative pickup from the producer Alexander Salkind.

The studios' increasing reliance on outside financing involved considerable peril for an inexperienced new generation of independent film financiers who had yet to discover how the industry worked. One of Columbia's negative pickups, *The Buddy Holly Story* (1978), offers an example. "It went way over budget," recalled its executive producer Fred Kuehnert. "We weren't bonded. The budget represented to me was most likely misrepresented but I didn't know any better. We got the picture finished but we were broke. We couldn't pay the taxes we owed on salaries. The creative team and the financiers were at each other's throats, and I was in between them. I vowed to never produce another film."[33]

In principle, the advent of tax-sheltered financing had the potential of providing a major source of new business for Film Finances because its completion guarantee offered an important safeguard to investors in such schemes. When in August 1974 *Barron's Financial Weekly* published a feature on what had become a popular new form of investment, it warned, "Investors should be especially wary of going into any co-financing deal unless the general partner has obtained a completion bond."[34] But what was striking was the attitude almost of reluctance that Bobby Garrett showed when an American tax-sheltered film inevitably came Film Finances' way.

In 1973, a documentary filmmaker, Bill Alexander, set up a New York–based production company, The Movie People, to make a feature film of a novel called *The Klansman*, about racial conflict in a small Alabama town. With James Bond director Terence Young and box office stars Richard Burton and Lee Marvin committed to the project, Alexander raised the $4 million budget through the combination of a distribution guarantee from Paramount and tax-sheltered investors from Atlanta, Canada, and Europe. Continuing to regard the US location itself as a significant risk, Film Finances required the production company not only to meet any overcosts up to $450,000 but also to hire a named representative, Richard McWhorter, to supervise the film on Film Finances' behalf. McWhorter, who had worked with King Vidor, Frank Capra, and Cecil B. De Mille, was one of the most experienced production managers in Hollywood.

After John Croydon had looked through the production papers with his usual thoroughness, he sent an exhaustive list of questions to McWhorter in Los Angeles. "Quite obviously in a letter of this sort it is quite impossible to detail all the questions that we would like to discuss," he concluded, "but I am sure you will appreciate that sitting here in London, without specific knowledge of local conditions, items such as we have mentioned above are virtually meaningless without the confirmation of a man with your knowledge and expertise."[35] After McWhorter visited Film Finances in London the following month, Croydon sent an even longer letter to summarize items of particular concern that had emerged out of their conferences.[36] At the same time, Bobby Garrett wrote to Young, "As you probably appreciate, the United States are more or less a strange territory as far as we are concerned, and the whole thing is very far from home. We are therefore relying upon you."[37]

But Garrett's idea of "home" was becoming an outdated concept in an increasingly international industry where the old divisions of "distributor," "producer," and "financier" were breaking down. In June 1974, *Variety* published an interview with one of the new breed of producers that gave a good summary of how the financial landscape of the international film industry was changing in the early 1970s. Martin Bregman was chair of a talent agency, Artists Entertainment Complex, that had turned into an independent production company, making the box office hits *Serpico* (1973) and *Dog Day Afternoon*

(1975). "Independent production, once a simple packaging of a film's creative elements to secure major distributor financing, is becoming more truly independent," explained *Variety*. "The trend, which has lately assumed significant proportions, is the result of producers' search for bigger and 'more meaningful' slices of a picture's profits and distributors' desire to limit 'their financial exposure' in picture production." During the 1960s, the traditional independent might have produced a picture for a fee plus a percentage of the profits, but now, explained Bregman, picture production involved "mixed bag" financing in which a producer had to assemble "a complex 'financial mix' with costs parcelled out to various jigsaw parts such as 'tax shelters,' advances and guarantees from overseas distributors."[38]

Film Finances' first serious effort to take advantage of the growing number of independently financed films being made in the United States occurred early in 1974 when it reached a partnership agreement with a Hollywood-based facilities business called Cinemobile. The agreement was that Cinemobile's recently established subsidiary, Cine Guarantors, would evaluate US productions that could be considered a fair risk and make itself responsible for any overcost up to 15 percent of the budget. Film Finances would then cover any claims that arose after that point.

Film Finances had first come to know of Cinemobile when John Croydon visited Los Angeles in 1969 to appraise the production plans for London Screenplays' *Cactus in the Snow*. The founder of Cinemobile, Fouad Said, was responsible for a much-fêted innovation that had been encouraging Hollywood filmmakers to break away from traditional, studio-based filmmaking. Earlier that year, he had won an Oscar for "the design and introduction of the Cinemobile series of equipment trucks for location motion picture production."[39]

Although *Cactus in the Snow* ended up being shot at Paramount studios, the original intention had been to shoot the film entirely on location using a Cinemobile bus. "There is no doubt that it is the most fantastic vehicle I have ever seen," commented Croydon in his report on the production. "It is so compactly designed that it can carry everything a unit is likely to want."[40]

Founded in 1965, Fouad Said's Cinemobile Systems was undergoing a period of rapid, exponential growth that coincided with but also—in its provision of more cost-effective filmmaking facilities that addressed the mood of the times—benefited from the financial crisis that gripped the Hollywood studios. In 1968, it provided location facilities for three features, but its acquisition that year by the Taft Broadcasting Company made possible a massive expansion of the business so that only three years later, in 1971, the number

The inventor of the Cinemobile bus, Fouad Said (*left*), talks with cinematographer Vilmos Zsigmond on the MGM backlot in 1970, during the production of *The Hired Hand* (1971). The mark IV Cinemobile bus, which can be seen in the background, took the equipment on location to New Mexico.

had risen to 102 features. They included *The Godfather* (1972), which was being shot on location in New York. It was the occasion for the *New York Times* to publish a profile of the company in which Said explained its success: "In the 1920s and 1930s, time was not that crucial and the style was to build Central Park in Los Angeles rather than travel the 3,000 miles. But today with better transportation, rather than bringing the location to the studio, it is more economical to bring the studio to the location. Instead of building a set for $8,000, you can rent it for $100. Also today's audiences are demanding realism in their films."[41]

By the end of 1972, Cinemobile controlled 75 percent of the US location facilities market and, in anticipation of a saturated market, was looking for other areas of film production into which it could diversify. In cutting costs and simplifying the filmmaking process, it had helped create a climate in which independent producers based in the United States could more readily contemplate the financing of their own films. Offering a facility for completion guaranties was a natural next step. The attraction of a partnership with Film Finances was not only its twenty years of production know-how but also the fact that, underwritten by Lloyd's, Film Finances enabled Cinemobile to guarantee much higher budgets than it could on its own.

"You and your organization exemplify the best because you are gentlemen to deal with and excellent businessmen," Cinemobile's director Bernard
Weitzman wrote to Bobby Garett in a letter dated 20 November 1973 to celebrate their final agreement.[42] A joint press release followed in the new year: "In
an unprecedented move, Taft's Cine Guarantors, Inc. of Los Angeles, and Film
Finances Ltd of London have formed a joint operation to provide completion
guarantees and production services on a full international basis. . . . For the
first time in the history of the industry a foreign producer planning to work in
the US will be able to arrange for completion bonding through Film Finances
in London and Cine Guarantors will handle the US end."[43]

But after many months went by, no business had resulted from the partnership. With the near total absence of any proposals from Cinemobile for
projects to guarantee, Richard Soames wrote on behalf of Film Finances to
Cine Guarantors in September 1975 to seek an explanation: "You will appreciate that since signing our mutual agreement, we have not, as yet, reinsured any
films for you; and we are naturally disappointed that practically no business
has been generated through this agreement."[44]

A few months later, in March 1976, Film Finances terminated the agreement.
It marked a significant change of attitude as Richard Soames began to take up
the reins. Film Finances was no longer going to sit back to wait for business to
come in, nor behave as though "abroad" was a dangerous place where it for-
ever had to tread carefully.

In the summer of 1976, Richard Soames and Bernard Smith went on a trip
to the United States to meet possible partners, whether banks, production
companies, or other completion guarantors. On their return they wrote a bull-
ish summary of their visit.[45] They reported that the chief banks prepared to
finance independent production welcomed Film Finances' guarantee but were
hesitant to support Film Finances' possible competitors. Indeed, one of them,
Chemical Bank, categorically stated that the only completion guarantee it would
be prepared to accept was Film Finances', although it "would be prepared to
accept a guarantee from a third party, if it was backed up by ourselves."[46]

One of the production companies they met, Trans-World Entertainment,
said that it would prefer "to deal direct" with Film Finances rather than go
through a third party. Another, the distributor Avco-Embassy, outlined its
intention to return to production financing after an absence of several years.
"It is their view that the American market is enormous but only for American
type production, but not all necessarily shot in the States. The financing would
require guaranties of completion but Avco are not too enamoured with the

November 20, 1973

Mr. Robert Garrett
Film Finances Limited
34 South Molton Street
London W1Y 1HA
England

Dear Robert:

I am in receipt of your note dated November 13, 1973. We
also are delighted with our new association and look forward
to working with your organization for our respective companies'
mutual benefit.

You and your organization exemplify the best because you
are gentlemen to deal with and also excellent businessmen.
We feel confident in relying upon your organization to
offer the film producers throughout our part of the world
a complete financial guarantee service on the most dependable
basis.

Thank you again for your confidence. Best regards to you
and your entire organization.

Sincerely,

Bernard Weitzman

A ⬛ BROADCASTING COMPANY ⬛ 8560 SUNSET BOULEVARD, HOLLYWOOD, CALIFORNIA 90069 • TELEPHONE: (213) 652-4800 • TELEX: 674124 • CABLE: FOUSAID

Letter from Cinemobile director Bernard Weitzman to Robert Garrett, 20 November
1973, regarding Film Finances' agreement with Cinemobile to guarantee independent
productions in the United States. The association was terminated three years later
without Film Finances guaranteeing any US-based films through the agreement.

existing companies and would like to deal direct with us," Soames and Smith reported.[47]

The overall picture the report offered was one of Film Finances being well placed to take advantage of the rapid growth of independent production in the United States, which appeared imminent: "In conclusion, we obtained the impression from everyone to whom we spoke, including the Bankers, that our presence as Guarantors of Completion in the States would be very welcome."[48]

In the aftermath of the trip, with the recommendation of Chemical Bank, Film Finances negotiated a partnership with Everett Rosenthal of FRP Productions, a New York–based facilities company that had, like Cinemobile, moved into completion guaranties. The basis of the arrangement was the same: that Film Finances, underwritten by Lloyd's, would guarantee to meet the over-costs of a film after FRP had met a first loss. The chief difference was that FRP turned out to be able to generate a steady flow of business in a way that Cinemobile had failed to do.

∾

At about the same time as Film Finances began to take a proactive attitude toward independent production in the United States, a huge opportunity for expansion opened up in Canada. "It was about '75," Soames recalled. "It was really irresistible. There were so many films being made. We were doing about twelve in England. The following year, we did twenty-five in Canada."[49]

In 1967, the Canadian government had created the Canadian Film Development Corporation (CFDC) to encourage an indigenous film industry. Over the next five years, the CFDC spent C$20 million (US$18.6 million) on film but also lobbied the government to introduce measures that would support a broader industrial infrastructure. "Since its first year of existence, the Corporation had known that it could succeed in creating an industry only if a significant number of films were made without its investment," wrote its first executive director, Michael Spencer. "Such films should be encouraged and applauded, I thought, because they lessened pressure on CFDC resources and expanded the financial base of the industry."[50]

In 1974, the Canadian government introduced a Capital Cost Allowance, which enabled investors to deduct from their taxable income 100 percent of their investment in Canadian-made feature-length films. The trickle of Hollywood companies moving across the border to take advantage of the incentive turned into a stampede after 1976 legislation closed down the loopholes that had allowed tax-sheltered financing in the United States.

Film Finances no longer waited to find a local company that would assume responsibility for the first loss, nor did it any longer seek to impose a surcharge for the perceived extra risk of operating in a foreign territory. Driven by the expansionist instincts of Richard Soames, it demonstrated a renewed confidence in the unique benefits that its guarantee was able to offer independent production as well as its unparalleled know-how and ability to acquire the necessary knowledge of local conditions.

The huge increase in the workload required a new way of working. There was no longer time to prepare painstaking, twenty-page reports that, after the manner of John Croydon, analyzed and anticipated every risk. "It became more of a people business in a way," commented Soames. "I was much more looking at the people involved than the detail of setup by setup."[51] The sheer volume of production required assessing the critical risk points of each proposition, weighing up the reliability of the specific individuals behind them.

The exponential growth in Canadian production was unprecedented, rocketing from three features in 1974 to sixty-six in 1979, with a number of these films being "Stars and Stripes" movies—in other words, films with an American story but produced in Canada to take advantage of Canadian investment opportunities.[52] Just to take as an example three films that were guaranteed by Film Finances in 1979: *Middle Age Crazy* (1980), starring Ann-Margret and Bruce Dern, was about a couple going through a midlife crisis, set in a Texas suburb but shot in Ontario. *The Changeling* (1980) was set in New York and Seattle but shot in the Canadian cities of Vancouver and Victoria. *City on Fire* (1979) was a disaster movie set in an unnamed midwestern US city but shot in Montreal, with an international cast of stars that included Leslie Nielsen, Shelley Winters, Ava Gardner, and Henry Fonda. As the tagline for the movie's poster put it, "What happened to them could happen to you . . . in any city anywhere!"

And the audience for these films could be found in any city anywhere, as was true of their producers, although increasingly, as the 1970s wore on, the preferred city for business was Los Angeles. Sid and Marty Krofft, who produced *Middle Age Crazy*, were examples of the city's magnetic pull. They were Canadians from Montreal but had long ago moved to the United States, where they had made their names in children's television. The executive producers of *The Changeling* were Andrew Vajna, who was from Budapest, and Mario Kassar, from Beirut. Both successful independent distributors, they formed

Bill Murray (*center*) in *Meatballs* (1979), the film that made him a star. One of many "Stars and Stripes" movies guaranteed by Film Finances, it happened to have been shot in Ontario, but with its nonspecific storyline, it could as easily have been a summer camp south of the border.

their independent production company, Carolco, after meeting at the Cannes Film Festival in 1975. What had brought them all to make their films in Canada was the extremely favorable investment climate that the government incentives had created, but they were ready, as opportunities in this newly globalized industry presented themselves, to move elsewhere.

At Film Finances' annual general meeting in October 1979, the chair, Bobby Garrett, announced Film Finances' most successful year in nearly thirty years of trading. But that success had come through the company making a decisive move away from Britain, where the local industry had been going through many years of stagnation. His summary of the twenty-four films that the company had guaranteed in the past year painted a picture of a business where it no longer made sense to imagine "home" as being in Britain. Home had to be wherever the company was making films: in that past year, one in Italy, one in South Africa, two in Mexico, five in the UK, five in the US, and ten in Canada. "Particularly cheering is our relationship with Canada," Garrett observed, "which country until recently produced modestly budgeted films, the majority being in French. Now thanks to tax concessions available to Canadian residents they are making often large-scale feature films aimed at an international market."[53] With Canada now responsible for the lion's share of the company's business, the decision was made to open a subsidiary there. Film Finances Canada Ltd. was incorporated in Toronto on 7 June 1979. Other overseas offices would soon follow.

∼

The key word that really summed up the drift of the decade was "international." Beyond Canada, there was a trend of European producers seeking to capitalize on the Hollywood studios' new readiness to cofinance production as well as their growing demand for product. A new phenomenon became apparent of European producers making not only American-style but also American-based films. Dino De Laurentiis led the way, negotiating presales to finance such box office hits as *Serpico* (1973), *Death Wish* (1974), and *Three Days of the Condor* (1975), and his mid-1970s move to Hollywood set a precedent that many other European producers followed.

"Leading company heads," reported *Variety* in May 1975, "have come to the conclusion, as De Laurentiis did before them, that production of an American film in the States is the only valid passport to the American market. At a time when American films are reconquering world audiences . . . thinking extends to the wholesome possibility of turning out genuine international product from a base on Yank soil."[54]

In Britain, Michael Deeley and Barry Spikings, who had run British Lion, persuaded EMI to adopt the same approach as they became joint managing directors of EMI after its takeover of British Lion in May 1976. "The cost of major American pictures," explained Deeley, "could to a great extent be recouped in the US domestic market, particularly now that network television was kicking in big prices. With a domestic market as small as we had in Britain we either had to make very cheap local films which could recoup domestically and in the British Commonwealth or, if we wanted to go international for the bigger revenues, we would have to lay off much of the financial risk and find co-funding partners around the world."[55] In this way, an iconic British company became the producer of such quintessentially American movies as *The Deer Hunter* (1978), *Convoy* (1978), and *The Driver* (1978).

Another British company that saw its future in international movies was Hemdale. Founded in 1967 by actor David Hemmings and his manager, John

Convoy (1978): British company EMI attempts a Hollywood-style movie.

Daly, the original purpose of Hemdale had been as a vehicle to protect the film star from very high rates of British personal taxation through investing his earnings in the entertainment industry. "Well, you've got to pay taxes one way or the other," Hemmings explained in an interview with the film critic Roger Ebert in 1969, "so why not [put] it back into the industry?"[56] Soon Hemdale had built up a stable of other British film stars and celebrities looking to protect their income in the same way.

Hemmings left in 1970, but Daly went on to build a company that had originally started out as a tax-sheltered investment fund into an international film financing, distribution, and production business. The scale of its ambition was notable from the outset. Becoming a quoted public company in the autumn of 1968, it began to grow through the acquisition of other businesses, as Hemmings put it, "like Jack's beanstalk on steroids."[57]

In the spring of 1978, Hemdale embarked on its most ambitious and expensive production, the wartime adventure film *The Passage* (1979), which Film Finances guaranteed. Raising the $5 million budget through a combination of tax-sheltered investment and presales, Hemdale promoted the film heavily at the Cannes Film Festival even as the production itself was being shot at the Victorine Studios down the road in Nice. At the same time, it used the occasion of the festival to show off the star of its next picture, Farrah Fawcett of TV's *Charlie's Angels*, who later that year was going to begin shooting a mystery thriller set in Acapulco called *Sunburn* (1979).

That year's festival marked a significant turning-point for the independent financing of films. "Indies Take Major Role in Pix Biz," declared a *Variety* article that took a look at what business had taken place over the fortnight of the festival. "In sheer numbers, spending, promotion, wheeling-dealing, and day-to-day visibility, the indie majors provided the leadership. Indie is the key term."[58] Sam Arkoff of American International Pictures explained the rationale for the independents' new prominence. They "were filling a big product void. The majors are welcoming independent activity and are more than willing to release their product since there is a need for a steady flow of films in all markets. The independent financier regards film-making as a business and realizes the viability

Farrah Fawcett in
Sunburn (1979).

British production company Hemdale's presale advertisement for *Sunburn* in *Variety*, 3 January 1979. Although the film was, in the words of *New York Times* critic Janet Maslin, a "breezy mish-mash" that did not fare well at the box office, Hemdale still made a large profit on presales, which far exceeded the production cost.

Romance and Riches (1936): Bobby Garrett's debut in the film industry was an accomplished and thoughtful, although not particularly successful, romantic comedy starring Cary Grant, made when Garrett was only twenty-five.

THE J. ARTHUR RANK ORGANISATION
presents

JEAN KENT
DIRK BOGARDE
JOHN McCALLUM
SUSAN SHAW

The Woman in Question

Screenplay by JOHN CRESSWELL · Produced by TEDDY BAIRD
Directed by ANTHONY ASQUITH

EAGLE-LION DISTRIBUTION

The Woman in Question (1950) was the first film to receive a completion guarantee from Film Finances.

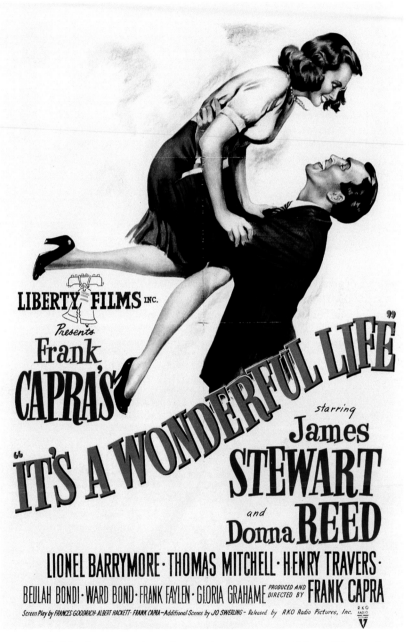

It's a Wonderful Life (1946): independent production company Liberty Films makes an early effort to challenge Hollywood's studio system.

SHARE CERTIFICATE

No. 65

No. of Shares 1,000

FILM FINANCES LIMITED

(Incorporated under the Companies Act, 1948).

AUTHORISED CAPITAL - £150,000
DIVIDED INTO 150,000 SHARES OF £1 EACH

This is to Certify that *Joseph Somlo*

of *19 Fresbury House, Rutland Gate, S.W.1* is/are the Registered

Holder(s) of *One Thousand* ————————————— Shares

of £1 each in the above-named Company, numbered *199,001* to *199,000* inclusive,

subject to the Memorandum and Articles of Association of the Company and that *1/-* is paid up on

each of such shares.

Given *under the Common Seal of the Company,*

this *18* day of *June* 19*54*

DIRECTOR.

Donald McKew SECRETARY.

A mark of Film Finances' success was when in 1954 it expanded its share capital
to £150,000. This certificate, dated 18 June 1954, was issued to a prominent
British-based film producer of the time, Joseph Somlo.

ROMULUS Presents

Humphrey **BOGART**
Katharine **HEPBURN**

in John Huston's
THE AFRICAN QUEEN

FILMED IN AFRICA IN COLOUR BY TECHNICOLOR

FROM THE NOVEL BY C.S. FORESTER

with
Robert
MORLEY

A HORIZON PRODUCTION · DISTRIBUTION CONTROLLED BY INDEPENDENT FILM DISTRIBUTORS

The African Queen (1951) demonstrated the potential of independent film
production.

The most startling and daring love story ever told!

Only amid the shameless glitter and streets of Paris could such a love be born! Kindled by a backstreet rendezvous, it swept from cabarets to artists' garrets until it flamed into a violence and passion that shocked the world!

ROMULUS presents **JOSÉ FERRER** in *John Huston's* **MOULIN ROUGE**

COLOR BY *Technicolor*

with ZSA ZSA GABOR · SUZANNE FLON

and introducing the fabulous COLETTE MARCHAND

A ROMULUS Production · Directed by John HUSTON · Screenplay by Anthony Veiller and John Huston · From the Novel "MOULIN ROUGE" by Pierre La MURE · Released thru UNITED ARTISTS

John Huston's *Moulin Rouge* (1952) became the first film guaranteed by Film Finances to be nominated for a Best Picture Oscar and confirmed United Artists' rebirth as Hollywood's champion of independents.

A collaboration between Romulus and Humphrey Bogart's own independent production company, Santana, *Beat the Devil* (1953) was the third John Huston film that Film Finances guaranteed.

STATEMENT OF PRODUCTION COST

Production Company........ EMBLEM PRODUCTIONS LTD.   Period....5 Wks. ended..10/11/62

Title of Film........ "LANCELOT AND GUINEVERE"

COST HEADING	Cost this Period	Total Committed Cost to Date	Estimate to Complete	Estimated Final Cost	Budget	Over (Red) Under (Black) Budget
	£	£	£	£	£	£
A STORY AND SCRIPT	33	10,394	11,257	21,651	21,600	51
B PRODUCER & DIRECTOR FEES	639	13,332	28,793	42,125	39,700	2425
C PRODUCTION UNIT SALARIES :—						
1. Production Management and Secretaries	610	4,003	232	4,235	2,686	1549
2. Assistant Directors and Continuity	419	5,208	30	5,238	3,634	1604
3. Technical Advisers		27		27		27
4. Camera Crews	1,182	11,632	1,259	12,891	7,910	4981
5. Recording Crews	1,157	2,793	1,658	4,451	2,494	1957
6. Editing Staff	1,907	5,629	2,629	8,258	4,086	4172
7. Stills Camera Staff	163	1,393		1,393	1,036	357
8. Wardrobe Designer and Staff	358	3,012	89	3,101	1,846	1255
9. Make-up Artistes	292	3,537	13	3,550	1,800	1750
10. Hairdressers	162	1,474	9	1,483	972	511
11. Casting		390		390	500	110
12. Production Accountancy	433	3,279	640	3,919	2,485	1434
13. Projectionists	53	503	347	850	410	440
14. Other Staff	26	1,348	22	1,370	750	620
15. Foreign Unit Technicians	2,536	10,704		10,704	4,118	6586
D SET DESIGNING & SUPERVISORY STAFF		14,456		14,456	11,060	3396
E ARTISTES :—						
1. Cast	267	57,114	26,943	84,057	79,469	4588
2. Stand-Ins and Doubles	2,075	8,382	10	8,392	5,318	3074
3. Crowd	6,467	36,998	40	37,038	8,650	28388
F ORCHESTRA & COMPOSER	4		3,050	3,050	2,850	200
G COSTUMES & WIGS	1,241	24,153	6,481	30,634	19,700	10934
H MISCELLANEOUS PRODN. STORES (Ex. Sets)	94	3,842	365	4,207	2,170	2037
I FILM & LABORATORY CHARGES	2,990	16,862	13,517	30,379	21,800	8579
J STUDIO RENTALS	231	26,286	2,270	28,556	21,795	6761
K EQUIPMENT	650	18,411	200	18,611	4,725	13886
L POWER		2,820	135	2,955	1,530	1425
M TRAVEL & TRANSPORT :—						
1. Location	9,749	49,276	387	49,663	12,570	37093
2. Other	337	6,512	482	6,994	6,111	883
N HOTEL & LIVING EXPENSES :						
1. Location	3,276	18,161		18,161	10,492	7669
2. Other	2,954	17,512	1,862	19,374	10,480	8894
O INSURANCES	7,794	7,665	120	7,785	10,000	2215
P HOLIDAY & SICK PAY SURCHARGES	437	10,063	390	10,453	7,055	3398
Q PUBLICITY SALARIES & EXPENSES		3,224		3,224	3,000	224
R MISCELLANEOUS EXPENSES	139	4,615	960	5,575	5,000	575
S SETS & MODELS :—						
1. Labour—Construction	248	29,430		29,430	20,090	9340
2. Labour—Dressing		4,261	25	4,286	1,840	2446
3. Labour—Operating	892	8,243	25	8,268	4,930	3338
4. Labour—Striking	1	2,162		2,162	750	1412
5. Labour—Lighting	239	9,456	30	9,486	5,697	3789
6. Labour—Lamp Spotting *7				8,528	1,413	7115
7. Labour—Foreign Unit Labour /8	1,318	8,528		23,105	19,574	3531
8. Materials—Construction /*.9	780	23,105		23,312	10,510	12802
9. Properties /*. .T	3,413	23,252	60	3,825	500	3325
	555	3,825				
T SPECIAL LOCATION FACILITIES /*						
TOTAL DIRECT COST :	40,525	517,292	104,330	621,602	405,106	216496
Y FINANCE & LEGAL CHARGES	268	27,543	30,452	57,995	51,070	6925
Z OVERHEADS		3	4,567	4,570	4,570	
TOTAL PRODUCTION COST ...£	40,793	544,818	139,349	684,167	460,746	223421

PRODUCTION CONTINGENCY .... 34,000 / 34000

£ 494,746 / 189421

Deferments.
Yugoslavia 73,367
Bermans 5,800
Theodora 69,395
148,562

Approved by.....

FORM S.P.C.

Copies of form S.P.C. can be obtained from Hepburn & Sons Ltd., 41/42 Wool Exchange, Coleman Street, London, E.C.2 Telephone : MONarch 5175

The color red dominates the final column of a costly weekly cost sheet for *Lancelot and Guinevere* (1963), starring and directed by Cornel Wilde.

The Romulus Films production *Room at the Top*, which Film Finances guaranteed in 1958, was nominated for six Oscars, winning the Academy Award for Best Actress (Simone Signoret) and Best Adapted Screenplay (Neil Paterson). The British cinema went on to enjoy a striking revival during the 1960s, and Film Finances was at the very heart of it.

Saturday Night and Sunday Morning (1960), one of several notable films that Film Finances guaranteed for Woodfall.

Dr. No (1962): the prototype for the longest-running film franchise in the history of the cinema.

The whole world loves **Tom Jones!**

ALBERT FINNEY   SUSANNAH YORK
HUGH GRIFFITH   EDITH EVANS
JOAN GREENWOOD in *"Tom Jones"*
also starring
DIANE CILENTO

with   and the guest appearance of   Screenplay by   Produced and Directed by
GEORGE   DAVID TOMLINSON   JOHN OSBORNE   TONY RICHARDSON   EASTMAN COLOUR   A WOODFALL
DEVINE   PRODUCTION

For once a poster's tagline wasn't an exaggeration: in 1963 the whole world really did love *Tom Jones*.

Cover of *Time* magazine, 15 April 1966, proclaiming London "the swinging city."

A generation younger than Film Finances' cofounder Bobby Garrett, Richard Soames had the energy and vision to embrace the huge change that the international film industry would undergo during the 1970s and 1980s.

The advent of the American Film Market in 1981 helped to put in place the infrastructure for independent film financing in the United States.

The Terminator (1984): rarely has a movie delivered so many bangs for the buck. Made for $6.5 million and guaranteed by Film Finances, this first *Terminator* was a model of cost-effective, lean filmmaking. Its sequel *Terminator 2*, at a production cost of approximately $100 million, was at the time of its release in 1991 the most expensive movie ever made (but not guaranteed by Film Finances).

Reply: 51 South Hill Park
London NW3

Dear Sirs,

I confirm that I have examined the schedule and to the best of my knowledge consider this to be adequate subject to unforeseen circumstances.

I also consider that the allocation of film stock is sufficient.

Yours faithfully,

Terry Gilliam

Film Finances Ltd.
34 South Molton Street
London W1

Letter from Terry Gilliam to Film Finances that gives an accurate depiction of the peril involved in guaranteeing a Gilliam movie—in this case, *Jabberwocky* (1977), which foreshadowed trouble to come in the 1980s with *The Adventures of Baron Munchausen* (1988).

May 9-15, 2000
$3.25 *(California)* $4.95 *(Canada)* $3.40 *(Elsewhere)* £3.50 *(U.K.)*

a **BPi** *publication*

FILM FINANCES 50TH ANNIVERSARY SPECIAL ISSUE

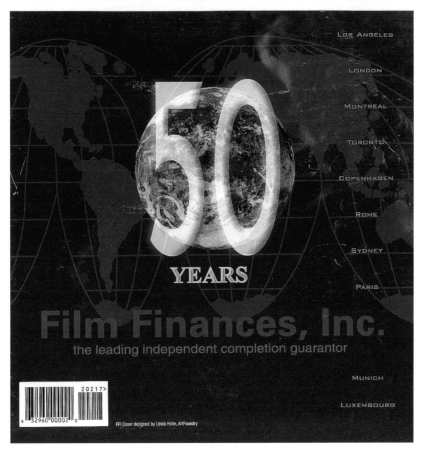

Fifty years of making Hollywood happen.

of investment with minimum exposure. He knows he can count on outside sales and TV programming either through the majors or independents."[59]

Although *Sunburn* turned out to be a flop at the US box office, Hemdale and its US coproduction partner, United Artists Theatre Circuit, still made a considerable profit on the venture through the presales it had made on the strength of Farrah Fawcett's name. The picture's failure meant that Hemdale had to cancel the next film it had planned to make with Fawcett, a Riviera comedy about jewel thieves called *Strictly Business*, but the way the international film industry had opened up meant that it had little trouble financing a busy production program. "There's such a big demand for films now," explained John Daly. "Opportunities exist with network TV, syndication, cable and the demand by foreign countries for independently financed films, so the climate is very much in favour of a company like Hemdale."[60]

At the end of 1978, Hemdale opened a Los Angeles office, from where it developed a production line of American movies presold on the strength of their box office stars. Just to take two of the early ones that were both distributed in the United States by Universal: the Western *Cattle Annie and Little Britches* (1981), starring Burt Lancaster and Rod Steiger, about two young women (Amanda Plummer and Diane Lane, in the title roles) who join an outlaw gang; and *Carbon Copy* (1981), starring George Segal and Denzel Washington, a comedy set in California about a white corporate executive who discovers that he has a black teenage son. Both of these films, as did most Hemdale productions, with their heavy reliance on presales financing, had completion guaranties from Film Finances.

If Bobby Garrett's antiexpansionist nature eventually had to yield to the sheer tide of new business that the 1970s internationalization of the industry led to, Richard Soames stressed the importance of timing, in which he felt that Garrett's caution had served as a useful check: "In retrospect, Bobby's resistance helped us in the sense that we didn't go in too early. And my wish to expand was not too late. So it was a good balance."[61] But it was Soames's can-do energy that made the critical difference. Even as Film Finances was facing the challenge of the rapidly growing business in Canada, Soames continued to make the most of the opportunities for expansion wherever they occurred.

The last challenge of the decade was Australia. "We have recently been approached by several Australian production companies," Soames wrote in February 1977 to Basil Appleby, a British producer who ran the Australian Film and Television School, which had been founded in 1973. "We wonder if there is a chance that you would be prepared to vet projects and be able to keep an

SAMSON PRODUCTIONS PTY. LIMITED

44 Liverpool Street, Paddington, N.S.W. 2021, Australia   Telephone 33 5412

Production Office   11 Young Street, Paddington.   33.4663.

Cables: SAMSONFILM, Sydney.

August 4, 1976.

Mr. Bernard Smith,
Managing Director,
Film Finances Ltd.,
34 South Molton Street,
LONDON.   W1Y 1HA.   ENGLAND.

Dear Mr. Smith,

Now that the dust has settled after our very hectic, but most worthwhile, round-the-world trip, I would like to take this opportunity to say how much Sue Milliken and I enjoyed our very constructive meeting with Richard Soames and yourself.

I wonder whether you have given further thought to the possibility of your Company becoming involved in Australian production financing. Since returning to Sydney, we have plunged into raising the production finance for our next feature, which we hope to film before the end of the year. As a consequence, we are giving serious consideration to the completion guarantee aspect of the financing, with particular reference to the kinds of terms which you outlined to us in London.

I would like to confirm with you now the basis on which you would provide a completion guarantee.

After satisfying yourselves about the efficiency of the organisational aspects of the production, you would agree to supply completion finance. If this is used, your funds would be recovered after recoupment of prime finance.

Your fee would be calculated as 6% of the negative production cost, less the 10% contingency which you would insist that the budget include, and also less your fee.

If you continue your involvement in further productions, a no-claim bonus system on your fee would operate.

One point on which I would like clarification is whether you put a limit on the amount of funds available per production as a completion guarantee. Is the completion guarantee, perhaps, calculated as a percentage of the negative picture cost?

If you believe that it is feasible for your company to involve itself in the Australian film production industry, I would be glad to send you the script, budget and schedule of our next project, with a view to negotiating a completion guarantee for it.

I look forward to hearing from you shortly.

With best wishes,

Yours sincerely,

TOM M. JEFFREY.

Samson Productions was the very first Australian production company to suggest to Film Finances, in 1976, the possibility of supporting Australian production. Its head of production, Sue Milliken, would five years later become Film Finances' Australian consultant.

eye on the progress of the film during shooting, acting on our behalf. If this is not possible due to your other commitments, would you be able to recommend anyone out there who would be competent to help us?"[62]

Among the other inquiries Film Finances had received was one from the producers of Peter Weir's *Picnic at Hanging Rock* (1975), Hal and Jim McElroy, who on a visit to London had invited Film Finances to look at the papers for their next production, *The Last Wave* (1977). Although in the end the Australian Film Commission and the South Australian Film Commission decided jointly to take the risk on the film's completion, the interest from producers that Film Finances had been receiving reflected the way in which a still comparatively young Australian film industry had reached an important turning point.

Through the first half of the 1970s, the principal investors in the industry had been government film commissions that had in effect themselves acted as completion guarantors for films that still had comparatively modest budgets. But toward the end of the decade, there was a swing toward much larger-budget films aimed at the international market, with Australian producers beginning to rely on international presales and coproduction deals.

Soames visited Australia in January 1980 to promote the benefits of Film Finances' guarantee at what was an obviously opportune time. When he learned ahead of the trip that the British producer David Puttnam was already there, Soames wrote in December 1979 to ask whether Puttnam might have any useful advice. Soames explained that he intended to meet "as many people in the industry as possible in the hope of establishing an understanding of the role of the completion guarantee and in general our operation. Although the situation is not the same as it was in Canada there do seem to be some parallels and as you may know we have been very involved in creating the climate and conditions for the boom in production there right from the start."[63]

After a successful visit, Soames made sure that Film Finances would be well placed to play an integral part in the production boom that occurred in the Australian film industry in the 1980s.

FRANCIS FORD COPPOLA
PRESENTS
THE OUTSIDERS
S. E. Hinton's
classic novel about youth.

GOING HOLLYWOOD

The 1980s

A changing of the guard was taking place at Film Finances. It had begun with the death in June 1977 of Bernard Smith, who had been managing director of the company since the early 1960s. The letter that Film Finances published in the British trade paper *Screen International* to announce the sad news touched on the extraordinary continuity that had been broken.

The Film Finances that Bernard Smith left behind—Bobby Garrett, John Croydon, Bill Croft (the company's finance director), Richard Soames, and Soames's assistant Elizabeth Byford—all signed the letter. Three of them— Garrett, Croydon, and Croft—had been with the company from the very beginning, but the ethos now was decisively different.

Bobby Garrett had founded Film Finances in 1950 with the sense of patriotic purpose felt by many British people during the grim austerity years that followed World War II, when the country was struggling to get back on its feet. Under Garrett's guidance, Film Finances assumed a quasi-institutional presence in a heavily subsidized and regulated British film industry.

But thirty years later, as the local industry, in the absence of any significant investment, languished in a backwater, it was clear that Film Finances' future lay in being not British but international. During the first six months of 1981, the company guaranteed forty-four films. Of these, only two were made in Britain, compared with nine in the United States, thirteen in Canada, and fifteen in Australia.[1] It was Film Finances' most profitable year, but on the basis of a now predominately overseas operation that the ever-cautious Bobby Garrett regarded as dangerously risky. As chairman of the company, he offered an august figurehead but otherwise played little part in an expansion that filled him with misgiving. "Garrett was against anything outside Calais," recalled Soames, who had after Bernard Smith's death replaced him as managing director

FILM FINANCES LIMITED

REGD. OFFICE: CANDLEWICK HOUSE, 116/126, CANNON STREET, E.C.4.
REGD. No. 478695 ENGLAND

CTORS
F. GARRETT CHAIRMAN
SMITH MANAGING DIRECTOR
A. CROFT, F.C.A.
DEAN, M.A., F.C.A.
SOAMES

34, SOUTH MOLTON STREET,

LONDON,

WIY IHA.

TELEPHONE: 01-629 6557/9.
CABLES: FILMGAR, LONDON, W.I.

28th June, 1977.

To all our friends:

We have to tell you that our colleague, Bernard Smith, died yesterday. He was 56 years of age. It was in the latter part of last year that Bernard was diagnosed as suffering from cancer and in spite of immediate remedial treatment, it was already too late.

Bernard was a relative newcomer to our Company – he had been with us only about 25 years – and he would become quite cross when asked if he was settling down and whether he would remain with us. It is to our infinite regret that he will not be so doing.

During the War Bernard flew as a navigator with 15 Squadron on operational duties over Europe. In 1943 Bernard's aircraft crashed and the whole of the crew save Bernard were killed. It was so typical of Bernard that since that time he had looked upon every new day of life as a happy and unexpected bonus. We all would like to think not that his life has been cut short but that we have enjoyed 25 years of his company.

We shall miss him.

Letter dated 28 June 1977 that was published in the British trade press to announce the death of Film Finances managing director Bernard Smith. It coincided with the passing of an era, as a once very British company became increasingly international.

and strongly advocated the company's foreign expansion.[2] The fundamental difference of attitude between Soames and Garrett set them on a collision course that was only finally resolved through a board meeting of directors that voted Garrett out of the chairmanship.

In October 1982, *Screen International* reported Garrett's resignation from the company he had founded. "It had been whispered in financial circles that there had been some boardroom bickering over the past year or two and that Bobby Garrett has not been seeing eye to eye on some matters with his managing director, Richard Soames."[3] Garrett, who had been ill for some time, died only a few weeks after he left Film Finances, on Christmas Eve 1982.

To help develop a company that was taking a decisively international direction, Soames found an important collaborator on the business side in Ron Aikin, who had been a partner at Harbottle & Lewis, the law firm that had looked after Film Finances' legal work since the mid-1950s. In 1978, Aikin left Harbottle & Lewis to become Film Finances' in-house legal adviser.

On the production side, Soames turned in 1980 to David Korda, who was a nephew of the film impresario Alexander Korda. After growing up in Hollywood, where his parents had moved during World War II, David Korda returned to Britain in the 1950s. He started out in the industry working for the producer Charles Schneer, who made fantasy and adventure films for distribution through Columbia, including most of the films of Ray Harryhausen. He went on to become a production manager and then worked as a line producer.

Richard Soames met him for the first time during the production of the Peter O'Toole film *Murphy's War* (1971), one of the films that had the backing of Dimitri de Grunwald's London Screenplays. It told the story of a submarine that was hiding out in the Orinoco River in Venezuela during World War II. "I worked on the film because the original producer of the film was fired," recalled Korda. "The film, frankly, was out of control. It was out of control not because they hadn't done their budget very well but because they had made ridiculous decisions about where to make the film and how to shoot it."[4] After abandoning location shooting in South America, the production finally did what it should have done in the first place and re-created the Orinoco in a large tank in Malta.

After producing two films for Peter O'Toole's production company Keep Films, Korda went on to work for Hemdale in Mexico on the films *Sunburn* (1979) and *Cattle Annie and Little Britches* (1981), which both had completion guaranties from Film Finances. He was, in his own words, "a practical, hands-on, organizational line producer," with experience of working around the world that Soames would have regarded as a particularly valuable qualification.[5] "When I met him on those films, we had a good relationship," Korda remembered. "I didn't want to put myself into the position of claiming on Film Finances, and I worked very hard to see that we didn't."[6]

In February 1982, a share in Film Finances was worth £3 ($5). But only two years later the value had increased to £9 ($12). During the same period, the cash reserves of the company had increased from £1.8 million ($3.1 million) to £9.2 million ($12.2 million). The company's dividend, which was 45 pence per share in 1979, had risen to 150 pence, or £1.50 ($2), in 1984. Richard Soames's determination to embrace international filmmaking had turned out to be extremely profitable.[7]

An important cause of Film Finances' success was the energy with which it seized the quite exceptional opportunities that the new decade presented. A variety of new distribution platforms, which had simply not existed before, all established themselves as significant presences in the entertainment marketplace: home video, satellite and cable television, and a proliferation of new TV channels that resulted from the deregulation of the telecommunications industries in the United States and Western Europe. Recognizing the underlying fundamentals of a rapidly growing market, with a massive demand for new product, financial institutions showed an increased readiness to invest in the entertainment industry. There had never been a better time to be an independent producer. Or a completion guarantor.

~

The pace of change was electrifying. No sooner had Film Finances opened a Canadian office than it was considering the possibility of doing the same in Australia. In 1978, the Australian government had introduced a 100 percent write-off for investors in Australian films. In the wake of the legislation, Film Finances had been receiving a growing number of inquiries from not only producers and financiers but also the newly established state film commissions.

Watching the developing situation closely was Joe Skrzynski, an investment banker at Sydney-based merchant bank Seldon & Associates. In December 1978, during a visit to London, he had a meeting with Ron Aikin at Film Finances to discuss the Australian industry's progress and to learn how the completion guarantee worked. Six months later, he wrote from Sydney to update Aikin on the latest news: "Since speaking with you, a stronger trend has emerged along the lines which I had predicted and that is there has been a swing to larger budget movies."[8]

While the films that had been produced in Australia with government support during the 1970s had been typically budgeted at between A$400,000 (US$200,000) and A$750,000 (US$375,000), now there were several projects with preproduction support from state film commissions that had budgets in excess of A$2 million (US$1 million). Such projects tended to be pitched at the international market. They relied on a funding strategy of preselling, international stars, and coproduction or distribution deals.

It was a situation that would require government film commissions, Skrzynski pointed out, "to re-examine the continued prudence of providing open-ended cost-free completion guarantees when their possible exposure begins to exceed $200,000 [in Australian dollars] per picture."[9] Rather than put public money at risk, there would be an incentive to turn instead to an organization like Film Finances, with its much greater experience and expertise.

Only a few weeks after receiving Skrzynski's update, Film Finances became involved in guaranteeing its first Australian-based picture. *The Earthling* (1980) had been set up through their business relationship with New York–based FRP Productions. The film was originally going to be made in the United States. It told the story of Patrick Foley, a man with terminal cancer who wants to die out in the wilderness where he was born. But on the trek out to a mountain valley where his father is buried, Foley meets a young girl whose parents have died in an avalanche. Reluctantly, he allows the child to travel with him. Soon after they reach the valley, Foley dies. The girl buries him and, with the survival skills that Foley has taught her, sets off back to civilization.

The production had been put together by New York financier Stephen Sharmat, whose company, Westchester Productions, specialized in packaging tax-sheltered deals for such Hollywood films as *Killer Elite* (1975), *Carrie* (1976), and *Semi-Tough* (1977). Sharmat took advantage of an expenditure recoupment scheme under section 51(1) of the Australian Income Tax Assessment Act to persuade the principal backer, American International Pictures—which at the time of the deal had just been acquired by Filmways—to move the production to Australia. With veteran Hollywood actor William Holden and child star Ricky Schroder engaged to play the leads, the child character was changed from a girl to a boy and the script adapted to accommodate the new Australian setting.

In August, Film Finances and FRP Productions signed a co-guarantor agreement under which FRP was liable for the first A$200,000 (US$100,000) of any overcost, and Film Finances for any additional sum required for completion after that. Directed by the British filmmaker Peter Collinson, best known

The Earthling (1980) was the first production that Film Finances guaranteed in Australia. It was essentially an American film that was shot in Australia to take advantage of local tax incentives.

for *The Italian Job* (1969), shooting commenced the following month with an Australian crew in the Blue Mountains of New South Wales. A locally based American producer called Mende Brown was engaged to oversee the production on behalf of the two guarantors.

It seemed so certain that the Australian industry was about to take off—as Canada had done previously—that, to protect its name, Film Finances instructed the Sydney-based law firm of Allen, Allen & Hemsley in October 1979 to incorporate a shelf company as Film Finances Australia before anyone from the London office had even set foot in Australia.[10]

"*The Earthling* is essentially an American film set in colorful Australian bush," wrote the Australian magazine *Cinema Papers*. "The fact that [it] captures the physical essence of Australia without its cultural fascination is a great pity, not only for Australians, but for those overseas who will only see one facet of Australia, namely the Barrington Tops National Park, where the film was shot."[11] It was hardly an effective calling card for a young film industry that was determined to assert its own Australian identity. And the mood that Richard Soames encountered when he finally arrived in Sydney in January 1980 for his first visit to Australia was one of skepticism. At a meeting with the Australian producers' association, he recalled "about twenty producers saying, 'Oh, you're just scammers, you shouldn't come here, and we know you'll just take a few fees and disappear.'"[12]

But the Australian Film Commission (AFC) appreciated the discipline that Film Finances could bring to its still fledgling industry. The AFC was chaired by Ken Watts, who had previously been a director of programs at the Australian Broadcasting Commission, and its director of project development was John Daniell. "They understood exactly what we were talking about," recalled Soames, "so they really embraced us to come there."[13]

Film Finances received even more support when a few months later Ken Watts announced the appointment of Joe Skrzynski as the AFC's "general manager" as of August 1980. Watts's accompanying statement marked a watershed moment of the New Australian Cinema gearing up to achieve its commercial potential: "In the first five years of the AFC activities, the industry has changed considerably. There is now a more solid base of experience and Australian films are well received at home and have achieved wide critical acclaim overseas. They have also attracted large audiences overseas."[14] After joining the AFC, Skrzynski masterminded an even more generous tax incentive, section 10BA, which in 1981 introduced a 150 percent tax write-off for investment in Australian films.

The incorporation of Film Finances Australia in April 1980 coincided with Soames's second visit to Sydney, when he continued discussions with the AFC and finalized negotiations over a completion guarantee for *Road Games* (1981), a Hitchcock-style thriller about a truck driver and a hitchhiker who encounter a serial killer on their journey through the Australian desert. The film was produced and directed by Australian director Richard Franklin with an attitude that suggested the new awareness among Australian filmmakers of the potential of the international market. Its production coincided with the release in America of *Mad Max* (1979), which offered a spectacular example of things to come. Over the previous ten years, Australian cinema had firmly established itself on the world stage with such films as *Picnic at Hanging Rock* (1975), *The Getting of Wisdom* (1976), and *My Brilliant Career* (1979). But although these films had won considerable critical esteem, they had made only a minimal impact on the international box office. Filmed on a budget of only US$350,000, *Mad Max* went on to earn a worldwide gross of nearly US$100 million.[15]

"I see our Australian landscape, geographically and culturally, as a backdrop for stories and ideas that should have universal relevance," Franklin commented

Emerging from the shadows . . . With films like *Picnic at Hanging Rock* (1975), the Australian cinema began to achieve an international prominence in the mid-1970s.

Road Games (1981) was the first production that Sue Milliken supervised for Film Finances in Australia. Her company, Samson Productions, in Pyrmont Street, Sydney, provided Film Finances with its first Australian home.

of *Road Games*. "I think it's insular to imagine that we concern ourselves with things that the rest of the world doesn't. And, if we do, then we have no right to want the rest of the world to look at what we do."[16] The casting of the American stars Jamie Lee Curtis (of *Halloween* [1978] fame) and Stacy Keach (a renowned stage and screen actor whose father and brother were also in films) was at the insistence of the US distributor Avco Embassy that the lead actors had to be of international standing.

Film Finances' guarantee was the linchpin in a complex jigsaw of financing that included subsidies from not only the Australian Film Commission but also two state governments (Victoria and Western Australia), foreign presales, and twenty private investors contributing to a tax-sheltered scheme that raised the lion's share of the budget (A$1,080,000 [US$1,229,749] out of a total budget of A$1,761,588 [US$2,005,844]).

Needing a local representative who had the necessary expertise to monitor the progress of the production, Soames turned to filmmaker Sue Milliken, who had begun her career in the 1960s as a continuity assistant with Fauna Productions on the *Skippy* TV series.[17] After working for the Australian Broadcasting Commission, she became a production manager and then a producer, setting up the company Samson Productions with her partner Tom Jeffrey. By

Jamie Lee Curtis hitching a ride in *Road Games* (1981).

coincidence, Milliken and Jeffrey had been the first Australian filmmakers to make contact with Film Finances several years previously, well before any tax legislation had been introduced.

Milliken would later remember meeting Soames for lunch at the Sebel Town House Hotel in Sydney's harborside suburb of Elizabeth Bay. Her impression was of "a tall, diffident Englishman with a sharp sense of humour and a brilliant business mind." A key asset was his command of "the awkward pause, into which many a guilty producer dropped information they had been planning to keep to themselves, just to break the silence." It was no accident, she thought, that for more than thirty years he had "remained on top in what has to be one of the planet's riskier businesses."[18]

Road Games, which began principal photography in the Melbourne Film Studio on 14 May 1980, was a challenging production that involved a location shoot over hundreds of miles of the Australian wilderness, but the answer to its problems relied on the same application of practical filmmaking principles that held true everywhere. At the end of the week, the shooting of an action scene that involved several cars had to be canceled because the vehicles, which had been delivered only the night before, all had mechanical problems that needed fixing. One of them had too little engine capacity to manage the boat trailer that it was required to tow in the scene. Although the model had been out of production for five years, a more powerful version had to be hurriedly found, purchased, and resprayed to the correct color.

Milliken had not been involved in the preplanning stage of the production to be able to ask the exhaustive, Croydon-style questions that might have saved the considerable extra cost that the lost shooting night entailed, but she was able to get the production to hire a dedicated vehicle manager, which helped alleviate further delays. "I suppose my effectiveness this far has been in the changes made," Milliken reflected at the end of her first week as a completion guarantor, "because if I had not been there enumerating the obvious I suspect they may have tried to muddle through without changes."[19]

Road Games was completed with a small overage of approximately A$30,000 (US$34,000), but its importance was to establish Film Finances as a long-term presence in the Australian film industry. It would go on to prove that it was not a scammer who would just "take the fees and disappear." No sooner had principal photography on *Road Games* finished than Film Finances asked Milliken to supervise another film, *Race for the Yankee Zephyr* (1981), to be directed by David Hemmings. More projects quickly followed, with Milliken playing an active role in building the relationships behind their acquisition. Samson

Productions' office, at 119 Pyrmont Street in Pyrmont, a suburb of Sydney, became the de facto base for Film Finances' fast-growing operation.

Driving the boom was the Division 10BA tax legislation. "Almost every producer has his or her story of the unknown and unmet country doctor ringing and wanting to invest fifty to one hundred thousand dollars," reported the Australian trade magazine *Film News*.[20] The industry "took off like a bush fire," Milliken recalled. "Suddenly there were about 40 feature films being shot a year, and every one of them had to be bonded. Film Finances was the only company operating, and I was it. So we just rolled into it without ever a conversation. We never discussed it. I just kept going."[21]

To the extent that there were any conversations, they were about how to cope with an extraordinary glut. "The work is flooding in here," Milliken wrote to Richard Soames in a telex, dated 12 February 1981. Its prime purpose was to request an assistant. "So far I am involved in 15 projects on your behalf plus a lot of time-consuming inquiries. Unless something really unforeseen happens, it's going to get worse from April on when there are more pictures shooting."[22] When a few days later Soames mailed her a schedule of the films that the company was looking at, he included a note with the comment, "Probably by the time you receive it, it will already be out of date."[23] His expansionist instinct was to make the most of what had become a very large wave.

"With regard to your very real concern over regulating production," Soames wrote to Milliken on 12 March 1981, "I feel that by our presence we are regulating it to the extent that we are not taking on pictures that we cannot live with, and to the extent that we are a deterrent to amateurs just trying it on. My view is that is the only criterion that can be applied."[24]

A comparison that he would have had in mind was how Film Finances had coped with the previous exponential boom in Canada. Soames advised, "Objectively, in our experience, after the first onslaught, production should settle down in a more orderly fashion and the amateurs will fall by the wayside. This actually seems to me to be happening already and I have a feeling that in 1982, from what I hear, there will be larger but fewer pictures."[25]

~

The ultimate prize for Film Finances was Hollywood. In October 1979, while the executive producer of *The Earthling*, Stephen Sharmat, was in Australia, he gave an interview to the Sydney magazine *The Bulletin*, which provided a succinct summary of the opportunities. The major studios, he explained, had cut their production to such an extent that there was "a tremendous dearth of product," which was pushing up the price that independent producers could get for Hollywood-style films. Whereas two years ago the sale of US TV rights to a movie might have fetched US$1 million, now it was US$3 million plus. He gave as an example the Burt Reynolds movie *Hooper* (1978), which he had recently financed. A network offered US$3.5 million, "but we waited six weeks and got $11 million." Such was the demand for content, he concluded, that "if you want a successful movie and you want to make money, you go USA."[26]

Film Finances had been "going USA" for some years now. It had started off modestly in 1977, through its association with Everett Rosenthal's New York–based FRP Productions, coguaranteeing productions that were mostly shot on the Eastern Seaboard. But by the turn of the decade, it was guaranteeing productions—sometimes in partnership but more often on its own—across America. "In the late 70s and early 80s, I was practically commuting between London and New York on a bi-monthly basis," recalled Ron Aikin, "leaving Heathrow at 11.30 a.m., attending a completion meeting in downtown Manhattan at 9.30 a.m., local time, courtesy of Concorde."[27]

The company's monthly schedule of the films that were under guarantee at this time offers a fascinating snapshot of a British company whose future now lay manifestly beyond Britain's shores. Take the schedule for April 1981, for example. Fourteen films were at various stages of production in Canada (including one of the most expensive films—at that stage in Film Finances' history—ever to have been guaranteed, *Quest for Fire*, with a budget of nearly US$11 million), eighteen in Australia, and eleven in the United States, but only one in Britain (*An American Werewolf in London*, with funding from PolyGram).

The American films included Wes Craven's *Swamp Thing*, shot in South Carolina; an Alan Arkin comedy, *Chu Chu and the Philly Flash* (San Francisco); a horror film, *Death Valley* (Arizona); a crime drama, *Vice Squad* (Los Angeles); and *Death Wish II* (also Los Angeles). Although some of these productions involved a local coguarantor, Film Finances no longer required such participation as a necessary condition. Its experience in the United States, Canada, and now Australia gave the company confidence that it could either supervise a production from a distance or, if necessary, appoint its own local representative—like Sue Milliken—to supervise the production on its behalf.

The chief issue was not location in itself but the intrinsic risk of a project, although, when the intrinsic risk was too high, location could provide a discreet means to decline a project. In November 1980, the London office passed on to Richard Soames the details of a call from Werner Herzog in Munich requesting a guarantee for his latest film: "Project entitled 'FITZCARRALDO'—

FILM FINANCES LIMITED			Year 1980/81.		at 1/4/81.	

FILMS: SHOOTING OR EDITING OR
ON WHICH WE HAVE GIVEN A LETTER
OF INTENT DURING CURRENT YEAR

U.S.A./U.K.

TITLE	PRODUCER	START DATE	BUDGET	GROSS FEE	NET FEE	SOURCE OF FINANCE	LOCATION
"FAST WALKING"	McWhorter	8/7	$3,500,000	$210,000	$105,000	Lorimar	Montana
"BIG BUCKS"	Green	14/7	$4,468,224	$224,520	$112,260	Hemdale	Mexico
"THE CHOSEN"	Landau	4/8	$3,554,000	$183,864	$91,932	Chemical	New York
"URGH"	White	10/8	$1,146,950	$30,450	$30,450	Lorimar	London/LA
"DAWN OF THE MUMMY"	Agrama	30/8	$492,000	$23,400	$23,400	Greyhound	Egypt
"CHU CHU AND THE PHILLY FLASH"	Weston & FRP	3/9	$7,057,876	$243,400	$170,361	Simon	L.A.
"DEATH VALLEY"	Kastner	17/11	$2,458,392	$123,693	$61,847	Slavenberg	Arizona
"AMERICAN WEREWOLF IN LONDON"	Folsey	2/2	$7,922,500	£169,354	£118,548	Polygram	U.K.
"BEATLEMANIA"	Landau	23/2	$4,176,000	$216,000	$108,000	American Releasing L.A.	
"SWAMPTHING"	Melniker	20/4	$2,745,355	$72,038	$72,038	Chemical Bank	Charleston, S.C.
"VICE SQUAD"	Howard	27/4	$2,663,621	$132,601	TBA	Avco	L.A.
"DEATH WISH - PART II"	Golan	4/5	$6,055,645	$313,223	$250,579	TBA	L.A.

List of US and UK films under guarantee by Film Finances at the beginning of April 1981, only one of which (*An American Werewolf in London*) was a British production.

about rubber, etc., in South America. Transporting ship from one river to another. Locations: Peru/Brazil/on Amazon. No Studio work. 2 ships involved. Prod. Werner Herzog—he is also director." The answer that was eventually returned once Soames had had an opportunity to consider the proposal did not need to go into any details as to why it might be a nightmare to guarantee. "Got back, and said 'no experience in S. America, v. sorry,' etc., etc."[28]

Yet the company's fundamental mode of operation was to carry a project forward if it possibly could. At about the same time as Film Finances turned down what would become the overbudget production disaster of *Fitzcarraldo*, Harbottle & Lewis lawyer John Stutter was trying—unsuccessfully, as it would turn out—to overcome its reservations about guaranteeing a series of operas to be directed by Franco Zeffirelli: *Cavalleria Rustica, I Pagliacci, La Traviata*, and *La Bohème*. "I know that you are constitutionally averse to saying no," Stutter cabled Ron Aikin, "and therefore hope that you might be persuaded (on good reason being shown) eventually to say yes."[29]

❦

The use of the completion guarantee in Hollywood at the beginning of the 1980s was still a rarity, but a number of overbudget disasters had made even the major studios receptive to its value. Most notorious of all was the $25 million overcost that United Artists had suffered on Michael Cimino's *Heaven's Gate* (1980). In its aftermath, United Artists had been offered the opportunity to back the Barbra Streisand production of the Isaac Bashevis Singer story *Yentl* (1983).

Streisand intended not only to appear in the film but also to direct it. "There was no star in the world with whom UA wanted to work more and hardly any project more risky," recalled the studio's then head of production, Steven Bach. The film had the potential to be a second *Fiddler on the Roof,* which had made a fortune for United Artists ten years previously, but the recent trauma the studio had suffered with *Heaven's Gate* undermined any enthusiasm. "What if she turns out to be the female Michael Cimino?" Bach recalled United Artists' chair, Jim Harvey, asking at a production meeting. "One, we agreed, was enough."[30]

The studio decided to go ahead with the $14 million movie but insisted that Streisand's company secure a completion bond. David Korda met the film's executive producer, Larry De Waay, to discuss the possibility. "I expressed our reservations on the intrinsic problem of not being able to remove director/producer," he wrote in a cable to Soames, updating him on the meeting. "De Waay

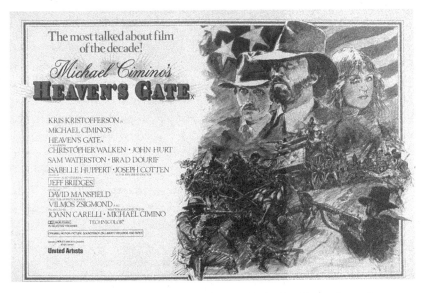

The massive overcosts of *Heaven's Gate* (1980) encouraged Hollywood to wake up to the need for financial discipline.

argues that Streisand is extremely co-operative and helpful and is as keen to show her financial responsibility as she is to make an artistic success. I explained our normal terms but said that in view of this unique situation this would not be acceptable."[31]

A cardinal rule for Film Finances was that no producer or director, no matter how powerful, should be exempt from its requirement to be the ultimate arbiter in deciding what was necessary for the delivery of a film. It insisted on the right to be able, in the worst case, to take over a production. In early summer 1981, Soames found himself having to explain the principle to Universal, when it inquired about the possibility of a completion guarantee for *ET*. The studio had previously cofinanced (with Columbia) Steven Spielberg's *1941*, which had gone massively over budget. Soames was dealing with Universal's director of business affairs, Mel Sattler, as well as lawyers representing Spielberg's new production company, Amblin Entertainment. "So I explained what we did," Soames recalled. "They just said, 'This is not acceptable.' I said, 'If it's not acceptable, it's not acceptable. That's just the way we work.' So, anyway, they walked away from it in the end."[32]

At a time when very few people in Hollywood even knew what a completion guarantor was, it was a challenge to explain the need for the ultimate control that, in the very last resort, Film Finances could exercise. "People don't like that concept," commented Soames, "until they realize that it's the last thing we ever want to do."[33]

A few months later, in February 1982, a feature article in the *New York Times* distilled Hollywood's unease over spiraling production costs and the huge license enjoyed by star directors that the box office returns of their films seemed no longer able to justify. The piece had been occasioned by the news that the director of the *Godfather* movies (1972, 1974) and *Apocalypse Now* (1979), Francis Ford Coppola, was facing the collapse of his independent production company American Zoetrope and, according to the *New York Times*, blamed his problems "on the fact that 'the studios,' not creative people, control the movies."[34]

"You can't let the inmates run the asylum," commented Freddie Fields, head of production at MGM. "I think Francis speaks with a forked tongue. He says that he can do a better job than the studios, but his little studio keeps going bankrupt." In Fields's view, the balance of power needed to shift back to the producer. "There was a time when it was a producer's medium, and I think all directors should work with a good producer to keep a step ahead of him, to help him plan. You go back to the days of Selznick and Spiegel. They knew what they were doing."[35]

But the trouble, according to director Blake Edwards, was precisely the fact that contemporary studio executives no longer seemed to know what they were doing. He lamented, "You have no creative people running the studios. There is nobody there who knows how to make a movie. It's appalling to me that the people in charge of studios don't even know the least thing about making a movie. Until you get some Thalbergs, we are not going to realize the full potential of the business."[36]

The *New York Times* piece coincided with the catastrophic release of Coppola's new movie *One from the Heart* (1981). The original distributor, Paramount, pulled out after Coppola organized a preview of the film at Radio City Music Hall in January 1982 without its authorization. Columbia released the film instead, but in only a handful of theaters. The total gross was $636,796 for a film that had ended up costing more than $25 million.[37]

One from the Heart had started out as a modest "old-fashioned love story," but the construction of an elaborate studio version of Las Vegas and Coppola's decision to reshoot several scenes resulted in expenditure that far exceeded the production's original budget.[38] It cemented the reputation for extravagance that he had established with his previous film *Apocalypse Now* (1979). Its original budget had been $12 million, but it ended up costing $31.5 million. "If

One from the Heart (1981)—Las Vegas on a soundstage.

there are nine easy ways to do something, Francis will manage to pick the 10th way," commented a Zoetrope colleague.[39]

Coppola himself seemed to revel in the risk. "The adventure of cinema is taking the next step," he told the *New York Times*. "Every one of my own personal future projects is dangerous."[40] The disastrous losses of *One from the Heart* bore out just how dangerous. It put him in a position where it seemed inevitable that he would have to give up "his little studio"—the old General Service Studios, at 1040 North Las Palmas Avenue in Los Angeles—which American Zoetrope had bought only two years before.

But this didn't prevent him from thinking about his next movie. He planned to direct a film version of the S. E. Hinton novel *The Outsiders*, about two rival gangs of teenagers growing up in Tulsa, Oklahoma. Although he was at the very nadir of his fortunes, with his company Zoetrope facing bankruptcy, Coppola still hoped to find financiers who would take the risk of lending him the money to make the film. No one in Hollywood could have much rated his chances: he was responsible for some of the most spectacular overcosts in film history and was the flag bearer—if not the godfather—of the movie brat generation that had fallen into such disfavor.

As a production accountant at Zoetrope, Kurt Woolner had direct experience of the financial troubles that Coppola was wrestling with at the time. He had joined Zoetrope soon after Coppola had bought General Service Studios. He worked on the Zoetrope film *The Escape Artist* (1982). But after the film had finished shooting, it was shelved because of Zoetrope's financial problems. A second film had to be shelved too, *Hammett* (1982), directed by the German filmmaker Wim Wenders.

About a year and a half later, Woolner was called back to the studio to help finish the two films. "They had limited funds," he recalled, "but they were going to stretch their dollars by offering a few people a chance to have more responsibility: 'Do your job plus another job.' It would be a saving for them and a way to get a couple of films finished." After *Hammett* had been completed, he was invited to work on the next film, *The Outsiders* (1983). The financing was to come from Warner Bros. and Chemical Bank, Woolner recounted, but they insisted that there should be a completion bond on the film, "which I, frankly, had never heard the concept of."[41]

❧

At the beginning of the 1980s there were no completion guarantors of any significant scale in Hollywood. But the rapid growth of independent production,

The Outsiders (1983) was a landmark film that helped not only the "Brat Pack" but also Film Finances to belong in Hollywood.

with the advent of video and cable and satellite TV, soon changed that. The insurance giant Fireman's Fund, which had long been Hollywood's largest provider of film production insurance, entered the guarantee business through a partnership with the newly established Completion Bond Company (CBC) in March 1981. Eager to make its mark, CBC began to bond some of Hollywood's most costly and high-profile independent productions, including some on which Film Finances had passed, such as *Yentl.* It boasted in its publicity of its readiness to take on "the 'tough' assignments—the high risk pictures that test determination and creativity," but it regarded Francis Ford Coppola as a risk too far.[42]

CBC "just rejected the project cold," remembered Woolner. "Said, 'We won't do it.'" It wasn't simply Coppola's reputation for exceeding budgets but also the sheer difficulty of controlling him should he do so again. "When a studio is financing a movie by Francis Ford Coppola," observed Woolner, "it's going to be a Francis Ford Coppola movie, so as a bond company you really have very little ability to influence the outcome . . . other than cajoling him and getting him to agree to be responsible."[43]

So Zoetrope turned to Film Finances. The first contact was made at the beginning of 1982. Before agreeing to go to Hollywood for discussions, David Korda outlined the stringent conditions that any guarantee would involve: "I do not want to put you to the trouble or expense of bringing me to California without making you aware of the above and of the fact that we do frequently reject projects where [we] believe we are not in a strong position to exercise control if need be."[44]

Zoetrope's president, Robert Spiotta, cabled back that Zoetrope was confident that it could meet the conditions and was still keen to negotiate. A script, budget, and shooting schedule were sent to Korda, who then flew from London in late February not to Los Angeles but to Tulsa, Oklahoma, where Coppola had already embarked on preproduction.

The new movie offered him an escape from the grim atmosphere of the Zoetrope studio in Los Angeles, where endless crisis meetings were taking place as the company struggled to stave off bankruptcy. "It was chaos incorporated time at Zoetrope," Coppola recalled, "like fighting a war. I used to be a great camp counselor, and the idea of being with half a dozen kids in the country and making a movie seemed like being a camp counselor again. It would be a breath of fresh air. I'd forget my troubles and have some laughs again."[45]

Shooting had been scheduled for the beginning of March, but there was a four-week delay while the difficult negotiations took place to secure the necessary funding, the success of which would depend on Film Finances' willingness to provide the completion guarantee.

Bob Storer, who was handling Film Finances' legal work at Harbottle & Lewis, recalled endless discussions about whether Film Finances should get involved. "His reputation had gone substantially," said Storer. "I was very aware that we were a big part of helping to see if an obviously hugely talented man could make a comeback."[46]

Having met the production team in Tulsa, David Korda sketched out an appraisal of the project on foolscap paper, enumerating one by one the factors at stake. The final point—Coppola's attitude—was the most important point of all. Ultimately, success depended on the will of the project's central figure. "When I met him, I was actually somewhat apprehensive," Korda recalled. "Here is a big director, and we're going to have to ask him to sign a letter saying he will behave himself. Some directors would just say, 'Go to hell.' They'd want nothing to do with anybody trying to police what they did. So I was apprehensive."[47]

But the Korda name turned out to be the perfect icebreaker. Not only had David Korda's uncle, Sir Alexander, produced a favorite movie of Coppola's, *The Thief of Bagdad* (1940), but he had completed it at General Service Studios, 1040 North Las Palmas Avenue, which Coppola's company American Zoetrope now owned. "When he found out that I was related to Alex, who had made his favorite movie ever, *The Thief of Bagdad*, he couldn't have been nicer."[48]

On 2 March 1982, Richard Soames telexed Robert Spiotta at Zoetrope Studios: "This is to confirm that we are in principle prepared to give a guarantee of completion."[49] The conditions included an "exceptional contingency." Zoetrope had to allow for the standard 10 percent contingency calculated on the basis of a $7 million budget—$700,000—but also an extra contingency of $1.5 million, which in effect was Coppola's fee as writer and director of the film. Not even this 30 percent contingency was enough to feel secure. So through their Lloyd's insurance broker, RTC, Film Finances took extra insurance cover up to $10 million. The information prepared for the Lloyd's reinsurers offered a neat explanation of why such a measure was deemed necessary: "This particular film is scheduled to shoot for 8 weeks mainly on location in Oklahoma. It is a simple picture but the Director is Francis Ford Coppola."[50]

Constitutionally averse as he was to saying no, Soames had been careful to stack the odds massively in favor of yes. "What is very interesting," observed Woolner, "is that Film Finances made an offer that David Korda later told me he thought was so severe that it would be rejected."[51]

1. Material – scripts manageable. + Locations easy little travel time except church

2. F.F.C. highly motivated + on the face of it determined to work to schedule + budget to make pictures for a price + within a specific time. – reputation to make.

3. Art director – Tavoularis very much limited – c.j. Small stage, no sets + builds only relatively minor modifications to Studio

4. Cameraman – not a "star" – chosen specifically because amenable + fast.

5. Tulsa – minimal distractions + he intent to stay

6. Retakes – problem of returning to Tulsa – could work both ways.

7. Danger areas –
   Schedule
   Bob Swarth fx.
   XX Calizpena children under 18
   XX Retakes
   Post production (but FFC wants to release by Oct.)

8. Zoetrope have 'reputation' to deal with – important to them.

9. Coppola's attitude – considers himself a 'practical' film maker – will study schedule + budget prior to signing letter.

David Korda's handwritten notes, February 1982, assessing the critical points of risk involved in guaranteeing *The Outsiders* (1983).

the OUTSIDERS

March 22, 1982

Film Finances, Ltd.
34, South Molton Street
London, WIY IHA England

      Re: Pony Boy, Inc. -- THE OUTSIDERS

Gentlemen:

      This letter consititues notice of my approval of
the final script and shooting schedule (ammended to include
7 weeks of shooting and one week of pick-ups) on THE OUTSIDERS
which I consider to be adequate. Moreover, I have determined
that the allocation of film stock as set forth in the budget
dated March 20, 1982 to be sufficient.

                        Very truly yours,

                        Francis Coppola

1006A NORTH QUAKER TULSA OK 74106 918 583 3470   1040 NO. LAS PALMAS AVE HOLLYWOOD 90038 213 463 7191

PONY BOY, INC.

Letter from Francis Coppola, 22 March 1982, approving the schedule and allocation of film stock for *The Outsiders* (1983).

During the production, which began shooting at the end of March, Woolner acted as the point of contact with Film Finances. Before meeting the guarantor, he went through the budget with Coppola, who checked that every area
was covered to his satisfaction. "As I was leaving," Woolner recalled, "he said,
'Tell the people at the bond company that my ability to make future films is
based upon my ability to do this film on budget.'"[52]

The two-month shoot went smoothly. Coppola had insured against the
unforeseen with a two-week period of rehearsals and careful preplanning.
David Korda remembered that in the large Tulsa schoolroom where he had his
office, Coppola had marked up the script on boards around the room, sequence
by sequence, showing what he thought were the most important points. "He
was very keen to say that he had studied it all and he knew that, if he needed
to, he could drop certain sequences."[53] The cinematographer Stephen Burum,
who had watched Coppola rehearse the young cast, was able to get the shots
in one or two takes.

The few mishaps that did occur during the production turned out to be
of a reassuringly minor order. One day, for example, Coppola had to see the
doctor after hurting his leg in a football game.[54] The overall impression he
gave to people was of a man who was finding moviemaking a happy, reward-
ing experience again. "He would work fifteen hours a day," recalled Korda.
"He shot from dawn to dusk, or even more. Then he would say, 'Fantastic.
Who's going to come to my place? I'm going to make dinner.' And he'd cook
for fifteen people."[55]

On 16 June 1982, Film Finances took out a full-page ad in *Variety* to mark
the completion of *The Outsiders* on schedule and on budget. "Of course doing
The Outsiders was a very big thing for Film Finances," observed Woolner. The
ad "was really an announcement to the industry that the completion bond was
there for bona fide mainstream movies, not just movies that were being
financed in Lexington, Kentucky, by dentists and doctors."[56]

Film Finances agreed to provide a second completion guarantee to Coppola
for *Rumblefish* (1983), which the director stayed on to shoot in Tulsa on a similar-
scale budget to *The Outsiders*. Once again it was agreed that the director's
fee would serve as an additional contingency, which turned out to be a wise
precaution. Principal photography, which began on 12 July 1982, ended three
weeks beyond schedule on 24 September.

At the end of a long postproduction period, which included many compli-
cated process shots, the film had swallowed up more than half the additional
contingency of Coppola's fee, but this extra allowance had been enough to

"outsiders"

FILM FINANCES LTD.

congratulates

FRANCIS FORD COPPOLA

and

the cast and crew

~~The Ponyboy Company~~

on

completing pcincipal photography

of

"THE OUTSIDERS"

on schedule and on budget

For information regarding Completion Guarantees
contact Richard Soames or David Korda at:-

34, South Molton Street,
London, WIY IHA.
Telephone: OI 629 6557
Telex: 298060 FILFIN.

W.O.

Proof for the full-page advertisement that Film Finances took out in *Variety*, 16 June 1982, to mark the completion of principal photography on *The Outsiders* (1983).

prevent any call on Film Finances' guarantee. A combination of the foresight and rigorous planning of Zoetrope's production team provided an effective containment that seemed to enable rather than hamper the creativity of a director who was kept carefully informed of the financial margins within which he could work.

Summing up their experience of working with Film Finances, Robert Spiotta told the *Wall Street Journal*, "You have to pay a fee up front, but unlike the studios that demand their pound of flesh, you end up having a lot more creative control over a project."[57]

The key to what turned out to be a successful relationship had been a mutual respect and confidence. Zoetrope observed undertakings that it had given relating to the budget, while Film Finances had been able to understand the creative challenges of the filmmakers, crucially because it brought to the process its own deep understanding of how films were made. As Woolner observed, not only did David Korda have a lifetime experience of the film industry through his family, but he had been a filmmaker himself before he came to Film Finances: "He had produced many films. For Francis, there was an element of trust there, and there was also an element of 'I know what they want.'"[58]

~

In July 1982, soon after *The Outsiders* had been completed, Film Finances took out another full-page advertisement, this time in the *Hollywood Reporter*: "Film Finances Ltd is proud to announce formation of Film Finances Inc, and merger with Lindsley Parsons and Completion Service Co."[59] Richard Soames knew Parsons as a "friendly rival," who, relying on insurance from Lloyd's underwriters, guaranteed only one or two films annually.[60] They'd first met through the John Carpenter film *Escape from New York* (1981), which Film Finances had considered but which Parsons eventually guaranteed. "We were friendly enough to just call each other if we needed something," Soames remembered. "And he called me and said, 'I can't make a go of this. The competition's cutting my rates. Can we do something together?'"[61] In 1982, "the competition" meant chiefly the Completion Bond Company, but the boom in production would soon attract several other new arrivals.

The merger marked the permanent arrival of Film Finances in Hollywood. Completion Service Co., which Lindsley Parsons had established in 1975, had its office on the border between Beverly Hills and West Hollywood at 9000 Sunset Boulevard. Parsons stayed on as vice president of what was effectively Film Finances' new American subsidiary.

Lindsley Parsons in the 1950s, when he was a prolific producer for Monogram Pictures and its successor Allied Artists.

Able to call on over fifty years of experience in the business, Parsons had started out at Monogram Pictures as a screenwriter of such early John Wayne Westerns as *The Man from Utah* (1934), *Paradise Canyon* (1935), and *The Oregon Trail* (1936). He and Wayne had first met when they were both college students in Los Angeles and, beyond the movie business, they remained close friends. After a stint as publicity director of Republic Studios, Parsons became Monogram's head of production. This B-picture background gave him the same practical, no-nonsense filmmaking expertise that John Croydon had been able to employ when Film Finances first established itself in the British film industry during the 1950s.

Film Finances was able to complement Parsons' knowledge of the Hollywood production scene with its much greater financial strength and reputation in the insurance market. When the merger took place, Parsons was working with Lloyd's of London and MGM on the Douglas Trumbull film *Brainstorm* (1983). Having spent $12 million, MGM had abandoned the production at the end of the previous year when the film's star Natalie Wood drowned in a boating accident.

Lloyd's, which was responsible for covering the loss, asked Parsons to report on whether it was possible to finish the film, which had been in the last weeks of principal photography when Wood died. Parsons devised a scheme of script revisions that successfully reassigned Wood's remaining lines to other characters. He then proposed a budget and shooting schedule and persuaded the director, Trumbull, to take part in the rescue plan. At first reluctant, MGM agreed to back the project when other studios made offers for the completed film. But once the merger had taken place, Parsons insisted that Film Finances should now be involved. He told the *Hollywood Reporter*, "I said the only way I can go on with the picture is if you take out a completion guarantee on it. Then I'd feel free to go out and finish it."[62]

"They say one of the troubles with the film business is that all your assets go home at night," commented David Korda. "I think the film business is all about relationships. Films get made in Los Angeles because of relationships. You know somebody who knows somebody else."[63] Parsons was an example of this. His immense value to Film Finances when it first opened its office in Los Angeles lay in his ease and familiarity with the Hollywood industry, from studio executives to the practical filmmakers.

In the autumn of 1982, Parsons was supervising the completion of *Brainstorm* but also advising on what would be the biggest project that Film Finances had guaranteed up to that point in its history, the $12 million production of *Iceman* (1984), which Norman Jewison and Patrick Palmer were producing for Universal. As a hugely respected and trusted Hollywood insider, Parsons was able to learn about the details of the project from a very early stage, even as it was taking shape.

In September 1982, he met the producers' chosen director, Fred Schepisi. Soon afterward, he was sent the budget and script. As the members of the crew were being chosen, Parsons reported back to Film Finances with detailed information on their suitability for a production that would be shot partly in the United States and partly in British Columbia, Canada. He knew that the proposed production managers, Bob Brown and Justis Greene, had both worked together on John Carpenter's *The Thing* (1982), which had been filmed in the same Canadian location. Parsons could report that they were "a combination highly recommended by both my Universal and Canadian contacts," that Greene would be especially useful to such a location because in a previous career he had been head of British Columbia's promotion office.[64] His local political connections had helped him solve several difficult problems on the Carpenter production.

Parsons's command of the Hollywood grapevine was second to none. And Film Finances backed up his obvious production expertise with its own financial muscle. To win Universal's backing, the company had to prove that it had the resources in a worst-case scenario to pay out sums equivalent to the $12 million of *Iceman*'s budget. It required Film Finances' broker, RTC, to negotiate in the Lloyd's market what was a significantly increased level of cover for the company. "I believe you are aware that this is the highest limit we have ever had to go on Completion Guarantees," the company's managing director, Freddy Hayward, wrote to Soames on 17 February 1983. "You could now, if you ever wished, show evidence of insurance coverage of $17,500,000."[65] And Hayward hoped to increase the limit further to $20 million at the next annual date of renewal.

In raising the extra cover, he stressed to Lloyd's insurers the company's long record of past achievement: "In 31 years of trading, Film Finances have never failed to deliver on any production they have undertaken."[66] An even more tangible measure of achievement was the company's decision in 1978 to opt for a "self-insured retention"—the proportion of a loss that an insured party undertakes to bear itself—of $1 million each year, which it chose to raise to $2 million from July 1983. Over the preceding five-year period, Film Finances had provided completion guaranties for 130 films but never paid out more than $2 million in a single year.

The insurance arrangements that were put in place at the time of *Iceman* marked the most significant turning point in the company's history since its founding in 1950. Film Finances had often worked with the big American film companies, but now it had established itself as a Hollywood insider, with the ambition to become an integral part of the Hollywood landscape.

∽

It was a landscape that was rapidly changing. Beyond the majors, an extraordinarily rich and diverse industry was sprouting up, taking advantage of the explosion of growth in the ancillary markets of pay TV and home video. In 1982, only a year after it had adopted a twenty-four-hour schedule, cable broadcaster Home Box Office (HBO) had nearly ten million subscribers and was screening two hundred movies a year.[67] The first US video store had opened in Los Angeles in December 1977. By mid-1983, there were more than six thousand video stores, and by mid-1985 more than fifteen thousand. "Five years ago if we had said videocassette rights would be worth 50 percent of the cost of a movie," Dino De Laurentiis told the *New York Times* in 1985, "everybody would have laughed."[68]

The first American Film Market took place in Westwood, Los Angeles, 21–31 March 1981. *Variety* hailed the event as a "hit before it starts."[69] Its success was a sign that the infrastructure for independent film financing in the United States had now properly arrived.

When Film Finances, Inc., opened for business in the summer of 1982, it was a tiny operation, which Lindsley Parsons ran with only one assistant, L. J. Van Cleave. As the company grew over the coming years, it would slowly rise up through the 9000 Sunset Boulevard building until eventually it occupied the entire fourteenth floor. The first stage of that journey began in July 1982 when Parsons and Van Cleave moved from Completion Service's tiny office on the fifth floor into four rooms on the eighth. Then, at the end of the year, the office nearly doubled in size when Film Finances leased an adjoining suite.

The extraordinary feat of the first few years was how a handful of people were able to keep pace with the rapid expansion of independent filmmaking in Hollywood. Richard Soames or David Korda or Ron Aikin or—after Aikin left Film Finances at the end of 1982—Bob Storer would drop by Los Angeles every few weeks but would soon have to set off again to some other part of Film Finances' now global empire, whether it was Toronto, Montreal, Sydney, or London. To accommodate the frequent to-ing and fro-ing of executives, Film Finances hired a permanent penthouse suite in the Beverly Wilshire Hotel. "You had to go up some stairs, and you enjoyed the use of the roof

Film Finances' US office at 9000 Sunset Boulevard, 2015.

garden," remembered Storer. "The occupant prior to us for five years who had it was Warren Beatty. It was quite a suite. . . . The whole ceiling was a mirror. And then there were sliding doors onto the roof."[70]

By the end of its first year of operation, in July 1983, Film Finances, Inc., had guaranteed sixteen films, but Lindsley Parsons had in addition overseen several other projects that had been guaranteed from London but were being shot in the United States or Mexico. These early projects included many well-known Hollywood names. There was John Carpenter's supernatural horror *Christine* (1983), based on the Stephen King novel. Richard Kobritz, who had produced the miniseries *Salem's Lot*, formed production company Polar Films to buy the prepublication rights from King and did a negative pickup deal with Columbia. There was *Romancing the Stone* (1984), which had been in turnaround at Columbia but which Michael Douglas bought to produce in Mexico as a negative pickup for 20th Century-Fox, forming a small company, El Corazon Producciones, for the occasion. "Friends at Columbia state they would have no qualms about Douglas's ability to bring film in on budget and schedule," Parsons was able to reassure Soames.[71]

But as notable as the familiar Hollywood names were investors from outside the industry. There was a Gold Rush atmosphere about independent production in Hollywood during the early 1980s that attracted many newcomers. The production company Zupnik-Curtis Enterprises was an example. A partnership between Washington, DC, property developer Stanley Zupnik and nightclub owner Tom Curtis, it had raised funding for two features through a syndicate of local investors with the support of the Maryland National Bank. *Fear City* (1984) was a thriller set in New York and directed by Abel Ferrara; and *Dreamscape* (1984) was a science-fiction horror film starring Max von Sydow, Christopher Plummer, and Dennis Quaid. "Because of the ancillary markets now available to film producers and distributors," Zupnik explained to the *Washington Post*, his investors "have a 75 percent chance of getting their money back."[72] After the two films had been completed, Zupnik-Curtis concluded a deal for their theatrical distribution in the United States with 20th Century-Fox and sold video rights to Thorn-EMI. The *Post* reported, "Zupnik says that with cable television needing 250 to 300 films per year, syndicated television, network television, video cassette and the foreign market, the demand for films is ever growing. He said independent producers, like himself, who can make more films at lower costs, are more able to supply that need than major studios with high overhead."[73]

The Maryland bank that had helped finance Zupnik-Curtis was so excited about the possibilities that its vice president Michael T. Flynn visited Film Finances in Los Angeles in April 1983 after the two films had successfully completed shooting. "As we discussed, we hope to be financing more films," he wrote to Soames on his return to Washington, "and I hope to also be able to expand our relationship with Film Finances."[74] Soames was receiving many similar letters from other bankers around the world who had noticed the

Michael Douglas and Kathleen Turner in *Romancing the Stone* (1984).

Hollywood boom in independent financing and were keen to learn how the guarantee worked.

~

But it wasn't only the banks that were keen to make the most of the new opportunities. After the establishment of Completion Bond Company in 1981 and the opening of Film Finances' Los Angeles office in 1982, three new completion guarantor businesses in 1983 alone joined the ranks of an increasingly crowded field: Rampart Film Services, Filmmaker Completion (The Americas), and Entertainment Completions.

The last of these was easily the most formidable. Opening offices simultaneously in London, New York, and Los Angeles, it had been set up by British merchant banker Nigel Cayzer, whose family had made a fortune in shipping and finance. Promising completion guaranties for film production worldwide, its glossy brochure boasted, "Now there's a new company to bring you happy endings."[75]

A glittering, illustrated who's who followed of the company's directors, which included the president of the British Film & Television Producers Association and a former vice president of Columbia Pictures, Kenneth Maidment; the screenwriter/producer Carl Foreman, whose credits included *High Noon* (1952) and *Bridge on the River Kwai* (1957); and Maxwell Aitken, the grandson of the newspaper baron Lord Beaverbrook.

But the field was dominated by the two main runners, Film Finances and Completion Bond Company, who between them shared 90 percent of the business. Most of the remaining competition would, one by one, fall by the wayside as the two major players engaged in an all-out battle for market share.

Fireman's Fund, which backed CBC, had dominated film production insurance in Hollywood since the days of silent movies and intended now to achieve the same dominance in the provision of completion guaranties. It would have been understandable if it regarded Film Finances' arrival in Hollywood as a trespass on its territory, but when it came to completion guaranties, Film Finances was the pioneer and CBC a newcomer.

In April 1983, "an open letter to the industry" from the vice president of the Fireman's Fund Insurance Companies, Richard T. Barry, was published in *Variety* to celebrate CBC's second anniversary. "The Completion Bond Company has already guaranteed some 30 motion pictures with an aggregate budget in excess of $250 million," it boasted.[76] By this time Film Finances, the industry

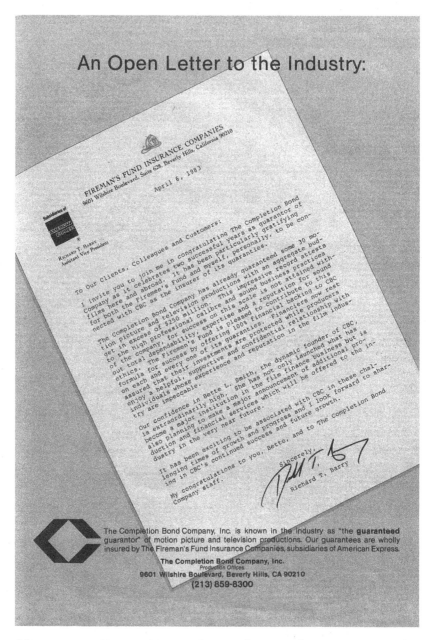

Advertisement in *Variety*, 11 May 1983, for Completion Bond Company (CBC), Film Finances' principal rival during the 1980s.

veteran, had guaranteed approximately eight hundred motion pictures, including some of the most celebrated ever made.

To make up for its lack of a comparable record, CBC made a selling point out of its relationship with both Fireman's Fund and entertainment broker Albert G. Ruben & Co., which had exclusive representation rights for Fireman's Fund. A producer or financier could go to CBC and, in a one-stop transaction, get not only a completion guarantee but also negative and cast insurance as well. Promoting itself as the "guaranteed guarantor," CBC was able to offer unbeatable commercial terms. When it issued a bond, at the same time it provided a "cut-through" undertaking that if for whatever reason it could not meet the guarantee, then Fireman's Fund would. It advertised heavily in the trade press in an effort to outdo the recognition that Film Finances already had through its reputation as the industry's oldest guarantor.

In 1985, CBC published a series of "advertorials" called "Completion Bond Communiques," in which its president, Bette L. Smith, expressed her views on the state of the industry. One of these offered a good summary of the essential reason for the existence of not only CBC but also the many other bond companies that had arrived on the scene during the 1980s.

> The global expansion of the entertainment industry has created new opportunities and wealth, as well as innovative financial arrangements and risks. The shift from studio financing and control to a mix of funding strategies which ranges from private investment to lender financing, to tax-based subsidies for production, has resulted in a variety of financial possibilities that are limited only by the creativity and ingenuity of motion picture producers and financiers.
>
> This multiplicity of financial strategies, coupled with legal and insurance arrangements which are often multinational in scope, has created a need for a professional third-party who can independently assess and guarantee that both the production and financial plans are sound, adequate and committed.[77]

In its efforts to take the lion's share of the market, CBC showed a readiness to take on several high-risk projects that Film Finances had declined to guarantee. They included *Jaws 3-D* (1983), which involved the challenge of not only difficult special effects in water but also a complex photographic process, and *9½ Weeks* (1986), which Soames felt needed a more experienced producer than was attached to the production.

When Film Finances did choose to pass on a production, it still kept a keen eye on how CBC fared in its place, perhaps inevitably taking some satisfaction if a production's fortunes seemed to bear out its own decision not to get involved. In October 1982, Parsons cabled to London the news he had learned through the grapevine that *Yentl* was "now $8,000,000 into guarantee and that CBC is also in deep trouble on Sergio Leone's *Once Upon a Time in America*."[78] Both were productions on which Film Finances had previously been approached to provide the completion guarantee.

Especially as the budgets being guaranteed were now in the many millions of dollars, one poor decision could mean disaster. A year later, in November 1983, Richard Soames explained in an internal memorandum why Film Finances had decided not to bond John Boorman's *The Emerald Forest* (1985): "We have passed on this project on a gut feeling rather than seriously studying the production papers. We do not consider the film will be controllable in the middle of a Brazilian Forest with Boorman directing."[79] Yet at the same time, as Film Finances now faced the serious competition of CBC, there was a pressure to bond a production if it possibly could. "Apparently the CBC have made an issue of the fact that we 'turned down' *Passage [to India]*," Richard Soames remarked in an interoffice cable. "I gather our position with regard to the film has been misrepresented and I will of course set the record straight when I meet Verity."[80] By "Verity," he meant Verity Lambert, who was the head of production at EMI.

The risks of providing a guarantee to such a notoriously perfectionist director as David Lean, who had been responsible for some of the largest overcosts in film history, were self-evident, but seriously studying the production papers—script, schedule, budget, and production plan—could always show the way in which it could be done. It was a question of making sure that there were terms in place to address the specific risks. There was no director who could not receive a guarantee if the circumstances were right—even Michelangelo Antonioni, whose *Red Desert* had cost Film Finances a fortune back in the 1960s. "There is a black-covered script written by Antonioni somewhere in the office and I cannot remember the name of the title," Soames cabled Lindsley Parsons's assistant, L. J. Van Cleave, at the Los Angeles office in April 1983. "I should be grateful if you could try and find it and let me know what it is."[81]

Van Cleave cabled back the title—*The Crew*—adding, "It's a story about a millionaire executive who, on his 50th birthday, takes his yacht out of Miami with a last-minute recruited crew of three 'flaky' characters who proceed to harass and terrorize him for reasons unknown. There's a hurricane, Towers [the executive] gets thrown out of the yacht, gets back into the yacht, and finally the lot of them docks in the Coral Keys."[82] It is the only mention of the project that can be found in Film Finances' archives, but presumably another

gut feeling about the difficulty of controlling the combination of Antonioni
and a hurricane deterred Soames from pursuing the project any further.

~

Whatever the risks of any individual film or the competition, the early 1980s
were unquestionably a boom time as a whole new infrastructure for independent filmmaking rapidly took shape. "This whole thing of Film Finances coming to LA was that the timing was really good," commented Richard Soames.
"There were several independent firms that had just started up, like Orion and
Hemdale."[83]

Orion was "basically a studio but without bricks and mortar," recalled
David Korda.[84] It had been formed in 1978 when United Artists boss Arthur
Krim had led a walk-out of his senior management, resenting the interference
of their corporate parent, Transamerica. "The basic goal of Orion," commented
Mike Medavoy, who became the new company's head of production, was "to
duplicate United Artists by creating a home where film-makers could realize
their visions without interference from executives."[85]

Fostering the independent spirit with which United Artists had been identified through most of its history was at the heart of the new venture. After a
two-year period during which it distributed its films in a joint venture with
Warner Bros., Orion established its own distribution network through buying
Filmways Pictures in February 1982. The following year, it raised production
finances through a public offering on Wall Street. At about the same time, the
Silver Screen Partners investment group was formed to fund the production of
films for HBO.

As many other investment initiatives followed, it became increasingly clear
that the completion bond had become the linchpin of independent film financing. As the *Entertainment Law Journal* pointed out in a long article in 1984:

> All of the financing methods used by independent producers are based on a
> common assumption: that the producer will complete, on time and especially
> on budget, the very movie that is promised to the distributor and other presale
> customers. If a producer were to go over-budget and run out of money before
> the movie is completed, the entire financial package would tumble like a house
> of cards. To protect against this possibility, all of those who advance production
> funds to independent producers—be they investors, lenders, movie financing
> companies like Silver Screen Partners, or distributors—require something called
> a "completion bond."[86]

Film Finances was providing as many as five or six completion bonds to Orion Pictures alone, but the other Hollywood distributors were also hungry for independent product. "We have to have about 20 pictures a year to satisfy our distribution requirements," the head of a major studio told Lindsley Parsons. "Here on the lot, we have the capacity to make six or seven—we just don't have the manpower to go beyond that. The other 12 or 13 have to be outside, independent productions, so it's worth a million dollars a picture for us to have a guarantee on them."[87]

Whether through Orion or any of the other Hollywood distributors, Film Finances helped facilitate the rise of many other independents that went on to become household names in 1980s Hollywood. In 1984, it provided the bond for the $23 million budget of *Rambo: First Blood Part II* (1985). Grossing a then staggering $300 million worldwide, the film provided the platform for Carolco to go on to dominate the action blockbuster movie.[88]

Also in 1984, Film Finances agreed to guarantee a joint venture between home video company Media Home Entertainment, which had achieved early success through the video distribution of the 1978 horror movie *Halloween*, and New Line Cinema, a small New York–based distributor of cult movies for college campuses that had recently moved into film production. "I remember

Sylvester Stallone flexes his muscles in *Rambo: First Blood Part II* (1985).

going with Richard [Soames] to meet the producer," recalled Bob Storer. "It was somewhere in a rather seedy part of Manhattan. We had to climb up seven flights to a little grubby office at the top. And that was where they were plotting *Nightmare on Elm Street.*"[89] The budget for the film was only $1.7 million, but *A Nightmare on Elm Street* (1984) went on to gross $25 million, spawning a successful franchise that would win New Line the nickname of "the studio that Freddy Built."[90]

The rapid rise in production drew not only independent filmmakers to Hollywood but also banks. The most prominent was the Rotterdam-based Slavenburg Bank, which was taken over by Crédit Lyonnais in 1983. Frans Afman, who headed the bank's entertainment division, had been discounting foreign distribution contracts since 1974, when Slavenburg Bank discounted the presales deals that independent producer Dino De Laurentiis had put together for the film *Three Days of the Condor* (1975). Afman went on to discount De Laurentiis's $24 million production of *King Kong* (1976) and Alexander Salkind's *Superman* (1978). Pushing the technique of presales to its limits, he turned the bank into the principal paymaster for the biggest independents making films in Hollywood during the 1980s, including Carolco, Cannon Group, Nelson Entertainment, and Hemdale.

A landmark moment indicating the revolution that had taken place in Hollywood film financing during the 1980s was when Arnold Kopelson, the producer of Oliver Stone's *Platoon* (1986), used the occasion of his acceptance speech for the Best Picture Oscar at the 1987 Academy Awards Ceremony to give a then unprecedented acknowledgment to the financiers who had made the film possible. He began with his backers at Hemdale: "My profound thanks to John Daly and Derek Gibson for sharing my passion for this property and giving me the money to make it when all others passed." He then went on to thank Orion Pictures and Vestron Video, as well as "Richard Soames for the Completion Guarantee. And Frans Afman of Crédit Lyonnais, for having the money in the Philippine jungle when I really needed it."[91]

A few years later, Kopelson, who had trained as a lawyer, would write an article on the independent film industry for the *Loyola of Los Angeles Entertainment Law Review*. Noting that during the 1980s, Crédit Lyonnais had become "the foremost lender to independent film-makers throughout the world," he explained the financing structure that Afman had put himself at the heart of: "Although he was a banker, Afman completely understood the power of independent distributors. He realized that contracts with well-financed distributors generally providing for the issuance of letters of credit, combined with

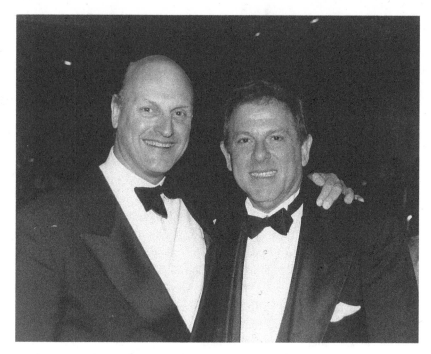

Crédit Lyonnais banker Frans Afman (*left*) with the producer of *Platoon* (1986), Arnold Kopelson, at the Academy Awards, 30 March 1987.

a contract with a major studio for domestic distribution rights, collectively supplied the entire negative cost of producing a film. More importantly, Afman recognized that [Crédit Lyonnais] would be fully secured in any loan it made to a filmmaker, if the distribution agreements were combined with a completion guarantee." He went on to explain that the completion guarantee "runs in favor of a bank or other financier and provides it with the certainty that the motion picture will be completed and delivered in compliance with the distribution agreements so that payments contracted under them will be achieved."[92]

The Terminator (1984), only one of the many iconic Hollywood films that Film Finances guaranteed during the decade, offered an example of how it provided not only an essential security to the financiers but also invaluable production expertise to the filmmakers. When writer-director James Cameron and producer Gale Anne Hurd took the project to John Daly at Hemdale in 1982, their experience of moviemaking was minimal. They had met when they were both working for Roger Corman at New World Pictures. Hurd was a production assistant, and Cameron was working in special effects. Hurd formed her own company, Pacific-Western Productions, so that Cameron could make *The Terminator*, which was the first full-length film he had directed.

Hemdale, which was taking a significant chance in backing such an inexperienced team, put together a financing structure whereby Crédit Lyonnais advanced $6 million of the $6.5 million budget on the security of distribution agreements with HBO, Thorn-EMI Video, and Orion Pictures. The film was originally going to be shot in Toronto during the summer of 1983, but the start date had to be pushed back to March 1984 and the location switched to Los Angeles when Dino De Laurentiis exercised his option to have the star, bodybuilder-turned-actor Arnold Schwarzenegger, appear in *Conan the Destroyer* (1984).

Although James Cameron and Gale Anne Hurd were responsible for the original conception of the film, Film Finances had the right to remove them from the production if necessary and, in view of their inexperience, made it a condition of the guarantee that Hemdale hire a line producer. Graham Henderson, who had worked as a production accountant on the Salkind *Superman* movies, was eventually appointed. The one production asset that was agreed to be "irreplaceable" was Schwarzenegger.

Principal photography began on 21 March 1984. After four weeks of filming, Cameron met with Lindsley Parsons, who discussed with him how the scenes could be revised to fit within the framework of the budget. "The meeting between Jim and Lindsley Parsons went very well," Hurd wrote to key production staff. "We must all co-operate and work together as closely as possible to effectively control this production. It is not helpful to work at cross-purposes since we are ultimately working toward the same goal: a terrific film that is all that it can be—while still on schedule and on budget."[93]

In achieving this goal, Parsons was a key ally. Accounting for the success of the film years later in a 2001 making-of documentary, Gale Anne Hurd observed, "We were doubly blessed in that Lindsley Parsons, who was the head of the LA branch of Film Finances, the completion bond company, believed in us." When she and Cameron decided, during the postproduction period of *The Terminator*, that additional photography was necessary, although it had not been provided for in the original budget, she recalled that Parsons "supported us every step of the way."[94] Describing him as an unsung hero, she commented in 2018 that he "knew what *The Terminator* was going to be and not a lot of people did. You absolutely need people to believe in you. You also need people to tell you when you're screwing up that you can listen to. Lindsley was all of that."[95]

This memo represents a firm bid for the creation of certain mechanical, prosthetic and special make-up effects for the feature film currently entitled "TERMINATOR"

For the sum of $350,000.00, my company will design, create, and construct all special effects necessary to bring to life the Terminator (not including stop-motion animation). Such mechanical, prosthetic and special make-up effects will be delivered to the set according to the needs of the production, and will be capable of performing such actions and fulfilling such requirements as specified by the director.

This proposal includes, but is not limited to, the following effects:

    (a) All prosthetics for all special make-up effects, including but not limited to the final directorial decisions regarding burns and/or scars on Reese; the chest appliance for insert shot of Matt when Terminator's fingers sink into his flesh (Scene 78); double masks as required, for stuntmen doubling principal actors.

    (b) All appliances necessary for bullet wounds on Terminator, when such wounds are exposed.

    (c) All appliances necessary for the various stages of Terminator's disintegration.

    (d) The functioning mechanical and prosthetic forearm effect on the Terminator (Scene 152), with exposed cables and hydraulics, when Terminator repairs himself.

In addition, my company will design, create and construct the three stages of separate, articulated, puppeted heads and matching appliances corresponding to Terminator's scripted disintegration. This includes, but is not limited to, the following:

    (1) The first stage of Terminator's disintegration, in which the eyebrows are singed, the lacerated, glass-imbedded eye (Scene 152) is removed to expose the glowing, red electronic eye beneath (Scene 158). These effects will include appliances and the puppeted head, with articulated eye, for full reveal.

    (2) The second stage of Terminator's disintegration (Scene 194), revealing the damaged scalp with metal plate beneath, the electronic eye and pale, damaged flesh. These effects will include appliances and a second puppeted head.

DESIGNS AND SPECIAL EFFECTS IN MAKE-UP

19201 PARTHENIA STREET, NORTHRIDGE, CALIFORNIA 91324 • (213) 886-0630

Stan Winston's tender "for the creation of certain mechanical, prosthetic and special make-up effects" for *The Terminator*, 24 March 1984.

(3) The third stage of Terminator's disintegration
(Scenes 232-246), after the motorcycle crash,
including a third puppeted head and necessary
appliances to reveal the glowing, red eye,
extreme damage to the left side of Terminator's
face, exposing cables, rotting flesh, etc.

Also included in this bid is the design and construction of the mechanical
Terminator(s) for use in all shots determined by the director (excluding
the stop-motion animation, armature and effects), and designed to fulfill
the requirements of the storyboarded shots, (including but not limited to
Scenes 248-256) in consultation with the director. A complete, additional
mechanical Terminator will be constructed to be utilized in the destruction
of Terminator (Scene 256) by the pipe bomb and the hydraulic press.

Included in this bid are the costs of all labor and materials necessary to
create the effects outlined above, with a payment schedule as follows:

Ten (10) equal payments of $35,000.00 each, payable
bi-weekly over a 20-week period, for a total, all-
inclusive payment of $350,000.00.

(Should the completed prosthetic, mechanical, and
special make-up effects be delivered on location in
Canada, no sales tax will be computed).

Not included in this bid are travel and living expenses (to be determined) for
a maximum of three special make-up effects technicians, as well as shipping,
freight and customs' charges (if any), should "TERMINATOR" be filmed on location
outside of the Los Angeles area.

Should this bid be accepted, it will be followed by a more formal agreement.

Sincerely,

STAN WINSTON

DESIGNS AND SPECIAL EFFECTS IN MAKE-UP

19201 PARTHENIA STREET, NORTHRIDGE, CALIFORNIA 91324 • (213) 886-0630

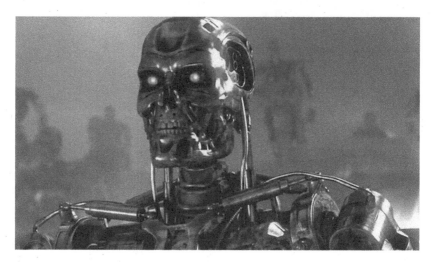

The Terminator pared to the bone.

The encouragement continued after the completion of the film. In the battle to get the film's distributor Orion to promote *The Terminator* as more than an exploitation movie, she remembered, "Our very first advocate was once again Lindsley Parsons from Film Finances, who came to us and said, 'This is a really good movie. You guys have put something on the screen here that is not only a good action movie, but it's an important action movie.'"[96]

The Terminator exhausted its contingency, but it was made more or less on budget, enabling Hemdale to remit its no-claims bonus from Film Finances back to Crédit Lyonnais.

～

With independent production taking off at an extraordinary pace in Hollywood, it soon became apparent that there was far too much work for Lindsley Parsons to cope with on his own. So in 1984, Kurt Woolner, who had been Film Finances' contact with American Zoetrope during the production of *The Outsiders*, was invited to join the company. "When I was hired, they'd done sixteen movies," he recalled. "My first year at the company, we did thirty-six movies in the LA office, my second year we did fifty, my third we did sixty."[97]

Woolner remembered learning the most important lesson on his first day, when Parsons called him into his office to welcome him to the company. "I know about 10 percent of what there is to know about this business," Parsons told him. "I get along because very few people even know 5 percent." A successful career as a completion guarantor depended on being as aware of what one did not know as what one did know. As Parsons put it, "I've seen everything that can go wrong on a movie, except for the next thing."[98]

Recognizing that something was wrong was the first step to putting it right. Woolner remembered Parsons giving the example of the Prince film *Purple Rain* (1984), which Film Finances guaranteed just before Woolner arrived at the company. The production began to fall further and further behind schedule. So Parsons visited the filmmakers in Minneapolis to try to help them rationalize their difficulties. When he looked at the script, he pointed out that the film was going to be far longer than had been estimated. "These musical numbers are only half a page," Parsons told them, "but each musical number is four or five minutes, so if you've got ten musical numbers, you're going to have forty minutes of musical numbers that comprise only three pages of script. You're going to have to cut stuff, otherwise you'll have an unreleasable movie."[99] Although it was a simple, obvious truth, no one on the production had even thought about it before. They recognized that they had to cut and, in doing so, brought the film back on schedule again. An invaluable resource that Film Finances offered a production was an expert overview, which from a

Prince adding unscripted time to *Purple Rain* (1984).

more distanced, objective perspective enabled the filmmakers to see the forest for the trees.

When Film Finances first opened the Los Angeles office, it hired the law firm Loeb & Loeb to do the legal work for the US films on a project-by-project basis. But as the business was growing so quickly in 1985, Steve Ransohoff, who had been the associate at Loeb & Loeb looking after the Film Finances account, was hired to work for Film Finances in-house. Lindsley Parsons, by this time, was well into his eighties. "He never hung up his hat," recalled Richard Soames. "He said to me, 'The only thing I'm not going to tell you, I'll tell you anything, I'm not going to tell you what my age is.' And he stayed until he died."[100]

Kurt Woolner and Steve Ransohoff, who were then both in their late twenties, quickly assumed the chief responsibility for running the Los Angeles office. "I would say certainly within six months of arriving at the company Kurt and I were running the business," commented Ransohoff, "and Lindsley was like having the encyclopedia on your bookshelf."[101] They were young enough to be able to grow with Hollywood's independent film industry, which was going through a key formative period in the 1980s. "Steve and I were unusual in that we were kids doing this," recalled Woolner. "We had the energy and the curiosity that comes with that."[102]

∾

Although Film Finances always sought to cultivate a positive relationship with filmmakers and prided itself on the wisdom and expertise it could provide, its ultimate position of authority meant that there were occasions when filmmakers, finding themselves at odds with the exigencies of a production, could make the mistake of treating the company like the Hollywood cliché of the philistine front office.

In 1987, Film Finances guaranteed Alex Cox's production of *Walker*, about William Walker, the nineteenth-century American mercenary who fought a war in Nicaragua and briefly became its president. As the understanding had been that the film was going to be made in Mexico, Film Finances was alarmed to discover that Cox had agreed with the Sandinista government to shoot the film in Nicaragua. It was at the height of the Reagan administration's efforts to overthrow the Nicaraguan government. There had been a US trade embargo in force against Nicaragua since 1985, so there was a serious question whether the film's distributor, Universal, could even legally accept delivery of such a film.

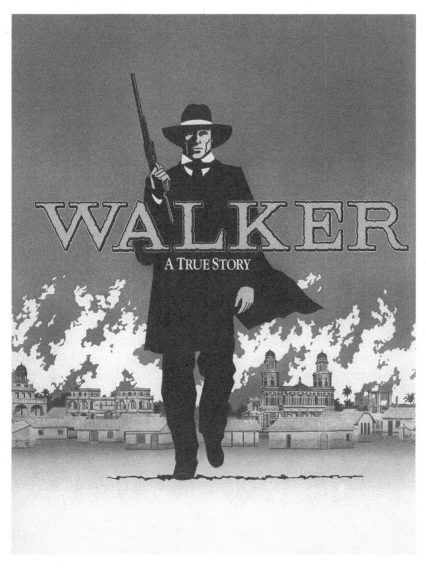

Walker (1987) became a renegade production when director Alex Cox made a deal with the Sandinista government to film in Nicaragua in defiance of a US trade embargo.

Steve Ransohoff and Kurt Woolner flew down to Nicaragua, where they met the film's producer Ed Pressman. He assured them that he was as surprised as they were when he had learned what had happened. They turned up at the set outside the capital, Managua, to tell Cox that he had to take the production back to Mexico, but he refused to talk to them. In what might have been a scene from one of the Spaghetti Westerns that Cox so admired, Ransohoff recalled that Cox got on a horse and rode off while the cast and crew declared that they were standing up for their director. Things went no better during the poolside dinner that had been arranged at the hotel that evening. Cox didn't show up, but a hostile cast and crew did, to berate the guarantors and to tell them to go home.

Cox later admitted in his published account of what happened that he and his producer Lorenzo O'Brien "planned to shoot in Nicaragua, of course, but we couldn't insist on this to potential insurers, to whom we had to present an image of flexibility rather than fanaticism."[103] In the end, Film Finances allowed the film to be completed in Nicaragua and was forbearing enough not to cancel the bond, although Cox showed little gratitude for the gesture. "If any experience demonstrates how absolutely useless and unnecessary a completion bond was, this was surely it," he commented. "Despite the difficulties they caused us, we continued shooting, on schedule and on budget, while they collected their percentage."[104]

Providing protection against the unforeseen could be a thankless task when the unforeseen did not actually happen. The often willful ignorance that filmmakers could show of what a bond actually involved was just one of the occupational hazards of being a completion guarantor. But there was perhaps little point in expecting filmmakers to understand the guarantor's point of view when they were engrossed in all the challenges of making a movie.

∽

After *Walker*, Film Finances might well have appreciated a break from maverick directors, but in the summer of 1987, even before it had signed off on *Walker*, Richard Soames agreed to guarantee one of the most maverick of them all. Terry Gilliam's *The Adventures of Baron Munchausen* (1988) would turn out to be by far the biggest challenge in the company's history.

It was not the first time that Film Finances had provided a bond for a Terry Gilliam film. In 1976, it had acted as the completion guarantor for *Jabberwocky* (1977), the first feature that Gilliam had directed as sole director. (He had previously been codirector, with Terry Jones, of *Monty Python and the*

Holy Grail [1975]). When the picture went six weeks over schedule, with a considerable overcost, Film Finances decided that to minimize any further overages, it would bring in an independent editor to complete the film after Gilliam had put together a rough cut. But it held off after a request from John Terry, the director of the National Film Finance Corporation, which was supporting the film. He wrote to Bobby Garrett, "It seems to us that the best hope of bringing this film to a satisfactory completion is by seeking and obtaining the full co-operation of those who have piloted the picture to its present state so that there is no loss of continuity or purpose."[105]

Having made this significant concession, Garrett was then upset to be told out of the blue that, although principal photography was over, Gilliam now needed to film a full-scale mechanical version of the Jabberwocky monster— further work that had not been discussed with Film Finances before filming began—and the producers therefore wished to add three extra weeks to the postproduction schedule. Garrett was adamant that Film Finances should not be responsible for the cost of this extra delay, but he was equally annoyed by the general manner of a director who—as he put it to John Terry—"took an unprofessional approach to the economics of film production."[106] Two weeks later, after further delays, he notified the producers of Film Finances' intention to take over the production. "I am sorry that it has come to this," he wrote to Terry, "but really for the last month we have been messed about and our patience is at an end and if we are to be effective, we must be so now."[107] But once again Garrett relented, allowing the producers to finish the film as they wished on the understanding that they would meet any overcosts beyond the sum that Film Finances considered adequate to complete the film.

Ten years later, the production troubles of *Jabberwocky* lay in a dusty file, and Garrett himself was long gone. But if his ghost had been present in Film Finances' boardroom, he might well have cried, "Beware the *Jabberwocky*!" It wasn't only *Jabberwocky* that Soames might have done well to consider. There was John Croydon's report on *Monty Python's Life of Brian* (1979), which Film Finances had considered but ultimately did not guarantee. After having attended a conference with the producer, Croydon reported that Terry Gilliam was "to have nothing whatsoever to do with direction, which in the light of the result of *Jabberwocky* is just as well!"[108]

Then there was Gilliam's 1984 film *Brazil*. Soames could hardly expect to get accurate details of any production difficulties from its rival, CBC, which had guaranteed the film, but he might have done well to pay some attention to a book that was published in 1987 at the very time that *The Adventures of*

Baron Munchausen was going into production. *The Battle of Brazil* chronicled the struggle between Gilliam and Universal boss Sid Sheinberg over Gilliam's director's cut of *Brazil*, which was significantly longer than the contractual length that Universal had agreed.[109] When Gilliam refused to edit it to meet Universal's commercial requirements, Sheinberg began to edit the movie himself. To get Universal to release his director's version, Gilliam mounted a long battle that included clandestine screenings of the movie to film critics and a full-page advertisement in *Variety* demanding that Sheinberg release his cut of the movie. "I will talk to Sid, I will get in a Jacuzzi and drink wine with Sid," Gilliam told the *Los Angeles Times*. "I will do anything to get this film released, except get in the editing room with him."[110] When Universal eventually caved in and released the Gilliam cut, the movie was a flop. Only later did it become a cult success.

Gilliam was an extremely high-profile, maverick artist whose identity lay in his uncompromising vision. With hindsight, this ought to have been a cause of serious concern, but Soames, as ever "constitutionally averse to saying no," was determined to make the new project work if he possibly could.

The proposed budget for *The Adventures of Baron Munchausen* was $23.5 million. "The film could have been made for the budget," maintained Soames, "if it was going to be shot in a Monty Python–esque way. When you had a horse, you didn't even have a horse. You had some clackers. So that works just as well in a funny way."[111]

The film was a coproduction of Monty Python's production company Prominent Features and Laura Film, the company of German producer Thomas Schühly, who was based at Cinécittà in Rome. Schühly, who had previously worked with the director Rainer Werner Fassbender and had been an executive producer of *The Name of the Rose* (1986), won Gilliam over with a buccaneering style that made anything seem possible. As Gilliam put it, "I'm willing to bend all sorts of rules and do outrageous things to make things happen, which is the connection between Thomas and me. I sensed that he was someone who would go all the way to get something done."[112]

Schühly's own account of how he sealed a distribution deal with Columbia was an example of just how far he would go. The original budget, he maintained, had been calculated at $35 million. "The problem was that when I started to discuss it with Columbia, Columbia would not go beyond 25, so I was given the clear hint from Columbia just to cut off ten. So I said, 'How can I cut it out?' They said, 'Just cut out production design.' So we just cut out production design, which meant everybody knew from the very beginning on

The Adventures of Baron Munchausen (1988)—Film Finances' biggest ever disaster.

that this cutting-out was just a fake."[113] Whether "everybody" included Gilliam is not clear. In interviews about the film, he professed the unworldly artist's traditional ignorance of such things: "I am not good with money. Let's be honest about it. But I am aware of money. I just don't know what it buys. And if somebody tells me that it buys what we've got on the page, I trust."[114] The recollection of Steve Abbott, who managed the business affairs of Prominent Features, suggests that there was a degree of wishful thinking: "I suppose Terry allowed himself to be lured to Italy to make the picture on what I would say now was a false promise. You know: 'We can do it for a few million less.'"[115]

Having manipulated the budget to suit Columbia, Schühly did not hesitate to say the things that he thought Film Finances wanted to hear—according to Soames, making the assurance that the film would indeed be shot in the Monty Python–esque way: "Our people in London thought, 'Well, OK, if they're going to do it like that, it's doable.'"[116]

The first outward signs of trouble occurred when the start date for shooting of 7 September 1987 was moved to the following week because the sets were not ready. There was a further week's delay when on 12 September a crane and some scaffolding collapsed. But perhaps the worst piece of news from Film Finances' perspective was David Puttnam's sudden resignation as head of Columbia on 16 September. Although the completion guarantee protected Columbia from any extra liability, as long as Puttnam remained in charge of the studio there was always the hope that, in the case of any production difficulties, he might grant some leeway. But once he had gone, it soon became apparent that a new, far less sympathetic dispensation would expect the letter of the contract to be observed.

Shooting finally began on Monday, 22 September 1987, but crawled along at a snail's pace. At the end of the first week, Richard Soames flew to Rome, where he discussed with Schühly and Gilliam what could be done to address the disastrous rate of progress. On 29 September, he faxed this letter to them both:

> Following my conversations with you yesterday, I must formally advise you immediately to revise the story board and method of shooting to manageable proportions in order to make the agreed schedule. You have both repeatedly stated to Film Finances that you could achieve this.
>
> On a simple analysis of the present rate of shooting you are averaging 10 set-ups per day which would give you, over the schedule of 79 days, 790 set-ups whereas the present story board indicates over 1500 set-ups. Secondly, you are

averaging 1 min 45 seconds screentime per day which would give you a total of 137 minutes screentime if you keep on schedule. This is already overlength and it does not take a genius to see how overlength it will be if you shoot the proposed story board in its entirety. Although you told me at our meeting that you had a "terrible" start, you also said that the last two days have been much better. However, in these two days you shot less set-ups than the average overall and more screentime. I do know you do not like these sorts of facts during an intensive creative process but they do not lie.

In any event, the bottom line of all the above is that you are two or three days behind after five days scheduled work and this is not acceptable progress.

I am prepared to rely on your explanation of the first week providing this week (Week 2) remains on schedule.[117]

But as the schedule continued to lag behind, the resulting necessity for script revisions created only further pressure. Although Kurt Woolner wasn't directly involved, he followed from a distance the unfolding drama of what was clearly going to be a major disaster for the company: "I remember Richard, who always spoke with a sense of humour, called me from Rome and he said, 'Boy, this is a problem.' And there was no humour at all. . . . It was really an out-of-control movie. And you know, out-of-control movies are not romantic or sexy. They're out of control. It's not like I'm going to bond this to fund an artist's genius vision. They're out of control. Money's pouring out of the door."[118]

When principal photography was finally completed in March 1988, the cost overage had escalated to $19.5 million, but Film Finances still faced a long and immensely complex postproduction period. The estimate for completion at this point was $7 million, which would have meant a $50 million movie. To take on the challenge of shrinking the cost of postproduction and expediting delivery, Film Finances turned to David Korda. He had left the company in 1985 to become head of production for the recently revived RKO Pictures but agreed to return to help contain a disaster that had now clearly become an existential threat to the company. "Richard asked if I would come back to do whatever I could to try to help out," Korda recalled. "And that's what I did. I suppose I spent nearly a year on that film, with Terry Gilliam. . . . It could almost have been our undoing. It was a terrible claim."[119] With his experience of overseeing productions as a past director of Film Finances, he had the ideal track record but also the advantage of being, as one memorandum from Steve Ransohoff put it, "our own man."[120]

Terry Gilliam faces the challenge of turning fantasy into reality during the
production of *The Adventures of Baron Munchausen* (1988).

At about this time, Film Finances' thoughts also turned to Thomas Schühly.
It was hardly surprising if within Film Finances there was considerable ani-
mosity toward the man perceived to be a prime cause of the disaster. There
were discussions about whether "Mad Dog Schühly," as one office memo styled
him, could be held to account. The unpaid part of his producer's fee had
already been held back to offset numerous breaches of the guarantee contract.
A lawyer was asked to consider the options. Could his credit as producer be
removed? Was there a case to answer for criminal fraud? Did he have any assets
against which a claim could be made in Italy or Germany? But the indignation
eventually gave way to the conclusion that it was better to cooperate than
engage in open warfare. The fear was that going after Schühly would compro-
mise the chief goal, which was to finish the picture. "Legally there is nothing
I can find that Thomas can do to frustrate delivery," wrote Film Finances'
Steve Ransohoff in summary of the situation, "but the unknown with him is
(and always has been) the problem."[121]

Film Finances believed that Terry Gilliam had a case to answer, too, but once
again it gave priority to the constructive relationship that it considered to be
in the interests of completing the film. Although it had withheld Gilliam's
director's fee on the basis that it had a legal claim against him, the company

The Queen of the Moon (Valentina Cortese) faces the Baron (John Neville) and his two companions Sally (Sarah Polley) and Berthold (Eric Idle) in *The Adventures of Baron Munchausen* (1988). The film became a ball and chain for Film Finances as it struggled to contain the expense of endless challenging shots such as this one.

agreed during the postproduction period to make a payment of $100,000 in return for two undertakings: (1) that Gilliam would acknowledge the company had not waived its right of action against him; and (2) that he would help Film Finances "in the economic and timely delivery of the picture to Columbia Pictures."

No one could have been too jubilant when the film was successfully delivered to Columbia in November 1988 approximately $22 million over budget. Among the articles that preceded the release of the film was an interview with Gilliam that appeared in the autumn 1988 issue of *Sight and Sound*. Replying to the question of whether he took into consideration how much something might actually cost when he storyboarded a film, he answered: "I sit there and I really think about it and I work out, 'It'll only take me a day to do that,' and then I think I know what I'm doing. And I've always been wrong. And each time I can convince myself that, 'No, I am right *this* time despite the past.' Strangely enough, because I believe it's possible, I am able to convince other people that it's possible. So we venture forth on these adventures that are just totally impossible. But it's too late by the time people have discovered the truth."[122]

It can have been scant consolation at the time, but if there was a silver lining to *Baron Munchausen*, at least it demonstrated the ability of Film Finances to manage a production disaster on the largest possible scale. What better way to demonstrate to the industry the importance of the completion guarantee? As Richard Soames explained to *Forbes* magazine in an article that preceded the release of *Baron Munchausen*, "Problems are our business."[123]

Film Finances was in the midst of the *Baron Munchausen* crisis when Nigel Cayzer headed a consortium of investors that bought the company in February 1988. Cayzer had come into the completion bond business in 1983 when he had set up Entertainment Completions, which he closed down with the acquisition of Film Finances.

But Film Finances' loss of independence would turn out to be brief. In May 1988, Cayzer sold the company to the financial services group Dominion International. The following year, Dominion International got into serious financial difficulties and, when the company went into receivership in early 1990, Richard Soames engineered a management buyout.

∾

Film Finances had weathered an extremely turbulent end to the 1980s, but its troubles were minor compared to those of the larger independent film industry that it existed to serve. The new markets of home video and pay TV that had promised such a bonanza earlier in the decade had dried up, as a glut of independently produced films drove down prices. According to Jake Eberts, the founder of the most well known of the British independents, Goldcrest, the tide had turned as early as 1985: "The independent sector was overcrowded and smaller companies too often found themselves producing films that got no more than a token theatrical release. The pendulum had swung back in favour of the major studios, who, after the dramatic decline in their fortunes in 1982, were now taking an ever greater share of every market."[124] As the decade progressed, home video became a gold mine for the majors, which took back the initiative from the independent video labels such as Vestron and Media Home Entertainment by creating their own video divisions. To some degree victims of their own success, the independents had also to contend with spiraling budgets that the rapid growth of the independent sector had caused. In 1984, Hemdale made *The Terminator* for $6.5 million; in 1991, Carolco, although not with a completion bond from Film Finances, made *Terminator 2* for reputedly more than $100 million.[125]

Whereas the studios had the capital resources and extensive film libraries to sustain them through lean times, the independents were extremely vulnerable to any sustained downturn. To take 1987 as an example, the box office was the best in Hollywood's history, but the winners tended to be studio films that the majors had the financial marketing muscle to make stand out from the crowd. High-concept, blockbuster movies like that summer's biggest hit, *Beverly Hills Cop II* (1987), left very few crumbs for the independents. "Wall Street is realizing something many Hollywood executives have long known," observed the *New York Times* in a piece that examined the independents' overreliance on the success of a small number of films. "Either because a film may have bombed or because they have not had enough movies in the marketplace, small entertainment companies at this point may be facing a long hot summer."[126]

The ecosystem of independent filmmaking that had developed through the 1980s, of which Film Finances was an essential part, was struggling to sustain itself through the second half of the decade. In the grim catalog of bankruptcies and takeovers that soon followed, one of the earliest casualties was the films division of the British conglomerate Thorn-EMI, which was sold to the Cannon Group in April 1986. Cannon, struggling with debt, then sold off EMI's film library in 1987 and its studio in 1988. But that was only the beginning of the shakeout. After a series of box office failures, the De Laurentiis Entertainment Group filed for bankruptcy in 1988 and was acquired by Carolco the following year.

In October 1989, under the headline "Now Showing, Survival of the Fittest," the *New York Times* reported on the continuing bloodbath of the independents: "Slaughtered by their lack of cash, their lack of size or their lack of good movies, Lorimar, Cannon, Tri-Star, New World, Atlantic, De Laurentiis, Vestron, Film Dallas, Island, Alive and half a dozen smaller companies have gone bankrupt or been reorganized or swallowed up by one of the bigger fish in the Hollywood sea." Speculating on who might be next, the article singled out Orion. "Orion is Hollywood's object lesson in the problems of being small," it warned. "Although Orion is respected for its taste and its willingness to tackle risky material (*Amadeus, Platoon, Mississippi Burning*), Hollywood wonders whether it can survive."[127]

It couldn't. In spite of achieving a big box office success the following year with *Dances with Wolves* (1990), Orion struggled through a series of debt and refinancing crises until eventually it filed for bankruptcy in December 1991.

Orion's troubles brought to a close an extraordinary decade of boom and bust, the repercussions of which would a few years later even bring down France's largest bank. Mired in financial scandal after funding Giancarlo Parretti's take-over of MGM, Crédit Lyonnais, the independents' most lavish source of funding, had to be bailed out by the French government. A state-owned company, the Consortium de Réalisation, was created to administer its assets and liabilities, which included a film library of about a thousand titles acquired from the independent production companies that had defaulted on their loans from the bank.

One Christmas holiday, Kurt Woolner found himself looking through old files from the early years of the US office. He recalled, "I was amazed that of all the companies we had worked with in the 1980s, every one had gone out of business." A decade of revolutionary change, the 1980s offered huge opportunity to independent filmmakers but at the same time mercilessly exposed their Achilles' heel. As Woolner put it, "You don't have the benefit, as the studios do, of having years and years of library . . . churning income for you every day. So studios have got a steady stream of income coming from the past many decades. These independent companies don't. Every project's a risk, and one project that goes bad can really put you back. It's why these companies all need a completion bond. A studio can weather a movie that goes three million over budget, but an independent company can't. That would derail their entire profits for the year, and maybe the year after."[128]

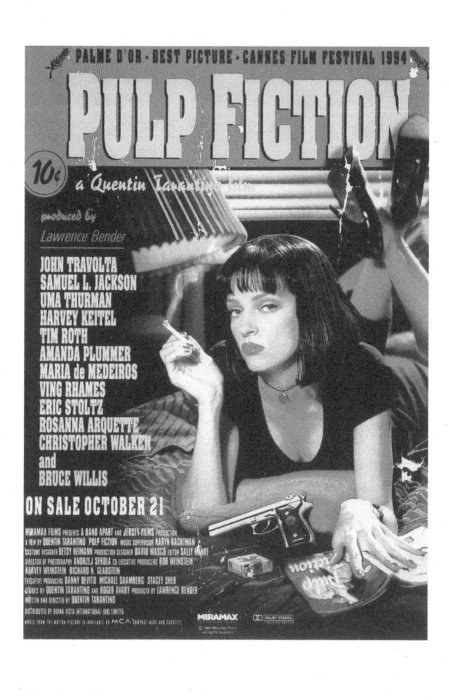

CHAPTER 5

INDIEWOOD

The 1990s

As a new decade began, perhaps the greatest challenge for Film Finances was fending off the fierce competition from Completion Bond Company (CBC). Film Finances had successfully established itself in Hollywood. Year after year it was growing, bonding ever more movies, but it was doing so under unrelenting pressure from an implacable rival. An early sign of the impact of this competition was how quickly the trend of new guarantee companies starting up had gone into reverse. Most would disappear as quickly as they had arrived. By the end of the 1980s, Film Finances and CBC were going head-to-head as the only two significant survivors.

The pressure of competition had been an ever-present factor from early on. Richard Soames was pleased to see New Line Cinema enjoy a huge success with the release of *A Nightmare on Elm Street*, which Film Finances had guaranteed in 1984. When New Line decided to make a sequel, it was only natural to expect that it would return to Film Finances for the completion guarantee. When it didn't, the head of New Line, Robert Shaye, in a letter dated 1 July 1985, made a point of writing to Soames to express his own personal regrets: "I'm sure you know the compelling economic factors which required us to at least try out the 'elsewhere.' Obviously, from a business co-operation and good faith perspective, there has never been a question from our side on the positive relationship we've enjoyed with you. I do want you to know that we shall endeavor, whenever possible, to continue our relationship in future."[1]

"Elsewhere," of course, meant CBC, which provided the bond for *A Nightmare on Elm Street Part 2: Freddy's Revenge* (1985).

"I too would like to continue our relationship in the future and wish you every further success," Soames replied. "As you know I was hoping that we would be involved with your other pictures, especially as I feel the success of

Robert Englund as Freddy Krueger in *Nightmare on Elm Street 2: Freddy's Revenge*
(1985). In spite of a successful collaboration with Film Finances on the first
Nightmare film, New Line Cinema went to Completion Bond Company for this
sequel—a foreshadowing of the rivalry between the two guarantors that escalated in
the early 1990s.

Elm Street was in some part due to our input into the production which was
not easy."[2]

The nightmare for Film Finances was to know that it didn't matter how
supportive or effective its contribution as a guarantor might be: cost would
always be a critical factor, and it had an undeterred rival that seemed always
ready to go lower.

The danger in such a highly competitive environment was to take on a
project that could turn out to be a risk too far. In a more leisurely climate, for
example, Film Finances might have weighed up much more carefully the decision to guarantee *The Adventures of Baron Munchausen* (1988).

Through the boom years of the 1980s, the price of a guarantee had remained reasonably stable at 5 to 6 percent of the budget. But the new decade
marked a watershed. When Bette Smith broke from Fireman's Fund in 1990,
selling CBC to the insurance group Transamerica, Tekla Morgan, her former
colleague at CBC, secured the backing of Fireman's Fund and Chicago-based

Near North Insurance Brokerage to establish a new completion guarantee business, International Film Guarantors, as a joint venture.

Now there were three well-resourced competitors battling for the same business. While CBC and Film Finances embarked on a fierce price-cutting war, International Film Guarantors played a waiting game that sought to capitalize on the financial strength of its insurance backing. "Let's have CBC and Film Finances duel to the death and we'll step in," commented Morgan, later explaining the strategy in an interview with *Variety*.[3]

James Shirras, who became Film Finances' in-house lawyer for the London office in 1993, but had over many years before then undertaken much of its legal work as a partner at Harbottle & Lewis, recalled the extraordinary intensity of the competition. "They charged very low rates. They'd undercut us anywhere, and they used to follow us around. If we made an offer to a producer, they'd immediately follow up with something cheaper."[4] As the two companies went after the same business, the prices quickly tumbled. "It was a clearly unsustainable battle," commented Kurt Woolner. "You know the saying, 'What doesn't kill you, makes you stronger?' We and the Completion Bond Company were pricing ourselves to the point of inevitable oblivion for one or both of us."[5]

The rivalry peaked in 1993 when Film Finances made a bid to guarantee a movie for a 1 percent bond fee with a limited contingency. "We knew the other would do it for 1 percent," remembered Woolner. "At that point it becomes a stupid business. And they [CBC] went out of business due to reducing incomes and a couple of movies that they rushed to do that they probably shouldn't have, so they had some pretty big losses. But honestly, I think, we were not far away from that point."[6]

The movies concerned were animator Richard Williams's *The Thief and the Cobbler* (1993) and Spike Lee's *Malcolm X* (1992). The large budget overruns that led CBC to take over these films were not only costly but also the cause of considerable bad publicity, as CBC was heavily criticized for interfering with the creative vision of two high-profile filmmakers. In the case of *The Thief and the Cobbler*, that interference went as far as firing Williams, a two-time Oscar winner, from a labor of love that he had been working on for more than twenty years. "I wouldn't have gone near it," Richard Soames told the *Los Angeles Times*.[7]

"CBC RIP," declared a *Variety* headline at the beginning of June 1993. Transamerica explained that while CBC would continue to honor its commitments on those films it had already guaranteed, it would henceforward write no new business. The *Variety* article went on to consider the impact CBC's demise would have on the independent film industry. It warned that unless producers were now prepared to accept higher rates, it might spell the end of the completion bond business. "The production community has gotten spoilt by artificially low rates," the head of the Chemical Bank's entertainment division told *Variety*. "They've got to understand the importance of this facility, and that the only way it's going to survive is if the rates and terms start making sense for everyone involved, including the providers."[8]

The fierce rivalry of CBC wasn't the only major challenge that Film Finances had to weather at the beginning of the 1990s. It had also to cope with the fallout of the near collapse of the Lloyd's insurance market after more than three hundred years. Between 1988 and 1992, Lloyd's suffered colossal overall losses of £8 billion (US$14 billion). Huge payouts to compensate victims of asbestosis claims combined with a series of catastrophic losses, including the Piper Alpha offshore oil platform disaster and the San Francisco earthquake of 1989, had a devastating impact on Lloyd's syndicates. Facing ruin, thousands of "Names" were forced by their losses to withdraw from the market. As the novelist Julian Barnes put it in a long feature for the *New Yorker*, "One of the pillars of British society has turned out to be made of Styrofoam."[9] Facing a bleak landscape of decimated insurance syndicates, Film Finances had to work carefully to stitch together a stable reinsurance program. A condition on which the underwriters insisted was that it raise its rates again.

A good omen for the surviving guarantors in the 1990s was the widespread understanding among Hollywood producers of the positive role that the completion bond had to play in the film industry when ten years before they barely even knew what a completion bond was. In the summer of 1991, the *New York Times* published a long feature article that set out why the guarantor was important.[10] Of the six hundred films that went into production in the United States during 1990, the article observed, Film Finances had bonded one hundred. Kim Jorgensen, who was an executive producer of *Out of Africa* (1985), explained, "To be in the completion bond business, one has to know about the entertainment field, to know the producers, directors, actors, cinematographers—everyone involved in making a picture—and the completion bond people are very good at this. I mean, they can tell you what caterers set up the fastest."[11] A production manager, Christopher Coles, commented, "Bond companies work in a subtle way, sort of like the Vatican—they work best when they're being indirect. Independents need the bond company not only for the bond but for the bond company's reservoir of knowledge. They have vast files of budget and cost reports."[12]

But it was not only the independents who valued the contribution of the guarantor. Kurt Woolner gave the example of United Artists asking Film Finances to bond *Rain Man* (1988) because of its concerns over Dustin Hoffman, whose previous film *Tootsie* (1982) had gone over budget partly because of the star's "arm wrestle of control," as Hoffman put it himself, with the director Sydney Pollack.[13] "The studio was afraid that they would not be able to control him," explained Woolner. "So it was like an insurance policy, to control Dustin. As it turned out, the movie finished a week ahead of schedule and a million dollars under budget."[14]

Although in practice the completion guarantor was extremely reluctant to use its power to take over a film, the fact that it even had such power was an extremely effective tool with which to concentrate minds. Francis Coppola's producer Fred Roos, with whom Film Finances had first worked when it had guaranteed *The Outsiders* (1983), explained the value to a producer of being able to call on a guarantor as the "bad cop" when it was necessary to persuade uncooperative talent to step into line: "You can say stuff like, 'Hey, you don't want to be making movies with a completion bond company. If you guys think I'm rough, there's always a worse situation around the corner.'"[15]

Yet for all the filmmaking experience and expertise that Film Finances had accumulated over forty years, its survival depended on its skill in negotiating the ups and downs of an intrinsically high-risk business. It may have weathered the storm of *Baron Munchausen*, but that did not prevent it only a few years later from having to meet the $10 million overcost of *Highlander II* (1991). No amount of expertise could make up for the uncertainty that lay in the infinite combination of situations and personalities that every movie represented. The key to survival ultimately lay in respecting the limits of knowledge that Lindsley Parsons had pointed out when he said, "I've seen everything that can go wrong on a movie, except for the next thing."[16]

∽

It was the exponential growth of independent financing and production that had brought Film Finances to Hollywood in the early 1980s, but a parallel factor in this switch of activity was the degree to which its home country, Britain, had turned into a backwater. The "British are coming!" the screenwriter Colin Welland famously declared in 1982 when he accepted his Oscar for *Chariots of*

Dustin Hoffman and Tom Cruise in *Rain Man* (1989), which on 26 March 1990 became the third film guaranteed by Film Finances to win the Academy Award for Best Picture.

Fire (1981). Goldcrest Films, which had helped develop the script for *Chariots of Fire*, was regarded as the great new hope for the British film industry. It had succeeded in luring City investors back into financing British films. But a series of expensive box office failures, involving huge overcosts, meant that the company was in serious trouble only three years later. The disastrous box office receipts of its American War of Independence epic, *Revolution* (1985), which cost $28 million to make but grossed less than $1 million on its US release, confirmed, in the cruelest possible way, that the British weren't coming at all.

Nor had Goldcrest made it possible for Film Finances to come to its rescue. David Korda recollected a telegram that Richard Soames had kept as a memento of the time when Film Finances' offer of assistance had been turned down. Goldcrest had approached Film Finances to inquire about completion guaranties for *Revolution*, *Absolute Beginners* (1986), and *The Mission* (1986). "I remember going through the production papers on these films. We had a careful look at them and we had concerns about the levels of the budget. Richard went back to Goldcrest and said, 'We're interested in doing this, but the budgets will have to be increased by a certain amount.'" Rather than agree to any increase, Goldcrest sent Soames a cable, saying, "Thank you very much. But if your figures are right, we don't deserve to be in this business."[17] Unfortunately for Goldcrest, the figures were right.

Goldcrest's founder, Jake Eberts, returned to the company in August 1985 in an attempt to turn around its fortunes. Its shares were then worth 75 pence (96 cents) each. But less than a year and a half later, in January 1987, shortly after Eberts had resigned as chief executive for a second time, the company, a shadow of its former self, was sold off to the property and leisure empire Brent Walker for only 6 pence (10 cents) per share.[18] At the beginning of 1989, Richard Soames contributed to a report prepared for Dominion International, the corporation that was briefly Film Finances' parent company, which set out the prospects for Film Finances' future growth. He observed that "virtually all our UK business is based on television. Since the demise of EMI and Goldcrest, no major UK film-maker has emerged. Accordingly, the budgets are small except where a foreign film is based in the UK. The key to our on-going business is the contract that we have with Channel Four."[19]

When Soames wrote this memorandum, the British cinema represented a small and dwindling part of its business. It was this sense of the industry's narrowing horizons that had led David Korda to leave Film Finances in 1985, when he accepted an offer to become head of production for RKO Pictures. To replace him as the effective head of the London office, Richard Soames, who was spending more and more of his time traveling overseas, turned to Jilda Smith, who had been working at Channel 4 as the financial controller of the *Film on 4* series but had previously been head of production at the National Film School, and before that had enjoyed a long and varied career as a production manager and line producer. When she died in 1988, an obituary was published in the London *Times*, which described her as "one of those in the film industry who get little recognition on screen but whose off-screen contribution is priceless."[20] In a summary that got to the heart of much of what Film Finances itself was about, the obituary singled out her forte as "controlling schedules, budgets and brilliant but spendthrift directors. If Jilda thought it would not work, she said so."

James Shirras remembered a person "who was extremely strong on detail. She tended to respect others who were similar. She really didn't like dilettantes." One of the films she did not think would work was *The Adventures of Baron Munchausen*. Shirras remembered having a conversation with Smith about the film before Film Finances gave the bond in which she said, "Well, I've read the script. It's completely impossible. I've told Richard we can't possibly do this."[21]

When Smith became ill, Soames invited Graham Easton to work for Film Finances as a consultant. At the time, Easton was finishing his second film as an independent producer, *Loser Takes All*, which he was coproducing with Christine Oestreicher. She had developed the project and put together the financing before inviting him to join her. An adaptation of a Graham Greene story that was released in the United States under the title *Strike It Rich* (1990), it was one of the first British films to have some production funding from Miramax. It was then still a small, little-known New York distribution company, but it was on the verge of becoming the trailblazer for 1990s independent filmmaking.

Easton had started out in the industry in the late 1960s. After working as a production manager and assistant director on a number of fantasy-adventure films produced by John Dark, including *The Land That Time Forgot* (1974) and *At the Earth's Core* (1976), in 1983, he was hired by the new head of production at Thorn-EMI, Verity Lambert, to oversee Thorn-EMI's in-house slate of feature films. When Thorn-EMI was taken over by the Cannon Group in 1986, Easton stayed on to work as the associate producer of *Superman IV* (1987) and then left to make his first film as an independent producer, *American Roulette* (1988).

After his brief taste of the precarious life of a British independent producer, "making a living but not making a living," Easton began to work for Film

Finances full-time.[22] In 1990, he joined the management buyout from Dominion International and became the managing director of the UK office. By this time, Richard Soames had moved to Los Angeles, which became the head office. Easton's own experience over the past decade had equipped him well to appreciate the paradoxical nature of a British industry that was experiencing economic circumstances as difficult as at any time in its history, yet on the other hand had undergone a revolution that enabled it to contribute significantly to the revitalization of independent filmmaking during the 1990s. The launch of Channel 4 in 1982 was, in Easton's view, "the start of the British film renaissance," even if that renaissance would begin to become apparent only in the following decade.[23] Its remit as a public broadcaster required it to commission rather than make its own programs, which resulted in it becoming an effective nursery for a new generation of independent producers.

Easton had been able to witness its beginning when in 1981 he became a production manager on *Giro City* (1982), one of the first Channel 4 feature films to be shot. It was a contemporary thriller starring Jon Finch and Glenda Jackson as two TV journalists who interview an IRA fugitive. The cinematographer was Curtis Clark, who brought with him an innovative approach to saving costs that he had pioneered on another film that had received funding from Channel 4. *The Draughtsman's Contract* (1982), made for the BFI Production Board on a budget of only £320,000 ($560,000), was the first major film in Britain to be shot on Super-16 (16mm film).[24] The process resulted in exponential savings in lab costs, but also the lightness of the equipment facilitated a much more time-saving way of working, with significant creative implications. The extraordinary achievement of *The Draughtsman's Contract* was to have made such an ambitious, visually striking feature film for so little money. Easton's six weeks working on *Giro City* constituted a radical departure from the industry he had known. "No one in the big old industry would ever have shot a feature film on 16mm," he commented. "You just didn't do it. . . . That really amazed me to be working with 16mm, shooting a feature with Glenda Jackson and Jon Finch. The way you made films, and the size of the crew. All of that was part of the revolution."[25]

Another novel experience was to witness the new permutations of financing. Channel 4 cofunded the £440,000 ($770,000) budget of *Giro City* with the cable TV company Rediffusion. It was a straightforward shared investment between two partners for which Film Finances provided the completion guarantee. But as the 1980s progressed—with the increasing availability of tax incentives, foreign sales, and video and pay-TV rights—the sources of financing

Mr. Neville (Anthony Higgins) prepares his next picture in *The Draughtsman's Contract* (1982), the first major movie in Britain to be shot on 16mm film. Such innovation in format contributed to Britain's independent filmmaking revolution of the 1990s.

became much more complex, and multiple. Easton was struck by the profound change that these new financing opportunities involved: "I can remember John Dark saying to me when I was talking to him about it afterwards, and about the other movies that were being made when you were putting together these patchwork quilts of finance, 'I don't understand how producers can make films when you get the money from more than one place. . . . Who's your boss? Who do you go to? Do you go to five different people?' I couldn't do that. We're making films for EMI. You know, everybody needs a boss. . . . I don't understand how you do it when you're dealing with three or four sources. I'm not set up for that."[26]

Although the National Film Finance Corporation was abolished in 1985, it was replaced the following year by British Screen Finance, a public-private partnership whose stakeholders included the Rank Organisation, Thorn-EMI, and Channel 4. "Despite the fact that we have some government support, the company is run on wholly commercial lines," commented its first chief executive, Simon Relph.[27] Its role, he emphasized, was to stimulate business. It was run on the basis that its investment in production should eventually return a profit. Supporting medium-scale British films with budgets up to £3 million

($4.4 million), British Screen had very modest resources by Hollywood standards, but it was able to operate with considerable speed and flexibility. Easton, who had represented Thorn-EMI on the British Screen board, remembered that its chief executive had the authority to commit up to £500,000 ($730,000) in any single production without having to refer the decision back to the board. The individual responsibility that Relph was able to exercise—and from 1991 onward his successor as chief executive, Simon Perry—"helped an extraordinarily diverse slate of British movies get made," observed Easton.[28]

The arrival of Channel 4 heralded a breakaway from the preconceptions of a highly structured, rigid industry, all the way from the development of a project and its financing through to production. Easton was also impressed by Channel 4's open, noninterventionist attitude: "People who were not old-style producers could go in [and] if they liked the project and thought it was interesting on a creative level they would back people with money, but not try to tell them how to make it."[29]

As far as Film Finances was concerned, the productions that it guaranteed for Channel 4 through the 1980s—which was most of them—were very small, low-budget films, but these films paved the way for important new business in the following decade, on both sides of the ocean. The success of the model was such that other TV companies in Britain followed Channel 4's example: Central Television, with its filmmaking arm Zenith Productions; Granada Television, which with a completion guarantee from Film Finances financed the Oscar-winning Jim Sheridan film *My Left Foot* (1989); and the British Broadcasting Corporation (BBC), which established its own filmmaking division, BBC Films, in 1990.

∾

During the course of the 1990s, Film Finances guaranteed approximately 1,500 feature films around the world. If one had to choose just one of them to capture the symbiotic, hybrid and international nature of the 1990s independent film industry, a good candidate would be *The Crying Game* (1992). It was a small British-made film, yet it was at the heart of the transformation of Miramax into the powerhouse that it became during the decade, fusing "arthouse" and "mainstream" into a new kind of cinema that would soon be dubbed "Indiewood." It was an example, too, of the flowering of the independent filmmaking culture that had begun ten years earlier with Channel 4.

The producer of *The Crying Game*, Stephen Woolley, had, in a personal and direct way, felt the impact of Channel 4 before it even began broadcasting. At the beginning of the 1980s, he ran the Scala Cinema in Charlotte Street, central London, in which Nik Powell and Richard Branson were the principal shareholders. He recalled that one day some Channel 4 executives came to look at the building: "They were wandering around, and I thought, 'Oh my gosh, there's Dickie Attenborough. What's he doing in our bar?'" Channel 4 bought the building, and the cinema had to move to King's Cross. "We closed the Scala Cinema in order for Channel 4 to begin broadcasting," Woolley recounted.[30]

Channel 4's chief executive, Jeremy Isaacs, commissioned Woolley to produce a series called *The Worst of Hollywood*, "a TV series about ten terrible movies," Woolley recalled, which was broadcast within weeks of Channel 4 going on the air for the first time.[31] The beginning of Channel 4 also coincided with the founding of Palace Pictures. A partnership between Nik Powell and Stephen Woolley, it started out as a video label to distribute the kind of films that Woolley was successfully programming at the Scala, but it soon afterward went into film production. Woolley's connection with Channel 4 was so close, he remembered, that "whenever, as a producer, I got rejected (which is more often than I care to remember), I always felt unjustly spurned."[32]

Woolley's long collaboration with the director Neil Jordan began through Channel 4, which had funded Jordan's first film, *Angel* (1982). "We had become very good friends on *Angel*," Woolley remembered, "because Channel 4 were only going to show it on television. I had seen it in a backstreet in Cannes—one of those marketplace screenings. So I said to Channel 4 and John Boorman, who was the producer . . . I wanted to show it in cinemas. I wanted to release it theatrically and release it on video. They had said, 'You can't do that because we're going to show it within the first few months of Channel 4 broadcasting.'"[33]

From the outset Channel 4 had the ambition, in the words of its first chief executive, Jeremy Isaacs, "to make, or help make, films of feature length for television here, for the cinema abroad."[34] It had hoped that some of its films might eventually be shown in British cinemas, too, but its immediate need for product to air on television during the first months of broadcasting resulted in an initial reluctance. "We could not justify showing in their stead a placard marked 'the film you should be seeing this evening is still in the cinema,'" explained Isaacs in a 1984 interview with the British film magazine *Sight and Sound*.[35]

Woolley approached Channel 4 with a plan that involved releasing the film in two London cinemas, the Scala and the Paris Pullman, but only for a short window so that a holdback on the television broadcast would not be necessary. "The result of this, of course, was that the film was nationally press shown," remembered Woolley, "and Neil Jordan quite rightly got stellar reviews. If the film had shown on television only, it would have got a handful of TV reviews. Instead, Neil Jordan made an auspicious debut as a film director, which he most patently was. I knew that the moment I saw *Angel* in a cinema in the backstreets of Cannes and I witnessed Chris Menges's incredible lighting and Stephen Rea's amazing performance."[36]

When, encouraged by Neil Jordan's mentor John Boorman, Woolley decided shortly afterward to become a producer, the first idea that Jordan brought to him was the original story that would eventually become *The Crying Game*, about an ex-member of the Irish Republican Army (IRA) who goes to London in search of the wife of a soldier he had been responsible for killing during the Troubles. Woolley liked the story, which "had echoes of *Angel*," and they discussed how it might develop, but Jordan struggled to work out what would happen after the character had got to London. The script, which was called "The Soldier's Wife," was dropped when Jordan suggested adapting some Angela Carter short stories. "So that's how *Company of Wolves* began," Woolley recounted. "But sat in the back room, in that locker of Neil's head, was this story, 'The Soldier's Wife.'"[37]

Company of Wolves (1984), and then *Mona Lisa* (1986), helped establish Neil Jordan as an important new director. But when he finally returned to "The Soldier's Wife" nearly a decade later, completing his unfinished script in 1991, the omens were not good. He might have cracked the conundrum of what should happen in London, but his three previous films—*High Spirits* (1988), *We're No Angels* (1989), and *The Miracle* (1991)—had all been unsuccessful.

"It was very bad timing," recalled Woolley. "And there were already things in that script people were responding negatively towards. Like an IRA terrorist as the protagonist. Like an IRA terrorist meeting a black woman. The idea of a love story between a black woman and a white guy was not good, and then of course the coup de grâce, which is the woman turns out to be a man. These were three taboos, three big major taboos."[38] The script was rejected by all the potential American investors that Palace approached and, according to Woolley, "especially by Miramax, who thought we should cast a woman in the role of Dil" (the woman who turns out to be a man).[39]

The plan had been to begin principal photography in mid-August 1991, but the lack of US financing forced Palace Pictures to postpone the production by several months and to reduce the budget from £2.8 million ($4.9 million) to

£2.2 million ($3.9 million). With the entire crew agreeing to accept a defer-
ment of their salary against the eventual US distribution of the film, "The
Soldier's Wife" eventually began shooting on 4 November 1991.

"Everything on the financing was right to the wire," Woolley recalled. It
was only when he went to the Venice Film Festival in September that he had
managed to put in place the last stitches of a patchwork quilt of what was
notably international financing: "I remember going with one aim only: to sign
everybody off. I went to a room in Venice in the Lido with all the distributors,
because I knew if I had French, Italian, Spanish, and German distribution,
plus Japanese—we had some interest in Japan weirdly, and we had a little
bit of interest from a Dutch financier—then I might with Film Four pull it
together."[40]

The European backing owed much to the network of connections that
Palace had built up during the 1980s as a film and video distributor. Through
acquiring and selling titles in Europe, it had become part of a group of European distributors: BAC Films in France, Senator in Germany, Lola in Spain,
and Academy in Italy. "We found that we were buying similar films and having a big success with those films in our territories," Woolley recalled. "We all
knew our markets. We were all producing as well in our own territories as well
as acquiring. So as an acquisitions team, we were formidable." In 1989, Palace
and these four distributors agreed on a plan jointly to buy European rights for
films. "Together we had the potential power of a mini-major in Europe," commented Woolley.[41]

But in practice no business was done by the new group until Woolley faced
the struggle of raising finance for what became *The Crying Game*: "With my
desperation on *The Crying Game*, I said, 'Look, guys, you've got to buy a film,
and this is it. You have to buy this one. This is impossible. You have to buy
it for your territories.'"[42] The group formed Eurotrustees in 1991, and the Ber-
liner Bank advanced £1.2 million ($2.1 million) on the basis of their guarantee
of distribution. The Japanese film financier Nippon Film Finance and Development Fund, Channel 4, and British Screen then supplied the remainder of
the £2.2 million ($3.9 million) budget, with Film Finances' completion guar-
antee providing the vital lynchpin for the separate investments.

Even if on this occasion no American distributor had come on board for *The
Crying Game* at the outset, the deal offered a good example of the intrinsically
global nature of the film industry. Through the 1990s, with the increased fluid-
ity and flexibility of financing, film was beginning to fulfill the potential it had
always had to cross national boundaries. "The film industry has always been a

global industry," commented Graham Easton. "So you're used to working with people outside your backyard, but their backyard is your backyard. . . . Whatever the individual specifics of a local film culture, there's a vast amount of shared attitude and approach."[43] When *The Crying Game* went into production, Palace's last big success had been *Scandal* (1989). Woolley remembered that the film, "which was a very British subject, attracted very little money from the UK and was reliant on an American advance, Dutch money, and international deals."[44]

Miramax, which had provided the American advance for *Scandal*, would eventually buy the North American rights for *The Crying Game*, in May 1992, but only after it had seen the finished film. By this time, Palace Pictures was collapsing. It had been in such serious financial trouble during the last stages of the film's production that it was agreed that investors would pay any remaining sums due under the budget not to Palace but to Film Finances, which would supervise the expenditure required to complete the film.

The release of *The Crying Game* in the United Kingdom, in the autumn of 1992, coincided with an IRA bombing campaign on the British mainland, which fatally undermined the appeal of the subject matter for a British audience. The film only became successful through the Miramax release in North America, but too late to save Palace.

Miramax, Woolley thought, was nervous about the film's prospects in the US: "It was odd when the film was released because there were no posters in either LA or NY—it was only released in two cinemas."[45] But what became a game-changer was the review that the *Variety* critic Todd McCarthy wrote when he saw the film at the Telluride Film Festival. On the one hand, the review lauded "an astonishingly good and daring film."[46] On the other hand, it offered a hardheaded analysis of the challenges that would be involved in selling a film that seemed to demand a discriminating rather than a mainstream audience.

> This Miramax pickup presents one of the toughest marketing challenges in recent memory. Title is unenticing, cast has no certified stars, and Irish Republican Army backdrop represents a turn-off for many.
>
> But more importantly, plot contains two major—and several other minor—convulsive surprises that, if revealed, would considerably spoil a first-time viewing experience, making it nearly impossible to describe the film in advance in meaningful detail.
>
> Distrib's main hope lies in amassing a collection of rave reviews the likes of which will make attendance mandatory for specialized audiences.[47]

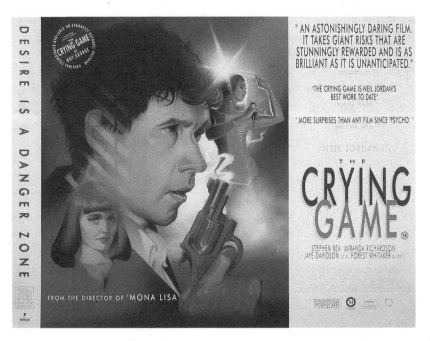

When *The Crying Game* was released in the UK in the autumn of 1992, it was received as just another drab British thriller and made little impression at the box office.

The review provided a kind of "marketing manual" as Miramax created a campaign that addressed, point by point, the risks that McCarthy had identified.

"Miramax got round the downbeat nature of the title," observed Woolley, "by coming up with the tagline on the poster, 'Play it at your own risk,' which put the emphasis on the word 'game' rather than 'crying.'"[48] Although she wasn't the main character, the US poster foregrounded Miranda Richardson to give the film the semblance of the star appeal that it didn't really have, and the IRA backdrop—being such a turnoff—was ignored. The plot twists were turned into a virtue by being heavily stressed to create a buzz around the film. Miramax's marketing campaign urged audiences not to reveal "the secret of *The Crying Game*," which, as a persistent subject of media comment, would end up becoming as iconic a movie mystery as *Citizen Kane*'s Rosebud.

And as for the rave reviews, which quickly followed, Miramax skillfully harvested them to create a critical reception that would help *The Crying Game* receive nine Golden Globe nominations in January 1993 and six Academy

Poster for the US release of *The Crying Game* (1992). The skillful promotion of Miramax transformed the film into a hit movie that caused Hollywood to reevaluate the commercial potential of independent movies. Any similarity that *Pulp Fiction*'s girl with the cigarette and gun bore only a little later was probably not purely coincidental.

Award nominations the following month, including for Best Picture. By the time the Oscars ceremony took place, on 29 March 1993, *The Crying Game* was playing on nearly eight hundred US screens. Industry wisdom, according to *Variety*, was that when it came to success at the US box office, "an arthouse movie had an absolute ceiling of $30 million."[49] *The Crying Game* went on to gross $62 million, smashing the previous records for such an "arthouse" film.[50]

Indeed, as Disney acquired Miramax at the end of April 1993, it caused the industry to reevaluate what "an arthouse film" actually meant. A year later, 20th Century-Fox created its own specialty division, Fox Searchlight Pictures, to fund independent films, and the other majors soon followed suit. In identifying the elemental, universal ingredients that could make even arthouse films popular, the Weinstein brothers massively increased the commercial potential of films that had previously been treated as niche products. As Bob Weinstein put it in an interview with *Rolling Stone*, "We helped to create that business—where these artistic films now go out into over 1,000 theaters. When we started out, in the early 80s, it used to be the art ghetto, literally. I'd look at Harvey and say, 'There are 30 theaters in the whole country that our movies can play in; 30 cities with one theater per city.' We tried to push that out."[51] In the same interview, Harvey Weinstein made the comment, "We're blue-collar guys with white-collar taste who believe that art is for everyone."[52]

Miramax had started out in music promotion and had its first big success as a distributor with the US release of the British-made *The Secret Policeman's Ball* (1979). The Weinsteins had hoped to build on this success to become filmmakers themselves. With funding from British sales company J&M Entertainment and the merchant bank Hill Samuel, in 1984 they coproduced, cowrote, and codirected *Playing for Keeps*, a comedy about three New York teenagers who turn a dilapidated mansion into a rock and roll hotel. Film Finances provided the completion guarantee. The film began shooting in September, with David Korda monitoring progress. After only a week of principal photography on a scheduled forty-day shoot, the novice filmmakers were in trouble. They were shooting footage far in excess of what had been allocated and had already made a substantial invasion into the contingency. At the end of the second week, Korda asked that measures be taken to redress the situation: "The production is not under control and we require an explanation from you of how the budget is going to be contained and what steps are being taken to reduce the overage."[53] About a week later, he explained to them the shortcomings of their proposed scene-cutting solution: "If your daily screen timings are accurate and represent cut material your average timing is in excess of three minutes so even if you complete your schedule in 40 days your film is already 120 minutes in length. Your comments please."[54]

More drastic script revisions had to be made, but close supervision was still required to minimize the substantial overcosts. Korda visited the location in Pennsylvania for the last few days of a shoot that finished a week over-schedule on 10 November 1984, and Richard Soames then flew to New York for a meeting about a week later to review the situation. Further difficulties were caused by the soundtrack. "Because Harvey and Bob knew the music world," recalled Film Finances' lawyer Bob Storer, "they decided the soundtrack was going to be the best soundtrack ever, and the film got finished but the soundtrack didn't."[55] The film was eventually delivered, but only after a lengthy delay in clearing the music.

The purpose of Film Finances was to enable filmmakers to realize their vision within the money available, not to seek to challenge or to modify that vision. It helped filmmakers realize their potential but couldn't create a successful film if the material was not there in the first place. When *Playing for Keeps* was finally released, it was not well received. "Even though there are big names like Pete Townshend and Peter Frampton on the soundtrack, they're wasted on the unimaginative scenario," commented the *New York Times* when the film was finally released. It was like "a below-average episode of the television series *Fame*" that "probably should have bypassed theaters altogether and gone directly to videotape or television, where its staleness might have been less conspicuous."[56]

If the debacle convinced the Weinsteins to stick to promoting films rather than directing them, it did not make them any more hesitant to impose their stamp on the films that they distributed, an issue that would become a source of increasing controversy as their influence over the industry grew, and the lengths they went to shape a commercial product often put them at odds with the artistic vision of the independent filmmakers who turned to Miramax for its support.

By contrast, Film Finances, which had no direct interest in the commercial prospects of the films that it guaranteed, was able routinely to offer dispassionate, even-handed advice that respected the original intentions of the filmmakers. Its key requirement was simply that the filmmakers themselves should respect the limits of the financing that they had secured. The value of the completion bond was to protect against the unforeseen but at the same time to afford access to the kind of practical filmmaking expertise that helped make a budget go as far as it possibly could go. As an international independent filmmaking community developed in the 1990s, encouraged by the growing prominence of the Sundance Film Festival and Miramax's own success as a distributor, Film Finances' unrivaled reservoir of practical production knowledge, accumulated now over five decades, was an important enabling element.

Behind the scenes, Film Finances' support had not only facilitated the breakthrough films of such major new independent filmmakers as Quentin Tarantino (*Reservoir Dogs* [1992], *Pulp Fiction* [1994]), Danny Boyle (*Shallow Grave* [1994], *Trainspotting* [1996]), Michael Winterbottom (*Welcome to Sarajevo* [1997]), Christopher Nolan (*Memento* [2000]), and Darren Aronofsky (*Requiem for a Dream* [2000]) but also helped build a framework of support for the work of such long-established filmmakers as Ken Loach, Mike Leigh, and Merchant-Ivory.

Notable was the breadth of different approaches that it could accommodate. Mike Leigh was a filmmaker who at the outset of each project did not even have a script that he could share, yet he had worked with Film Finances on all his films since *High Hopes* in 1988. In 2014 he took part in a study afternoon at the BFI Southbank with Graham Easton, his principal contact at Film Finances, in which they explained the nature of their collaboration. "I really do," said Leigh, "go out on location, and it's always on location, with very rare sorties into a studio, and make the film up as I go along. Now we can only do that because I am protected by Film Finances." It was Easton's "understanding, intelligence, sensitivity and practical help," he explained, that made a significant contribution to the successful outcome of each production. "The important thing is that because Graham has always been on the production at every stage, without ever interfering with it, we have been able to make these films in a way that is completely pragmatic."[57]

Easton then gave the guarantor's point of view: "The financiers want the security of the completion bond. But once it's there it's a resource for the producer and the film-makers to use." In assessing a project, the aim of the guarantor was to make sure that the production plan, schedule, and financing reflected "the will and the understanding and the ambitions of the people setting out to make the film." But no matter how well planned a production might be, once it had begun, the budget limitations meant that Film Finances had to manage the progress of the production on a daily basis. "You're always working to a finite resource," Easton said. "It's for the film-makers to decide where the priority is within that resource, but we have to help them do that."

Palme d'Or winner in 1996, *Secrets and Lies* was one of the many Mike Leigh films that were made with Film Finances' assistance.

According to Easton, the advantage that Film Finances had in sorting out any problems when things went wrong lay in the fact that it was "at one remove from all the muck and the bullets, so it could go into the trenches but with a clear view."[58] Its detachment enabled it to see the individual tree in the wood in a way that was often more difficult for the filmmakers themselves, grappling with the problems up-close.

Although Film Finances had the legal right to take control of a production if necessary, over its seventy years it had done so on only a handful of occasions. Its experience had repeatedly been that the best answer to most problems lies in finding a solution that involves the filmmakers themselves. Much of its authority lay in the fact that, although it possessed huge theoretical power, it rarely asserted it. In Film Finances' long relationship with Merchant-Ivory Productions, Richard Soames was amused by Ismail Merchant's habit of "using the guarantor as a real bad guy," a kind of embodiment of a mythical Front Office. When he was visiting the set of the Merchant-Ivory film *The Bostonians* (1984), Soames recalled Merchant insisting that he should meet the teamster captain.

> So I said, "Fine." But then Ismail said to the guy, "This is Richard Soames. He's the boss. And he says you've got to get rid of two teamsters." Ismail had never even consulted me about it. He used to do the same thing with James Ivory all the time. Once there was some huge bust-up with Jim about the editor for some reason. Ismail said, "Look, Richard says we've got to get rid of this editor." I had no idea what he was talking about. "You've got to get rid of him, Jim." And Jim was screaming. "Richard says so, so you do it." I think the editor went in the end, but it had nothing to do with me at all.[59]

A major test of Film Finances' commitment to the principle of creative independence came with Merchant-Ivory's production of *The Golden Bowl*, which was shot in England and Italy during the autumn of 1999. The French bank Société Générale was advancing the $14.1 million budget on the strength of a $7.6 million guarantee from the French distributor TF1 and $6.5 million from Miramax. Although there was a significant overage on the production of the film, the really serious problems began only in the following spring when, after editing had been completed at Merchant-Ivory's house in Claverack in the Hudson Valley, the film was screened for Miramax.

Harvey Weinstein complained that the film was too long and he felt that Uma Thurman's acting was over the top. He "publicly told her that he hadn't

Heat and Dust (1983), according to Richard Soames, "really brought Merchant-Ivory to everyone's attention. That's when we came in."

liked her performance," recalled James Ivory, and that it could be improved only
if the director listened to Weinstein's suggestions.[60] Weinstein tried to enlist
Thurman's support to persuade Merchant-Ivory not to showcase the film at
Cannes and to rework it, but she resisted the pressure. "It didn't matter to me
who was right and who was wrong," she recalled. "James Ivory is an auteur, an
artist, and win, lose or draw, you don't turn your back on a film-maker."[61]

After the film was screened at Cannes to mixed reviews, Miramax exercised
its contractual right to "make suggestions." While the agreed delivery date was
put back to allow Miramax to work on an alternative version, the French distributor TF1 confirmed that it would accept the director's cut version of the
film, unless Merchant-Ivory reached an agreement with Miramax on a version
that was acceptable to both parties.

Harvey Weinstein's intervention served only to entrench Merchant-Ivory's
mood of resistance. "With all his messing about with it," recalled James Ivory,
"experimentally shortening, staging a sneak preview in a New Jersey mall,
stomping and threatening, affronting Uma, trying to frighten the French
co-financiers with dire predictions of failure (the French stood firm), and so
forth—we still refused to go along with his suggested changes, as was our

Director James Ivory in conversation with Uma Thurman in 1999, during the
production of *The Golden Bowl* (2000).

contractual right. He then said that he would take the movie straight to television and not give it a theatrical release in the United States at all."[62]

When Miramax soon afterward offered a million dollars to be let out of its obligation to distribute the film in North America, Merchant-Ivory immediately accepted. There was a degree of heroic madness about a decision that made no business sense whatsoever, as James Ivory himself later acknowledged. "How much better it would have been for us if we'd told Harvey what Julie Taymor is supposed to have said when he used the same threat about her *Frida*. 'Fine. I don't care. At least it will be my cut of the movie on TV, not yours.' After she'd called his bluff, he backed down."[63] The logic of the situation dictated that Weinstein would probably have backed down in the case of *The Golden Bowl*, too, rather than damage the commercial potential of a film for which Miramax had paid a lot of money.

Instead, Merchant-Ivory had now created a massive challenge for itself to make up for the loss of the $6.5 million that Miramax had originally offered. After Miramax's reversion payment for $1 million, there was still a large hole that had to be filled in order to pay back the balance of the production loan that the Société Générale had advanced. And the task of finding an alternative US distributor was seriously undermined by the perception of the film, after Miramax's withdrawal, as "damaged goods."

Lionsgate eventually picked up the US rights but for only $1 million. "They will endorse Merchant-Ivory's belief that the creative integrity of independent film-makers must be respected and maintained," said Merchant when he announced the deal in September 2000.[64] It was a thinly veiled dig at Miramax, but the cost for Merchant-Ivory of defending its creative integrity was turning out to be very high.

"It nearly broke us," admitted Ivory.[65] Merchant-Ivory's last commercially successful film had been *The Remains of the Day* (1993). The three films they had released subsequently, *Jefferson in Paris* (1995), *Surviving Picasso* (1996), and *A Soldier's Daughter Never Cries* (1998), had all been box office disappointments, so there was very little fat to spare.

After immediately realizable funds had been committed toward the outstanding amount of the production loan, there was still a $1.5 million shortfall, which Ismail Merchant proposed to cover by selling rights to the Merchant-Ivory film library. The Société Générale agreed to accept this arrangement only on the basis that, in the interim, Film Finances provide it with an absolute guarantee of repayment of the $1.5 million.

As the film had already been completed and delivered, Film Finances had no contractual obligation to do so, but it still agreed to give the guarantee. Partly it was a question of showing the company's loyalty to a long-term partner. When Richard Soames sought to persuade Film Finances' reinsurers to support the decision, he made the point that Merchant-Ivory "have always been great supporters of Film Finances, and we have guaranteed at least 15 of their films."[66] But it was a question, too, of standing up for the principle of creative freedom in independent filmmaking, which after all was the lifeblood of Film Finances' business.

The premiere of *The Golden Bowl* took place at the Curzon Soho on Thursday, 2 November 2000. The following night there was a screening of the film at the Barbican Centre, when Ismail Merchant and James Ivory took part in a Q and A. The moderator explained to the audience how the production had been threatened by the financing troubles that followed Miramax's withdrawal as a distributor, but that it was luckily saved "by some miracle." When he turned to Ismail Merchant to explain, Merchant made the audience laugh with the comment that he had managed to sort out the difficulties through the use of "an Indian rope trick."[67]

Standing behind this "Indian rope trick," of course, was Film Finances. But it was used to being the elusive Pimpernel figure, who slipped quietly away from the scene after having pulled off some fantastic rescue. Over its seventy-year history, only in exceptional circumstances—such as the occasion of a major anniversary—did it ever presume to take center stage. The 1990s was the decade in which independent movies became "cool," but what Film Finances did was really beyond fashion, if still important in any age in which an expensive art form required a coherent, sensible plan.

∾

One index of how cool movies had become in the 1990s was the decision of rock business giant PolyGram, the entertainment division of the electronics conglomerate Philips, to expand its music interests into the film business. Establishing its base in London, it was the first European "major" of any size since the Rank Organisation. In 1988, it had taken equity shares in the UK production company Working Title and the LA-based Propaganda Pictures.

In his account of PolyGram Films, its British president, Michael Kuhn, explained the logic of this new commitment to the film industry: "The movie business had changed significantly since the beginning of the 1980s in that two very significant revenue sources had developed in the meantime; pay television

00135

Tatler &
Merchant Ivory Productions

INVITATION TO THE
PREMIERE PARTY FOR

THE GOLDEN BOWL

on Thursday 2 November from 9.45pm
at St Martins Lane
45 St Martin's Lane WC2

TATLER
Laurent-Perrier

The Golden Bowl is a
BVI/Miramax release

ADMIT ONE

Dress: smart
Invitation strictly personal

A smudgy but well-earned invitation to the premiere of Merchant-Ivory's *The Golden Bowl* on 2 November 2000. Although Miramax reverted the US rights, it continued to be the distributor of the film in the UK.

and home video."[68] Kuhn estimated that, by the beginning of the 1990s, a "third or more of all revenues from movies came from home video," and PolyGram was well placed to take advantage.[69] "Unlike most film studios at the time, we had a worldwide distribution system capable of distributing bits of plastic to the public, but we were only using it for one bit of plastic—the music carrier."[70]

In pursuit of its vision of building "a studio without a lot," PolyGram set up the distributor Gramercy in 1992 as a joint venture with Universal.[71] At the same time, to ensure a supply of product, it acquired the US production company Interscope Pictures and bought out the remaining shares of Working Title and Propaganda Pictures. It nearly bought Palace Pictures too.

The structure that PolyGram put in place—of semiautonomous production units that relied on PolyGram for production finance and international distribution—was grafted onto the hybrid industry of small independent companies that had emerged during the 1980s. Its corporate and financial power gave these constituent elements global reach. It anticipated the specialty divisions that the Hollywood majors would, one by one, starting with Disney's acquisition of Miramax, establish through the 1990s.

When James Shirras joined Film Finances in the early 1990s, the London office, he recalled, was guaranteeing not more than fifteen films a year. Following the abolition in 1985 of the National Film Finance Corporation (NFFC) and the curtailment of capital allowances that had been available to the film industry since 1979, a much diminished British film industry had experienced a long lull in which it had been chiefly reliant on British Screen Finance and Channel 4 for any activity or direction. But the arrival of PolyGram created a renewed confidence, which increased exponentially in 1996 when the government proposed investing funds from the new National Lottery in the British film industry and invited consortiums to be formed to bid for funding on a franchise basis.

"The introduction of the lottery money was a game-changer," recalled Shirras. "It was an enormous amount of money compared to anything that had been available since the glory days of the NFFC."[72] The accompanying effort to rationalize the industry led a few years later to the establishment of the UK Film Council in 2000, which had the express remit of creating a "sustainable" film industry.

Equally significant in the 1990s was the government's renewed commitment to tax relief as an instrument of film policy. In 1992, it introduced legislation to permit expenditure on the production or acquisition of British films to be written off over a period of three years.[73] The measure in practice encouraged the higher-budget productions financed by Hollywood. But further legislation, which followed in 1997, focused on indigenous British production, enabling investors to claim a 100 percent write-off on British-made films with budgets up to £15 million ($25 million).[74] It was a "real shot in the arm for the UK film industry," observed Wilf Stevenson, the director of the British Film Institute.[75]

The UK office had in the early 1990s been involved in a growing number of European coproductions, but it guaranteed comparatively few British-originated and UK-financed films. Now it was transformed into a buoyant, bustling business again. "By the late '90s, we were doing thirty or forty or fifty films a year from this office," recalled Shirras. "In some years we would have done sixty films a year."[76]

As the company approached the turn of a new century, it enjoyed an unrivaled reputation as a cornerstone of filmmaking in the English-speaking world. With forty employees now spread throughout eight global offices, it guaranteed well over two hundred movies a year with budgets that ranged from $100,000 all the way up to $100 million.

Although it was nearly two months after the company's actual fiftieth birthday on 24 February, the mayor of West Hollywood declared 17 April 2000 "Film Finances Day," and a special issue of the *Hollywood Reporter* was published to celebrate the occasion.[77] The issue featured an interview in which Richard Soames and Steve Ransohoff outlined how the business had changed and identified some of the key challenges of the future. "In the old days, one of our deals used to fit in one manila folder. Now, we have up to 15 folders for a given picture," commented Ransohoff. "The number of financing sources, the number of people involved in the deals and their level of sophistication have also increased. Typically, a movie would have two funding sources, but now it could be 15."[78]

Soames highlighted the arrival of computer-generated imagery, or CGI, which, after its use over the past decade in a few highly publicized landmark films such as *Jurassic Park* (1993), *Toy Story* (1995), and *Titanic* (1997), was now well on its way to become a ubiquitous new process whose implications, from both a technical and a cost standpoint, still needed to be fully understood. Ransohoff welcomed the advent of digital films being made for very low budgets, stating, "We are very excited about this, because it will increase demand for films and will allow some really talented film-makers with 'marginal' projects to get them off the ground."[79]

Another revolutionary change that was already clearly on the horizon was the rise of productions tailored for Internet distribution. At the turn of the millennium, the technology that would lead to the rise of today's streaming giants was already in place. As significant was the way independent filmmaking was spreading around the world as more and more countries offered subsidies to attract film production. It had become a truly global business, in which the completion guarantor was ready to go anywhere. Richard Soames chose a characteristically buccaneering metaphor to summarize Film Finances' role: "I think of Film Finances as a small and efficient vessel in a shark-infested sea—a wild sea with swells and gales. We know our way through these treacherous waters in every country in the world. Nobody on the ship needs to be told what the job is, because they know it instinctively."[80]

WINNER
People's Choice Award
TORONTO
INTERNATIONAL FILM FESTIVAL 2008

TIME

"A BUOYANT HYMN TO LIFE,
AND A MOVIE TO CELEBRATE."
RICHARD CORLISS

WHAT DOES IT TAKE TO FIND A LOST LOVE?

A. MONEY   B. LUCK

C. SMARTS   D. DESTINY

A DANNY BOYLE FILM

slumdog millionaire

www.foxsearchlight.com

AFTERWORD

The New Millennium

When Film Finances first gave scholars access to its historical archive in 2012, it imposed a "thirty-year rule." For reasons of discretion and confidentiality, it stipulated that any papers after 1980 should remain private. This afterword offers a necessarily brief overview of recent decades, specifically the years since the new millennium began, which have been as eventful as any period in the company's history.

With the retirement of Richard Soames in 2008, the responsibility for guiding the company through the "treacherous waters" of international film production passed to a third generation as Steve Ransohoff and Kurt Woolner took over as joint CEOs. Although each era in Film Finances' existence presented its own unique set of challenges, the underlying reality remained the same. As Soames had observed in 1984, soon after he had taken over from Bobby Garrett, "The very fact that there are problems with pictures is the reason that we're in business."[1]

At the beginning of the new century, International Film Guarantors (IFG) was Film Finances' chief competitor. While Film Finances bonded annually a far greater number of films around the world, IFG had taken advantage of the growing trend for the Hollywood majors to collaborate with one another on high-budget pictures.

"Because there are a lot of split-rights deals and the studios are willing to give up ownership to get these event-type pictures," explained its chairman Michael Segal in 1995, "the studios need bonds to protect themselves since they're not in total control."[2] In 1999, IFG made the headlines of the trade papers when it bonded the $100 million Arnold Schwarzenegger film *End of Days* (1999), then the largest independently financed film ever to receive a completion guarantee. IFG went on to guarantee many other big-budget pictures, including *Lara Croft: Tomb Raider* (2001), *Lord of the Rings: The Fellowship of the Ring* (2001), *Iron Man* (2008), and *Terminator Salvation* (2009).

"The perception in the industry was that we could do the smaller independent films, but the bigger-budget films had to go to IFG," recalled Kurt Woolner.[3]

For a while, this perception was close to the truth. When Film Finances rebuilt its insurance program at Lloyd's in the early 1990s, the insurers were reluctant to give the company the backing to guarantee films with budgets in excess of $20 million, but in the years that followed, the confidence was built up with the Lloyd's insurers that allowed Film Finances to guarantee larger-budget films.

In 2003, Andrew Lloyd-Webber's Really Useful Group bought back the film rights for *Phantom of the Opera* from Warner Bros. and instead made the film independently with a guarantee from Film Finances.[4] With an $80 million budget, it was the biggest project that Film Finances had guaranteed up to that point. But only five years later, in 2008, the company went on to guarantee *Twilight*, which was its first $100 million movie. "The fact that we did that," observed Woolner, "really made it clear that we could do those films."[5]

In 2012, Film Finances bonded *The Hunger Games* film series, which, with a total production budget of more than $400 million, was the biggest independently funded feature project in history. It was a powerful message to the industry that there was effectively no upper limit on the budgets that Film Finances could guarantee.

It was a development that had far-reaching implications for its main competitor, IFG, which had become a subsidiary of Fireman's Fund in 2005. The advantage had now decisively shifted in Film Finances' favor. "They couldn't get into our business," commented Woolner, "because they didn't have the bandwidth to do all these independent films, but suddenly we were in their business."[6]

In 2013, Fireman's Fund made the decision to close down IFG and to underwrite Film Finances' guarantees instead. After IFG was gone, Film Finances enjoyed an 80 percent share of the completion guarantee market. It issued guarantees for approximately two hundred productions per annum, which was more than all the feature films produced by the major Hollywood studios put together. The combined budgets of the films it guaranteed in 2018 was $2 billion, more than triple what it had been in 2000, with an average cost of $14.3 million. The new millennium saw the entrenchment of the tax incentive as a permanent feature of global production, as governments around the world became increasingly aware of the capacity of the international film industry to generate high levels of spending in their economies. By 2020, there were approximately one hundred jurisdictions that were offering production incentive schemes.[7]

In Europe, cinema admissions rose 39 percent between 1999 and 2019.[8] But the major structural shift was to come from video on demand, which, with the advent of streaming, increased exponentially from €388.8 million ($515.9 million) in 2010 to €11.6 billion ($13.2 billion) in 2020.[9]

A significant milestone was the year 2006, when the UK government introduced a new system of tax relief for the film industry. The legislation replaced previous incentives that, although they had attracted substantial investment, had given rise to complex financing structures, with high levels of tax avoidance resulting from the exploitation of legislative loopholes. A measure of the new system's success was the extension of the relief to high-end television in 2013 and later to other sectors in the UK creative industries. It became a model for comparable schemes in other countries keen to encourage inward investment. The German Federal Film Fund (DFFF, from its German name Deutscher Filmförderfonds) was launched in 2007. France's Tax Rebate for International Productions and Italy's Credit for Foreign Films followed in 2009. The Czech Republic introduced the Film Industry Support Program in 2010, and Hungary launched its Film Fund in 2012. By the end of the decade, there was hardly a European country that couldn't boast some form of fiscal incentive.

The introduction of such schemes was accompanied by a corresponding increase in the demand for the completion guarantee. It enabled national film organizations to safeguard the commitment of public money, but it also provided—in a production landscape where often multiple partners were seeking to take advantage of incentive schemes in more than one country—a means to underpin a complex collaborative process in such a way that the individual participants had an assurance that the picture would cohere as a whole.

Rupert Everett's 2018 film *The Happy Prince*, which chronicled Oscar Wilde's last year in Paris, was a German, Italian, and Belgian coproduction. The number of producers was well into double figures. Although the story was set mostly in France, filming took place not only in France but also in Germany, Italy, and Belgium to take advantage of the tax incentives and other grants available in those three countries. The legal and financial complexity of such productions required Film Finances not only to monitor the progress of the production itself but also to provide the ultimate touchstone for what it was that multiple parties had agreed.

Perhaps the most significant feature of the new millennium has been the huge, often disruptive technological change of an industry making the transition from analog to digital delivery methods. In a fast-changing landscape, the rise of streaming revolutionized the way in which audiovisual content was being produced and consumed. In 2015, Netflix released its first original feature-length film, *Beasts of No Nation*, which Film Finances guaranteed. The advent of streaming also facilitated the growth of the international TV series. In 2015, Film Finances guaranteed the first of several series of *Narcos*. *The Night Manager* (2016), *Das Boot* (2018), and *My Brilliant Friend* (2020) followed. By 2019, as combined revenues for the global entertainment market passed $100 billion for the first time, revenue from streaming had already overtaken that of the box office.[10] It was a trend that subsequent events would only accelerate.

∽

The growing global demand for content meant that in its seventieth anniversary year of 2020, Film Finances had good reason to look to the future with more than the usual degree of confidence. But the fact that the very purpose of a completion guarantor is to guard against the unforeseeable offered some warning against complacency. "I've seen everything that can go wrong on a movie, except for the next thing," Lindsley Parsons told Kurt Woolner on his first day as a guarantor back in the 1980s.[11] Four decades later, a global pandemic resulting from a new strain of coronavirus called COVID-19 bore out this eternal truth. Instead of celebrating its anniversary, Film Finances found itself suddenly facing an existential threat as the international film industry ground to a halt.

When Tom Hanks announced on 11 March 2020 that he and his wife had tested positive for coronavirus, he was in Australia filming Baz Luhrmann's Elvis Presley biopic. The Warner Bros. production shut down immediately and didn't resume for six months. In the same week, Netflix, Amazon, and Disney all announced that they would suspend production.

Countries around the world went into lockdown. By the beginning of April 2020, the entire international film industry was at a standstill, with no certainty as to when it might be able to resume production. Film Finances' position was potentially catastrophic. Although it immediately imposed a COVID exemption in line with the rest of the insurance industry—excluding any risk that arose from COVID or the fear of COVID—the pandemic had caught in midstream more than twenty productions that the company had the responsibility to deliver in the usual way for the original amount of money. For the first time in its history, Film Finances faced the kind of perfect storm that had always been a theoretical possibility but no one imagined would ever actually happen. The next few months offered the ultimate test of the company's raison d'être. It faced the challenge of getting more than twenty films around the world back into production and safely completed, knowing that the combined overcost resulting from their simultaneous delay had the potential to sink the business.

"Mission Impossible?" asked the headline of an article that the director Alex Cox wrote for *The Guardian* at the beginning of July. It described some of the difficulties that the industry was facing. "Productions remain on hold or in pre-production limbo." The crisis had "decimated film and television."[12] Cox was the director who had once described the completion bond as unnecessary, but that summer it was the essential lifeline for those twenty independent feature films that Film Finances managed to nurse back into production.[13]

With the insurance industry refusing to cover COVID-related risk for new production, the UK government in early August 2020 introduced what it called a Film and TV Production Restart Scheme, which provided enough support for the industry to start production again; the scheme underwent further modifications but was still in effect more than a year later.[14]

In the United States, representatives of the entertainment industry urged the federal government to provide temporary support of a similar kind. A letter sent to the US Senate leadership in February 2021 summarized the scale of the crisis:

> Our industries, especially independent film producers, have struggled to restart productions due to our inability to secure insurance against the risk of losses resulting from shutdowns or illnesses of key cast members. Without federal protection against these unprecedented risks, private banks are unable to justify financing many independent film productions and some major studios will not risk investment in high budget, large cast productions. The job loss numbers suffered in these impacted industries since March have been staggering. The pandemic has impacted 464,000 film and television jobs in the United States to date. Roughly 400 film and television productions were canceled last year.[15]

As production slowly began to pick up again, with elaborate procedures in place to manage the COVID risk, the challenge for Film Finances in 2021 became how to manage the so-called new normal.

It is impossible to insure against an unknown risk until such time as that risk can be assessed and quantified through experience. Some risks—such as nuclear explosions—involve events so catastrophic that they are effectively uninsurable. But most risks can be insured once they are understood. Back in the 1950s, Film Finances used to insist on an additional weather contingency for productions that involved location shooting. But the requirement was dropped as soon as reliable protocols had been developed to manage the unpredictability of filming outdoors. In a similar way, as the nature of COVID-19 became clearer, insurers began to grapple with the challenge of making it a containable risk.

The first policies for COVID-19 were introduced at the end of the summer of 2020.[16] Costing approximately 10 percent of a film's budget, they were too expensive and limited in their coverage to make any great difference. But the process of developing systems to cope with the rapidly mutating virus continued into 2021, offering the hope that more-affordable insurance would eventually follow.

∼

With its overview of multiple productions around the world—in which it repeatedly encounters situations that any individual producer faces rarely, if at all—Film Finances has been at the heart of the efforts to address this latest crisis for the independent film industry. But the pandemic is only one of many crises that it has faced over a long and—until now—mostly unsung history. Although the company continues to accumulate a vast repository of knowledge and experience, which this book briefly samples, it remains a behind-the-scenes, invisible presence.

In *Kingsman: The Secret Service*, which Film Finances guaranteed in 2014, the agent Galahad explains to his new recruit that the nature of Kingsman is for its achievements to remain secret: "A gentleman's name should appear in the papers only three times. When he's born, when he marries, and when he dies. And we are, first and foremost, gentlemen."

Although it is forty years after Bobby Garrett died, those words evoke the ethos that this alumnus of Bletchley Park—"a real gentleman" who "still wears a bowler hat"—sought to imbue in the company he founded in 1950, only a stone's throw from Kingsman's Savile Row headquarters. Galahad describes Kingsman as "an independent, international intelligence agency operating at the highest level of discretion, above the politics and bureaucracy that undermine the integrity of government-run spy organizations." It was the successful command of such independent intelligence that provided the foundation for Film Finances' first seven decades.

Acknowledgments

I would to like express my gratitude to Maureen Duffy, who first suggested the idea of a book to celebrate Film Finances' history more than ten years ago, and Steve Ransohoff, who then enthusiastically supported the idea and did what was necessary to make it happen.

In the years that followed, many other people offered their help. I would like to thank them all individually, with apologies to anyone I may inadvertently have left out: David Adger, Rozemyn Afman, Ron Aikin, Angela Allen, Christopher Bestehorn, Tom Craig, Penelope Craig, Neil Calder, Dinah Drazin, Graham Easton, Charles Fairey, Wes Fleuchaus, Laurence Harbottle, Ruth Hodgson, Ahmed Khamouch, Antonia Klopfer, David Korda, Mike Leigh, Dennis Lloyd, Emma Mager, Thoko Mavolwane, Sheila McMahon, Sue Milliken, Nathalie Morris, Ali Mosref, Jean Munif, Jennifer Nadin, Olivia Parkes, Richard Paterson, Linda Pather, Schuyler Ransohoff, Angeria Rigamonti di Cutò, Julian Rose, Lori Meek Schuldt, James Shirras, Chandra Silver, Richard Soames, Ruby Soames, Michael Spencer, Pierre Spengler, Bob Storer, Ama Tasca di Cutò, Jackie Teoh, Matthew Toro, Kurt Woolner, and Stephen Woolley.

Notes

PREFACE

1. Those six Best Picture Oscars were awarded to *Tom Jones* (1963), *Platoon* (1986), *Rain Man* (1988), *Slumdog Millionaire* (2008), *The King's Speech* (2010), and *12 Years a Slave* (2013).

2. For a helpful mapping of the landscape, see David Cook, "Orders of Magnitude 1: Majors, Mini-Majors, 'Instant Majors' and Independents," in *Lost Illusions: American Cinema in the Shadow of Watergate and Vietnam, 1970–1979*, by David A. Cook (University of California Press, 2002), 301–36; and Justin Wyatt, "The Formation of the 'Major Independent,'" in *Contemporary Hollywood Cinema*, ed. Stephen Neale and Murray Smith (Routledge, 1998), 74–90.

3. I remember that very soon after the cataloging had finished—in yet another example of the constantly evolving relationship between independent and major—De Lane Lea was acquired by Warner Bros.

4. "The Film Finances Archive," special issue, *Historical Journal of Film, Radio and Television* 34, no. 1 (March 2014).

CHAPTER 1. IN THE BEGINNING

1. Quoted in Martin Gilbert, *Winston S. Churchill: Finest Hour, 1939–1941* (Heinemann, 1983), 612.

2. Business proposal, 3 August 1949, box 100, General Collection, Film Finances Archive, London.

3. The allotment of shares is listed in Film Finances' first minute book, paragraph 22, box M104, Film Finances Archive. The dollar equivalent of British currency figures is taken from the Pacific Exchange Rate Service of the Sauder School of Business at the University of British Columbia.

4. "Every Rank Studio Is Dark for First Time since He Entered Pix Industry," *Variety*, 19 April 1950.

5. Report on Production Costs, no. 27, 24 February 1951, box 1, Films Collection, Film Finances Archive.

6. Report on Production Costs.

7. GPO form for "New or Additional Service," 18 September 1950, box 100, General Collection, Film Finances Archive.

8. Business proposal.

9. John Croydon curriculum vitae, box 9, General Collection, Film Finances Archive.

10. John Croydon to Peter Hope, 8 June 1950, box 6, Films Collection, Film Finances Archive.

11. Robert Garrett to Bill Cullen, 10 July 1950, box 100, General Collection, Film Finances Archive.

12. Robert Garrett to Bill Cullen and Peter Hope, 11 July 1950, box 100, General Collection, Film Finances Archive.

13. Robert Garrett to Alessandro Tasca di Cutò, 29 February 1952, box 101, General Collection, Film Finances Archive.

14. Alessandro Tasca di Cutò to Robert Garrett, 6 March 1952, box 101, General Collection, Film Finances Archive.

15. Robert Garrett to Sir Michael Balcon, 6 August 1954, box 34, General Collection, Film Finances Archive.

16. "Bell Tolls for Indie Producers," *Variety*, 19 May 1948.

17. "Bankers Cautious," *Variety*, 11 May 1949.

18. "Milton Gordon's Candid Picture," *Variety*, 13 October 1954.

19. "Milton Gordon's Candid Picture."

20. "Milton Gordon's Candid Picture."

21. Howard Thompson, "An Independent Operator Takes Inventory," *New York Times*, 2 March 1952.

22. "Top Grossers of 1952," *Variety*, 7 January 1953.

23. Thompson, "An Independent Operator Takes Inventory."

24. John Huston, *An Open Book* (Knopf, 1980), 253.

25. Huston, *An Open Book*, 254.

26. Michael Powell to Robert Garrett, 31 July 1954, box 135, Films Collection, Film Finances Archive.

27. John Croydon to Robert Garrett, 16 August 1954, box 135, Films Collection, Film Finances Archive.

28. Croydon to Garrett, 16 August 1954.

29. Maurice Foster to John Croydon, 17 September 1954, box 135, Films Collection, Film Finances Archive.

30. John Croydon to Robert Garrett, 20 September 1954, box 135, Films Collection, Film Finances Archive.

31. Michael Powell to Film Finances, 27 July 1954, box 135, Films Collection, Film Finances Archive.

32. Tino Balio, *United Artists: The Company That Changed the Film Industry*, vol. 2, *1951–1978* (University of Wisconsin Press, 2009), 73.

33. Michael Conant, "The Impact of the Paramount Decrees," in *American Film Industry*, ed. Tino Balio (University of Wisconsin Press, 1976), 354.

CHAPTER 2. SWINGING LONDON

1. Chairman's Speech for Annual General Meeting, 2 March 1967, box 36, General Collection, Film Finances Archive.

2. Chairman's speech.

3. Robert Evans, *The Kid Stays in the Picture*, rev. paperback ed. (Faber, 2003), 112.

4. Beatty quoted in Mark Harris, *Scenes from a Revolution: The Birth of the New Hollywood* (Canongate, 2009), 21–22.

5. Tony Richardson, *Long Distance Runner: A Memoir* (Faber, 1993), 109.

6. Richardson, *Long Distance Runner*, 109.

7. John Croydon to Maurice Foster, 1 October 1959, box 276, Films Collection, Film Finances Archive.

8. John Croydon to Robert Garrett, 30 May 1960, box 310, Films Collection, Film Finances Archive.

9. Croydon to Garrett, 30 May 1960.

10. Robert Garrett to Michael Holden, 9 August 1962, box 346, Films Collection, Film Finances Archive.

11. Robert Garrett to George Ornstein, 9 August 1962, box 346, Films Collection, Film Finances Archive.

12. Crist review quoted in Balio, *United Artists*, 244; Bosley Crowther, review of *Tom Jones*, *New York Times*, 13 October 1963.

13. Crowther, review of *Tom Jones*.

14. Financing agreement between Danjaq, S.A. and United Artists, 10 April 1962, box 328, Films Collection, Film Finances Archive.

15. John Croydon to Robert Garrett, 16 December 1961, box 328, Films Collection, Film Finances Archive.

16. Undated memorandum, box 389, Films Collection, Film Finances Archive.

17. Robert Garrett to A. J. Winter, Bank of America, 11 August 1964, box 389, Films Collection, Film Finances Archive.

18. Robert Garrett to Harry Saltzman, 4 January 1965, box 389, Films Collection, Film Finances Archive.

19. Piri Halasz, "You Can Walk Across it on the Grass," *Time*, 15 April 1966.

20. Evans, *Kid Stays in the Picture*, 115.

21. Evans, *Kid Stays in the Picture*, 115.

22. Robert Garrett to Howard Harrison, 26 August 1964, box 92, General Collection, Film Finances Archive.

23. Robert Garrett to Elmo Williams, 19 May 1965, box 92, General Collection, Film Finances Archive.

24. Robert Garrett to Jay Kanter, 18 January 1966, box 23, General Collection, Film Finances Archive.

25. Robert Garrett to Gerry Blattner, 24 February 1966, box 23, General Collection, Film Finances Archive.

26. Unsigned memorandum, 9 September 1966, box 23, General Collection, Film Finances Archive.

27. Zanuck quoted in Mark Harris, *Scenes from a Revolution*, 132.

28. Harris, *Scenes from a Revolution*, 244.

29. Robert Garrett to Alessandro Tasca di Cutò, 7 February 1964, box 92, General Collection, Film Finances Archive.

30. "Commentary by Observer," *Daily Cinema*, 15 November 1967.

31. "Commentary by Observer."

32. Antony Thorncroft, "Film Studios Enjoy a Boom—Thanks to American Money," *Financial Times*, 21 September 1967.

33. Peter Hope to David Dickson, 15 December 1967, box 68, General Collection, Film Finances Archive.

34. G. D. Dean to Robert Garrett, 19 August 1969, box 68, General Collection, Film Finances Archive.

35. "MGM-EMI Sans Borehamwood," *Variety*, 29 April 1970.

36. Stefan Kanfer, "Hollywood: The Shock of Freedom in Films," *Time*, 8 December 1967.

CHAPTER 3. GLOBAL EXPANSION

1. Shenson quoted in Alexander Walker, *Hollywood, England: The British Film Industry in the Sixties* (Orion, 2005), 451.

2. Vincent Canby, "The Rise of the German Cinema," *New York Times*, 20 April 1980.

3. Interview with Richard Soames, 19 May 2009, Cannes.

4. Soames interview.

5. Soames interview.

6. Lee Steiner to Robert Garrett, 22 July 1970, box 503, Films Collection, Film Finances Archive.

7. Pauline Kael, review of *Cabaret*, *New Yorker*, 11 February 1972.

8. Cy Feuer to John Croydon, 13 March 1972, box 503, Films Collection, Film Finances Archive.

9. John Croydon to Cy Feuer, 6 June 1972, box 503, Films Collection, Film Finances Archive.

10. Soames interview.

11. Soames interview.

12. Soames interview.

13. Filmed interview with Alessandro Tasca di Cutò, undated, Film Finances Archive.

14. Robert Lindsey, "Hollywood Scenario: Boom and Bust," *New York Times*, 26 September 1975.

15. "Banks Back Films for Cinerama," *The Times* (UK), 8 January 1970.

16. Tad Szulc, "Financial Close-Up of a Movie Cliff-Hanger," *New York Times*, 1 April 1968.

17. A. H. Weiler, "Fellini Meets Bergman," *New York Times*, 27 October 1968.

18. Robert Garrett to Dimitri de Grunwald, 4 March 1969, box 45, General Collection, Film Finances Archive.

19. Bernard Smith to Sandy Howard, 25 March 1969, box 45, General Collection, Film Finances Archive.

20. *Hollywood Reporter*, 9 July 1969.

21. John Croydon to Robert Garrett, 21 October 1969, box 478, Films Collection, Film Finances Archive.

22. Croydon to Garrett, 21 October 1969.

23. John Croydon to Robert Garrett, 22 October 1969, box 76, General Collection, Film Finances Archive.

24. "London-Based Farflung Consortium Now Has Distribs Deals in 59 Lands," *Variety*, 11 March 1970.

25. "London-Based Farflung Consortium."

26. "London-Based Farflung Consortium."

27. The Tax Reform Act of 1976 amended the legislation so that investors in such schemes could claim only the amount for which they were personally liable.

28. Dan Dorfman, "New IRS Tax-Shelter the Last Picture Show?," *New York Magazine*, 27 September 1976.

29. Jim Watters, "His Money Talks in Hollywood," *New York Times*, 5 September 1976.

30. "His Money Talks."

31. Richard Albarino, "Risk in Shabby Tax Shelter," *Variety*, 14 August 1974.

32. Aljean Harmetz, "Studios Are Picking Up More Films from Independents," *New York Times*, 26 June 1978.

33. Luke Ford, "Producer Fred T. Kuehnert," accessed 16 March 2021, https://www.lukeford.net/profiles/profiles/fred_kuehnert.htm.

34. David A. Loehwing, "Son of Comeback," *Barron's Financial Weekly*, 26 August 1974.

35. John Croydon to Richard McWhorter, 25 October 1973, box 97, General Collection, Film Finances Archive.

36. John Croydon to Richard McWhorter, 22 November 1973, box 97, General Collection, Film Finances Archive.

37. Robert Garrett to Terence Young, 22 November 1973, box 97, General Collection, Film Finances Archive.

38. Richard Albarino, "Bregman Views New Financing," *Variety*, 19 June 1974.

39. Academy Awards Database, accessed 9 September 2021, https://www.oscars.org/oscars/awards-databases-0.

40. Croydon to Garrett, 21 October 1969.

41. "Cinemobiles Cutting Costs on Location," *New York Times*, 27 August 1971.

42. Bernard Weitzman to Robert Garrett, 20 November 1973, box 115, General Collection, Film Finances Archive.

43. Press release enclosed with a covering note from Cinemobile dated 15 January 1974, box 115, General Collection, Film Finances Archive.

44. Richard Soames to Michael Plotkin, 26 September 1975, box 115, General Collection, Film Finances Archive.

45. Report, "USA Trip Commencing 23rd August, 1976," 2 September 1976, box 5, General Collection, Film Finances Archive.

46. "USA Trip."

47. "USA Trip."

48. "USA Trip."

49. Soames interview.

50. Michael Spencer, *Hollywood North: Creating the Canadian Motion Picture Industry* (Cantos International Publishing, 2003), 143.

51. Soames interview.

52. "Capital Cost Allowance / The Tax Shelter Years: 1975 to 1982," *Canadian Film Encyclopedia,* accessed 26 August 2021, https://cfe.tiff.net/canadianfilmencyclopedia/Browse/bysubject/capital-cost-allowancethe-tax-shelter-years-1975-to-1982.

53. "Chairman's Speech for 29th Annual General Meeting," 12 October 1979, box 74, General Collection, Film Finances Archive.

54. Hank Werba, "Italo Prods Rediscovering America," *Variety,* 7 May 1975.

55. Michael Deeley, *Blade Runners, Deer Hunters, and Blowing the Bloody Doors Off: My Life in Cult Movies* (Faber, 2010), 133.

56. David Hemmings, interview by Roger Ebert, *Chicago Sun-Times,* 6 April 1969.

57. David Hemmings, *Blow-Up and Other Exaggerations* (Robson Books, 2004), 239.

58. "Indies Take Major Role in Pix Biz," *Variety,* 7 June 1978.

59. "Indies Take Major Role in Pix Biz."

60. "Hemdale—A Force from Britain," *Screen International,* 17 March 1979.

61. Soames interview.

62. Richard Soames to Basil Appleby, 1 February 1977, box 48, General Collection, Film Finances Archive.

63. Richard Soames to David Puttnam, 11 December 1979, box 48, General Collection, Film Finances Archive.

CHAPTER 4. GOING HOLLYWOOD

1. "Chairman's Speech for 31st Annual General Meeting."

2. Soames interview.

3. "Garrett Leaves Film Finances," *Screen International,* 30 October 1982.

4. Interview with David Korda, 9 July 2009, London.

5. Korda interview.

6. Korda interview.

7. These figures come from a judgment made in a court case that the minority shareholders brought after Bobby Garrett's departure to challenge the new management of the company: *Smith and Others v. Croft and Others,* [1986] 1 W.L.R. 580 (Ch.).

8. Joe Skrzynski to Ron Aikin, 8 May 1979, box 48, General Collection, Film Finances Archive.

9. Skrzynski to Aikin.

10. Ron Aikin to Ambrose Dunne, 18 October 1979, box 49, General Collection, Film Finances Archive.

11. Jim McCullogh, "The Earthling," *Cinema Papers,* no. 30 (December/January 1980/81): 508.

12. Soames interview.

13. Soames interview.

14. "Skrzynski Appointed," *Cinema Papers*, no. 28 (August/September 1980): 224.

15. "Mad Max," The Numbers, accessed 4 August 2021, https://www.the-numbers.com/custom-search?searchterm=Mad+Max.

16. "Richard Franklin," interviewed by Scott Murray and Tom Ryan, *Cinema Papers*, no. 28 (August/September 1980): 245.

17. Soames interview.

18. Sue Milliken, *Selective Memory: A Life in Film* (Hybrid Publishers, 2013), 96.

19. Sue Milliken to Richard Soames, 20 May 1980, box 698, Films Collection, Film Finances Archive.

20. "The Only Game in Town," *Film News*, February 1981, 1.

21. Sue Milliken, interview, The Knowledge, Centre for Screen Business, July 2007, www.aftrsmedia.com/CSB.

22. Sue Milliken to Richard Soames, 12 February 1981, box 48, General Collection, Film Finances Archive.

23. Richard Soames to Sue Milliken, 17 February 1981, box 48, General Collection, Film Finances Archive.

24. Richard Soames to Sue Milliken, 12 March 1981, box 48, General Collection, Film Finances Archive.

25. Soames to Milliken, 12 March 1981.

26. Sharmat quoted in David Haselhurst, "Film Financier Seeks $100 Million in Australia," *The Bulletin*, 9 October 1979.

27. Ron Aikin, letter to author, 13 April 2009.

28. Unsigned memorandum, 27 November 1980, box 86, General Collection, Film Finances Archive.

29. John Stutter to Ron Aikin, 21 November 1980, box 86, General Collection, Film Finances Archive.

30. Steven Bach, *Final Cut: Dreams and Disaster in the Making of "Heaven's Gate"* (Faber, 1986), 390.

31. David Korda to Richard Soames, 15 September 1981, box 86, General Collection, Film Finances Archive.

32. Soames interview.

33. Soames interview.

34. Coppola quoted in Robert Lindsey, "Who Wields the Power in Hollywood?," *New York Times*, 14 February 1982.

35. Fields quoted in Lindsey, "Who Wields the Power in Hollywood?"

36. Edwards quoted in Lindsey, "Who Wields the Power in Hollywood?"

37. "One from the Heart (1981)," Box Office Mojo, accessed 4 August 2021, https://www.boxofficemojo.com/title/tt0084445/?ref_=bo_se_r_1.

38. Aljean Harmetz, "Four Studios Discuss Release of Coppola Film," *New York Times*, 22 January 1982.

39. Aljean Harmetz, "Coppola Risks All on $22 Million Movie," *New York Times*, 2 February 1981.

40. Aljean Harmetz, "Coppola: Will He Break Even?," *New York Times*, 18 March 1980.

41. Interview with Kurt Woolner, 17 April 2016, London.

42. Advertisement, *Variety*, 5 December 1984.

43. Woolner interview.

44. David Korda to Robert Spiotta, 19 January 1982, box 753, Films Collection, Film Finances Archive.

45. Coppola quoted in Aljean Harmetz, "Making 'The Outsiders,' a Librarian's Dream," *New York Times*, 23 March 1983.

46. Interview with Bob Storer, 4 August 2009, London.

47. Korda interview.

48. Korda interview.

49. Richard Soames to Robert Spiotta, 2 March 1982, box 753, Films Collection, Film Finances Archive.

50. Cover/debit note, 82/44/0288, RTC Ltd, 14 April 1982, box 753, Films Collection, Film Finances Archive.

51. Woolner interview.

52. Woolner interview.

53. Korda interview.

54. Daily production report, 11 April 1982, box 753, Films Collection, Film Finances Archive.

55. Korda interview.

56. Woolner interview.

57. Stephen J. Sansweet, "Insurers Help Keep Movies within Budget," *Wall Street Journal*, 13 October 1982.

58. Woolner interview.

59. Advertisement, *Hollywood Reporter*, 13 July 1982.

60. Soames interview.

61. Soames interview.

62. Parsons quoted in *Hollywood Reporter*, 25 April 1991.

63. Korda interview.

64. Lindsley Parsons to Richard Soames, 15 October 1982, box 786, Films Collection, Film Finances Archive.

65. Fred Hayward to Richard Soames, 17 February 1983, box 786, Films Collection, Film Finances Archive.

66. RTC cover/debit note 83/44/0041, 24 February 1983, box 786, Films Collection, Film Finances Archive.

67. Tony Schwartz, "Hollywood Debates HBO Role in Film Financing," *New York Times*, 7 July 1982.

68. De Laurentiis quoted in Aljean Hartmetz, "De Laurentiis to Market Own Films," *New York Times*, 4 October 1985.

69. "L.A. Film Market," *Variety*, 18 March 1981.

70. Storer interview.

71. Lindsley Parsons to Richard Soames, 15 April 1983, box 194, General Collection, Film Finances Archive.

72. Elisabeth McAllister, "Washington Investors Go Hollywood with Zupnik-Curtis Films," *Washington Post*, 1 August 1983.

73. McAllister, "Washington Investors Go Hollywood."

74. Michael T. Flynn to Richard Soames, 27 April 1983, box 188, General Collection, Film Finances Archive.

75. Entertainment Completions brochure, unnumbered box called "Competitors," General Collection, Film Finances Archive.

76. Advertisement, *Variety*, 11 May 1983.

77. "Completion Bond Communique" advertisement, *Variety*, 4 December 1985.

78. Lindsley Parsons to Richard Soames, 13 October 1982, box 194, General Collection, Film Finances Archive.

79. Richard Soames, internal memorandum, 15 November 1983, box 184, General Collection, Film Finances Archive.

80. Richard Soames, internal memorandum, 23 January 1984, box 188, General Collection, Film Finances Archive.

81. Richard Soames to L. J. Van Cleave, 14 April 1983, box 194, General Collection, Film Finances Archive.

82. L. J. Van Cleave to Richard Soames, 14 April 1983, box 194, General Collection, Film Finances Archive.

83. Soames interview.

84. Korda interview.

85. Mike Medavoy, *You're Only as Good as Your Next One* (Simon & Schuster, 2002), 95.

86. Lionel S. Sobel, "Financing the Production of Theatrical Motion Pictures," *Entertainment Law Reporter* 5, no. 12 (May 1984).

87. Parsons quoted in Steve Taravella, "Movie Producers Buy Bonds to Guarantee Film Completion," *Business Insurance*, 14 May 1984.

88. "Rambo: First Blood Part II," The Numbers, accessed 5 August 2021, https://www.the-numbers.com/custom-search?searchterm=Rambo%3A+First+Blood+Part+II.

89. Storer interview.

90. "A Nightmare on Elm Street (1984)," The Numbers, accessed 5 August 2021, https://www.the-numbers.com/custom-search?searchterm=Nightmare+on+Elm+Street.

91. Arnold Kopelson, 1986 (59th) Academy Awards acceptance speech for Best Picture, 30 March 1987, Academy Awards Acceptance Speech Database, http://aaspeech esdb.oscars.org/.

92. Arnold Kopelson, "One Producer's Inside View of Foreign and Domestic Pre-Sales in the Independent Financing of Motion Pictures," *Loyola of Los Angeles Entertainment Law Review* 12, no. 1 (1992), https://digitalcommons.lmu.edu/elr/vol12/iss1/2.

93. Gale Anne Hurd, memorandum, 23 April 1984, box 861, Films Collection, Film Finances Archive.

94. Hurd quoted in *Other Voices: Creating "The Terminator,"* directed by Van Ling (MGM Home Entertainment, 2001), video.

95. Hurd quoted in Adam Holmes, "The Terminator Almost Got a Happy Ending," CinemaBlend, 22 October 2018, https://www.cinemablend.com/news/2459920/the-terminator-almost-got-a-happy-ending.

96. *Other Voices.*

97. Woolner interview.

98. Woolner interview.

99. Woolner interview.

100. Soames interview.

101. Interview with Steve Ransohoff, 1 October 2015, London.

102. Woolner interview.

103. Alex Cox, *X Films: True Confessions of a Radical Filmmaker* (I.B. Tauris, 2008), 133.

104. Cox, *X Films,* 150.

105. John Terry to Robert Garrett, 25 October 1976, box 595, Films Collection, Film Finances Archive.

106. Robert Garrett to John Terry, 3 November 1976, box 595, Films Collection, Film Finances Archive.

107. Robert Garrett to John Terry, 15 November 1976, box 595, Films Collection, Film Finances Archive.

108. John Croydon to Robert Garrett, 16 March 1978, box 122, General Collection, Film Finances Archive.

109. Jack Mathews, *The Battle of Brazil* (Crown, 1987).

110. Gilliam quoted in Jack Mathews, "Director vs. Studio Chief: The Battle to Release 'Brazil,'" *Los Angeles Times,* 5 November 1985.

111. Richard Soames, interview for documentary *The Madness and Misadventures of Munchausen* (New Wave Entertainment, 2008).

112. Gilliam quoted in Andrew Yule, *Losing the Light* (Applause Books, 1991), 10.

113. Thomas Schühly, interview for *Madness and Misadventures of Munchausen.*

114. Terry Gilliam, interview for *Madness and Misadventures of Munchausen.*

115. Steve Abbott, interview for *Madness and Misadventures of Munchausen.*

116. Soames, interview for *Madness and Misadventures of Munchausen.*

117. Richard Soames to Thomas Schühly and Terry Gilliam, 29 September 1987, box 1253, Films Collection, Film Finances Archive.

118. Woolner interview.

119. Korda interview.

120. Steve Ransohoff to Nigel Cayzer, 28 March 1988, box 1253, Films Collection, Film Finances Archive.

121. Steve Ransohoff to Carla Vissat, 19 April 1988, box 1253, Films Collection, Film Finances Archive.

122. Gilliam quoted in David Morgan, "The Mad Adventures of Terry Gilliam," *Sight and Sound* 57, no. 4 (Autumn 1988): 238–42.

123. Lisa Gubernick, "Miss Jones, Get Me Film Finances," *Forbes,* 26 December 1988.

124. Jake Eberts and Terry Ilott, *My Indecision Is Final: The Rise and Fall of Gold-crest Films* (Faber, 1990), 449.

125. Anne Thompson, "Time and Money on *Terminator 2*," *Entertainment Weekly*, 5 April 1991.

126. Geraldine Fabrikant, "Small Studios' Tough Season," *New York Times*, 6 July 1987.

127. Aljean Harmetz, "Now Showing, Survival of the Fittest," *New York Times*, 22 October 1989.

128. Woolner interview.

CHAPTER 5. INDIEWOOD

1. Robert Shaye to Richard Soames, 1 July 1985, box 002A, General Collection, Film Finances Archive.

2. Richard Soames to Robert Shaye, 11 July 1985, box 002A, General Collection, Film Finances Archive.

3. Morgan quoted in Matt Rothman, "Morgan Breaks IFG Bond," *Variety*, 20 December 1992.

4. Interview with James Shirras, 16 July 2015, London.

5. Woolner interview.

6. Woolner interview.

7. Patricia Apodaca, "Insurance Risky in the Film Business," *Los Angeles Times*, 23 June 1992.

8. "CBC RIP," *Variety*, 1 June 1993.

9. Julian Barnes, "The Deficit Millionaires," *New Yorker*, 20 September 1993.

10. Michael Angeli, "My Name Is Bond. Completion Bond," *New York Times*, 11 August 1991.

11. Jorgensen quoted in Angeli, "My Name Is Bond."

12. Coles quoted in Angeli, "My Name Is Bond."

13. Hoffman quoted in Susan Wloszczyna, "Hoffman Dishes on His Directors, for Better or for Worse," *USA Today*, 25 December 2012.

14. Woolner quoted in Angeli, "My Name Is Bond."

15. Roos quoted in Angeli, "My Name Is Bond."

16. Parsons quoted in Woolner interview.

17. Interview with David Korda, undated.

18. Eberts and Illot, *My Indecision Is Final*, 646.

19. Richard Soames and Nigel Cayzer to Anthony Richards, 3 February 1989, box R506249814, General Collection, Film Finances Archive.

20. Jilda Smith obituary, *The Times* (UK), 22 December 1988.

21. Shirras interview.

22. Interview with Graham Easton, 27 October 2017, London.

23. Easton interview.

24. Budget figure from Alexander Walker, *National Heroes: British Cinema in the Seventies and Eighties* (Harrap, 1985), 261.

25. Easton interview.

26. Easton interview.

27. Relph quoted in Andrew Spicer, "The Independent Producer and the State: Simon Relph, Government Policy and the British Film Industry, 1980–2005," in *Beyond the Bottom Line: The Producer in Film and Television Studies*, ed. Andrew Spicer, Anthony McKenna, and Christopher Meir (Bloomsbury, 2016), 75.

28. Graham Easton, email to author, 12 January 2020.

29. Easton interview.

30. Interview with Stephen Woolley, 9 January 2018, London.

31. Woolley interview.

32. Woolley interview.

33. Woolley interview.

34. Jeremy Isaacs, *Storm over 4: A Personal Account* (Weidenfeld & Nicolson, 1989), 25.

35. Isaacs quoted in "British Cinema: Life before Death on Television," *Sight and Sound* 53, no. 2 (1984): 118.

36. Woolley interview.

37. Woolley interview.

38. Woolley interview.

39. Woolley interview.

40. Woolley interview.

41. Woolley interview.

42. Woolley interview.

43. Easton interview.

44. Woolley interview.

45. Woolley interview.

46. Todd McCarthy, review of *The Crying Game*, *Variety*, 11 September 1992.

47. McCarthy, review of *The Crying Game*.

48. Woolley interview.

49. Leonard Klady, "Where Have All the Independents Gone?," *Variety*, 23 January 1995.

50. Alissa Perren, *Indie Inc.: Miramax and the Transformation of Hollywood in the 1990s* (University of Texas Press, 2013), 63.

51. Bob Weinstein quoted in John Colapinto, "The Big Bad Wolves of Miramax," *Rolling Stone*, 3 April 1997.

52. Harvey Weinstein quoted in Colapinto, "The Big Bad Wolves."

53. David Korda to Harvey Weinstein, Bob Weinstein, and Alan Brewer, 2 October 1984, box 176, General Collection, Film Finances Archive.

54. David Korda to Alan Brewer, 10 October 1984, box 176, General Collection, Film Finances Archive.

55. Storer interview.

56. Caryn James, "Film: 'Playing for Keeps,' a Rock-and-Roll Resort," *New York Times*, 4 October 1986.

57. "The Bottom Line: Behind the Scenes of Film Finances," BFI Southbank, 10 May 2014.

58. "Bottom Line."

59. Soames interview.

60. Ivory quoted in Peter Biskind, *Down and Dirty Pictures: Miramax, Sundance, and the Rise of Independent Film* (Bloomsbury, 2004), 394.

61. Thurman quoted in Biskind, *Down and Dirty Pictures*, 395.

62. Ivory quoted in Robert Emmet Long, *James Ivory in Conversation: How Merchant Ivory Makes Its Movies* (University of California Press, 2005), 243.

63. Ivory quoted in Long, *James Ivory in Conversation*, 243.

64. Merchant quoted in Mike Goodridge, "Lions Gate Takes Over US on The Golden Bowl," *Screen Daily*, 21 September 2000.

65. Ivory quoted in Long, *James Ivory in Conversation*, 243.

66. Richard Soames to Adam C. Barker, Sedgwick, Detert, Moran & Arnold, 26 October 2000, box 4073, Films Collection, Film Finances Archive.

67. As described in an email to James Shirras, 6 November 2000.

68. Michael Kuhn, *One Hundred Films and a Funeral* (Thorogood, 2002), 10.

69. Kuhn, *One Hundred Films and a Funeral*, 46.

70. Kuhn, *One Hundred Films and a Funeral*, 46.

71. Kuhn, *One Hundred Films and a Funeral*, 48.

72. Shirras interview.

73. Finance (No. 2) Act, 1992, c. 48, sec. 42.

74. Finance (No. 2) Act, 1997, c. 58, sec. 48.

75. Stevenson quoted in Eric Boehm, "Brits Bow Pic Tax Break," *Variety*, 3 July 1997.

76. Shirras interview.

77. "Film Finances 50th Anniversary," special issue, *Hollywood Reporter*, 9–15 May 2000.

78. Ransohoff quoted in "Film Finances 50th Anniversary," 4.

79. Ransohoff quoted in "Film Finances 50th Anniversary," 12.

80. Soames quoted in "Film Finances 50th Anniversary," 20.

AFTERWORD

1. Soames quoted in Martin Grove, "30 Minutes with Richard M. Soames," *Show Business Insiders' Newsletter*, 7 March 1984.

2. Claudia Eller, "It's Game Is Bond. Completion Bond," *Los Angeles Times*, 26 May 1995.

3. Woolner interview.

4. Michael Fleming, "Lloyd Webber Back on 'Phantom' Prowl," *Variety*, 9 January 2003.

5. Woolner interview.

6. Woolner interview.

7. See Olsberg-SPI, *Global Film Production Incentives: A White Paper by Olsberg-SPI*, 4 June 2019, 4, https://www.o-spi.com/projects/global-film-production-incentives-white-paper.

8. UNIC: Union Internationale des Cinémas / International Union of Cinemas, *UNIC Annual Report 2020*, 5, https://www.unic-cinemas.org/fileadmin/user_upload/Publications/UNIC_AnnualReport_2020.pdf.

9. Christian Grece, *Trends in the VOD market in EU28* (European Audiovisual Observatory, January 2021), 6.

10. Pamela McClintock, "Fueled by Streaming, Global Entertainment Market Hit Record $100 Billion in 2019," *Hollywood Reporter*, 11 March 2020. According to the Motion Picture Association, the total revenue of the global market for entertainment in 2019 was $101 billion, of which the box office accounted for $42.2 billion, home and mobile entertainment $48.7 billion, and physical entertainment (i.e., DVD and Blu-ray) $10.1 billion.

11. Woolner interview.

12. Alex Cox, "Mission Impossible?," *The Guardian*, 3 July 2020.

13. Cox, *X Films*, 150.

14. "Film and TV Production Restart Scheme," GOV.UK, updated 12 October 2021, https://www.gov.uk/government/publications/film-tv-production-restart-scheme.

15. Diane Haithman, "Entertainment Industry Coalition Asks Senate to Address Need for Pandemic Risk Insurance," *The Wrap*, 19 February 2021. The signatories of the letter, dated 19 February 2021, included the Motion Picture Association, the Independent Film & Television Alliance, the Directors Guild of America, the Producers Guild of America, the American Coalition for Independent Content Production, and the Screen Actors Guild.

16. See Jill Goldsmith, "Reopening Hollywood: Two Firms Take First Steps Toward COVID-19 Insurance for Indie Industry Desperate to Yell 'Action!'" Deadline Hollywood, 9 September 2020, https://deadline.com/2020/09/covid-insurance-indie-film-tv-producers-production-restart-repoening-hollywood-1234572564.

Illustration Credits

Grateful acknowledgment is made to the following individuals and organizations for the permission to use illustrations (C followed by a number indicates a page in the color insert):

Alamy Ltd for *Romance and Riches* poster, C1 (Everett Collection, Inc. / Alamy Stock Photo); *The Woman in Question* poster, C2 (Everett Collection, Inc. / Alamy Stock Photo); *Convoy* poster, 90 (CD/Prod.DB / Alamy Stock Photo); *The Earthling* poster, 102 (TCD/Prod.DB / Alamy Stock Photo); *Road Games* poster, 105; *The Crying Game* UK poster, 172 (TCD/Prod.DB / Alamy Stock Photo); *The Crying Game* US poster, 173 (TCD/Prod.DB / Alamy Stock Photo).

Christopher Bestehorn and Antonia Klopfler for photograph of John Croydon, 11; photograph of John Croydon and Alberto Cavalcanti, 12.

Eric Demarcq for photograph of 9000 Sunset Boulevard (© Eric Demarcq, 2015; permission granted under "Creative Commons" rights), 126.

Don Camp for the photograph of Frans Afman and Arnold Kopelson, 136.

Historic Images for photograph of Lindsley Parsons 123.

Los Angeles Times Photographic Archives (Collection 1429), UCLA Library Special Collections, Charles E. Young Research Library, UCLA, for 1970 photograph of Fouad Said and Vilmos Zsigmond on MGM backlot with a film crew and Cinemobile bus, 83.

Jennifer Nadin for photograph of Bobby Garrett, 3; photograph of Bobby Garrett, Anthony Havelock-Allan, Sidney Salkow, and Erwin Hillier during the production of *Shadow of the Eagle*, 5.

The Ronald Grant Archive for *Reach for the Sky* poster, 18; *It's a Wonderful Life* poster, C3; *The African Queen* poster, C4; *Beat the Devil* poster, C6; *Oh—Rosalinda!!* production still, 26; *Moulin Rouge* poster, C5; *The V.I.P.s* poster, 32;

Saturday Night and Sunday Morning poster, C9; *Room at the Top* poster, C8; *Tom Jones* production photograph 40; *Tom Jones* poster, C10; *Dr. No* poster, C9; *The Red Beret* poster, 46; *The Ipcress File* poster, 48; photograph of Harry Saltzman, 49; *Zulu* production still, 49; *Darling* production still, 37; *Isadora* production photograph, 56; *Easy Rider* poster, 58; *Midnight Cowboy* production still, 59; *Cabaret* poster, 60; *Shalako* production still, 73; *You Can't Have Everything* production still, 75; *The Great Gatsby* production still, 79; *Meatballs* production still, 88; *Sunburn* production still, 91; *The Outsiders* poster, 96; *Picnic at Hanging Rock* production still, 104; *Road Games* production still, 106; *Heaven's Gate* poster, 111; *One from the Heart* production still, 113; *The Outsiders* poster, 115; *Romancing the Stone* production still, 128; *Rambo: First Blood Part II* production still, 134; *The Terminator* poster, C14; *The Terminator* production still, 140; *Purple Rain* production still, 141; *Walker* poster, 143; *The Adventures of Baron Munchausen* poster, 147; *The Adventures of Baron Munchausen* production photograph, 150; *The Adventures of Baron Munchausen* production still, 151; *Pulp Fiction* poster, 156; *Nightmare on Elm Street 2* production still, 158; *Rain Man* production still, 162; *The Draughtsman's Contract* production still, 168; *Secrets and Lies* poster, 177; *Heat and Dust* poster, 179; *The Golden Bowl* production photograph, 180; *Slumdog Millionaire* poster, 188.

Richard Smith for photograph of Bernard Smith, 14.

Ruby Soames for photograph of Richard Soames, C12.

Time USA LLC for the cover of *Time*, 11 April 1966, C11 (From TIME. © 1966 TIME USA LLC. All rights reserved. Used under license. TIME and TIME USA LLC. are not affiliated with, and do not endorse products or services of, Film Finances).

Index